STUDENT SOLUTIONS MANUAL

of
ODD NUMBERED EXERCISES and PROBLEMS
to accompany

MANAGERIAL ACCOUNTING
CONCEPTS FOR PLANNING, CONTROL, DECISION MAKING

Fourth Canadian Edition

Ray H. Garrison
Professor Emeritus
Brigham Young University

Eric W. Noreen
University of Washington
and
Hong Kong University of Science & Technology

G. R. (Dick) Chesley
St. Mary's University

Raymond F. Carroll
Dalhousie University

Toronto • New York • Burr Ridge • Bangkok • Bogotá • Caracas
Lisbon • London • Madrid • Mexico City • Milan • New Delhi • Seoul
Singapore • Sydney • Taipei

McGraw-Hill
Ryerson Limited

A Subsidiary of The McGraw-Hill Companies

Student Solutions Manual
to accompany
Managerial Accounting: Concepts for Planning, Control, Decision Making
Fourth Canadian Edition

ISBN: 0-07-560641-0

1 2 3 4 5 6 7 8 9 10   8 7 6 5 4 3 2 1 0 9

Printed and bound in Canada

Cover Photo: *Cirque du Soleil: Al Seib*
Costume Designer: *Dominique Lemieux*

Contents

Managerial Accounting and the Business Environment

Exercise 1-1 (10 minutes)

1. Managerial accounting; financial accounting
2. Planning
3. Directing and motivating
4. Feedback
5. Decentralization
6. Line
7. Staff
8. Controller
9. Budgets
10. Performance report
11. Precision; nonmonetary data

Exercise 1-3 (10 minutes)

1. The characteristics of the JIT approach include the following:

   - Reducing the number of suppliers and requiring suppliers to make frequent deliveries of defect-free goods.

   - Creating a continuous flow of product through the plant, minimizing the investment in raw materials, work in process, and finished goods.

   - Making production operations more efficient by redesigning workstations and improving the plant layout by creating individual product flow lines.

   - Reducing setup time.

   - Reducing defects.

   - Cross training employees so that all are multi-skilled and can perform all functions required at a particular workstation.

2. A successful JIT system requires suppliers who are willing to make frequent deliveries of defect-free goods in small quantities. This often requires weeding out unreliable suppliers and working intensively with a few, ultra-reliable suppliers.

Problem 1-5 (20 minutes)

1. No, Sarver did not act in an ethical manner. In complying with the president's instructions to omit liabilities from the company's financial statements he was in direct violation of the IMA's *Standards of Ethical Conduct for Management Accountants.* He violated both the "Integrity" and "Objectivity" guidelines on this code of ethical conduct. The fact that the president ordered the omission of the liabilities is immaterial.

2. No, Sarver's actions can't be justified. In dealing with similar situations, the Securities and Exchange Commission (SEC) has consistently ruled that "...corporate officers...cannot escape culpability by asserting that they acted as 'good soldiers' and cannot rely upon the fact that the violative conduct may have been condoned or ordered by their corporate superiors." (Quoted from: Gerald H. Lander, Michael T. Cronin, and Alan Reinstein, "In Defense of the Management Accountant," *Management Accounting,* May, 1990, p. 55) Thus, Sarver not only acted unethically, but he could be held legally liable if insolvency occurs and litigation is brought against the company by creditors or others. It is important that students understand this point early in the course, since it is widely assumed that "good soldiers" are justified by the fact that they are just following orders. In the case at hand, Sarver should have resigned rather than become a party to the fraudulent misrepresentation of the company's financial statements.

Problem 1-7 (30 minutes)

1. Adam Williams has an ethical responsibility to take some action in the matter of GroChem Inc. and the dumping of toxic wastes. In accordance with the "Standards of Ethical Conduct for Management Accountants," management accountants should not condone the commission of acts by their organization that violate the standards of ethical conduct. The specific standards that apply are as follows.

   - **Competence.** Management accountants have a responsibility to perform their professional duties in accordance with relevant laws and regulations.

   - **Confidentiality.** Management accountants must refrain from disclosing confidential information unless legally obligated to do so. However, Adam Williams may have a legal responsibility to take some action.

   - **Integrity.** Management accountants have a responsibility to
     - refrain from either actively or passively subverting the attainment of the organization's legitimate and ethical objectives.
     - communicate favourable as well as unfavourable information and professional judgments or opinions.

   - **Objectivity.** Management accountants must disclose fully all relevant information that could reasonably be expected to influence an intended user's understanding of the reports, comments, and recommendations.

Managerial Accounting

Problem 1-7 (continued)

2. The first alternative being considered by Adam Williams, seeking the advice of his boss, is appropriate. To resolve an ethical conflict, the first step is to discuss the problem with the immediate superior, unless it appears that this individual is involved in the conflict. In this case, it does not appear that Williams' boss is involved.

   Communication of confidential information to anyone outside the company is inappropriate unless there is a legal obligation to do so, in which case Williams should contact the proper authorities.

   Contacting a member of the board of directors would be an inappropriate action at this time. Williams should report the conflict to successively higher levels within the organization and turn only to the board of directors if the problem is not resolved at lower levels.

3. Adam Williams should follow the established policies of the organization bearing on the resolution of such conflict. If these policies do not resolve the ethical conflict, Williams should report the problem to successively higher levels of management up to the board of directors until it is satisfactorily resolved. There is no requirement for Williams to inform his immediate superior of this action because the superior is involved in the conflict. If the conflict is not resolved after exhausting all courses of internal review, Williams may have no other recourse than to resign from the organization and submit an informative memorandum to an appropriate member of the organization.

   (CMA Unofficial Solution, adapted)

Problem 1-9 (20 minutes)

1. If all automotive service shops routinely tried to sell customers parts and services they didn't really need, most customers would eventually figure this out. They would then be reluctant to accept the word of the service representative that a particular problem needs to be corrected—even when there is a legitimate problem. Either the work would not be done, customers would learn to diagnose and repair problems themselves, or customers would hire an independent expert to verify that the work is really needed. All three of these alternatives impose costs and hassle on customers.

2. As argued above, if customers could not trust their service representatives, they would be reluctant to follow the service representative's advice. They would be inclined not to order the work done even when it is really necessary. More customers would learn to do automotive repairs and maintenance themselves. Moreover, customers would be unwilling to pay as much for work that is done because customers would have reason to believe that the work may be unnecessary. These two effects would reduce demand for automotive repair services. The reduced demand would reduce employment in the industry and would lead to lower overall profits.

Cost Terms, Concepts, and Classifications

2

Exercise 2-1 (15 minutes)

1. Product; variable
2. Opportunity
3. Prime
4. Period
5. Product; period; fixed
6. Product
7. Conversion
8. Period; variable
9. Sunk
10. Fixed; product; conversion

Exercise 2-3 (20 minutes)

1. Schedule of cost of goods manufactured:

ECCLES COMPANY
Schedule of Cost of Goods Manufactured
For the Year Ended December 31

Direct materials:

Raw materials inventory, January 1	$ 8,000	
Add: Purchases of raw materials....................	132,000	
Raw materials available for use	140,000	
Deduct: Raw materials inventory,		
December 31	10,000	
Raw materials used in production		$130,000
Direct labour		90,000
Manufacturing overhead:		
Rent, factory building.....................................	80,000	
Indirect labour...	56,300	
Utilities, factory	9,000	
Maintenance, factory equipment	24,000	
Supplies, factory..	700	
Depreciation, factory equipment....................	40,000	
Total overhead costs		210,000
Total manufacturing costs		430,000
Add: Work in process, January 1		5,000
		435,000
Deduct: Work in process, December 31		20,000
Cost of goods manufactured.............................		$415,000

2. The cost of goods sold section would be:

Finished goods inventory, January 1	$ 70,000
Add: Cost of goods manufactured	415,000
Goods available for sale	485,000
Deduct: Finished goods inventory,	
December 31	25,000
Cost of goods sold	$460,000

Exercise 2-5 (10 minutes)

	Cost	Cost Behaviour	
		Variable	Fixed
1.	Small glass plates used for lab tests in a hospital..	X	
2.	Straight-line depreciation of a building...........		X
3.	Top management salaries		X
4.	Electrical costs of running machines..............	X	
5.	Advertising of products and services		X
6.	Batteries used in manufacturing trucks..........	X	
7.	Commissions to salespersons	X	
8.	Insurance on a dentist's office		X
9.	Leather used in manufacturing footballs........	X	
10.	Rent on a medical centre...............................		X

Exercise 2-7 (10 minutes)

1. No. It appears that the overtime spent completing the job was simply a matter of how the job happened to be scheduled. Under these circumstances, an overtime premium should not be charged to a customer whose job happens to fall at the tail end of the day's scheduling sheet.

2. Direct labour cost: 9 hours x $20 .... $180
    General overhead cost: 1 hour x $10........................... <u>10</u>
    Total labour cost .... <u>$190</u>

3. A charge for an overtime premium might be justified if the customer requests that the work be done on a "rush" basis. Generally, no overtime premium should be charged on emergency work if the company solicits for that kind of work in its advertisements.

Managerial Accounting

Problem 2-9 (30 minutes)

1. Mr. Richart's first action was to direct that discretionary expenditures be delayed until the first of the new year. Providing that these "discretionary expenditures" can be delayed without hampering operations, this is a good business decision. By delaying expenditures, the company can keep its cash a bit longer and thereby earn a bit more interest. There is nothing unethical about such an action. The second action was to ask that the order for the parts be cancelled. Since the clerk's order was a mistake, there is nothing unethical about this action either.

   The third action was to ask the accounting department to delay recognition of the delivery until the bill is paid in January. This action is dubious. Asking the accounting department to ignore transactions strikes at the heart of the integrity of the accounting system. If the accounting system cannot be trusted, it is very difficult to run a business or obtain funds from outsiders. However, in Mr. Richart's defence, the purchase of the raw materials really shouldn't be recorded as an expense. He has been placed in an extremely awkward position because the company's accounting policy is flawed.

Problem 2-9 (continued)

2. The company's accounting policy with respect to raw materials is incorrect. Raw materials should be recorded as an asset rather than as an expense when delivered. If the correct accounting policy were followed, there would be no reason for Mr. Richart to ask the accounting department to delay recognition of the delivery of the raw materials. This flawed accounting policy creates incentives for managers to delay deliveries of raw materials until after the end of the fiscal year. This could lead to raw materials shortages and poor relations with suppliers who would like to record *their* sales before the end of the year.

The company's "manage-by-the-numbers" approach does not foster ethical behaviour—particularly when managers are told to "do anything so long as you hit the target profits for the year." In practice, such "no excuses" pressure from the top too often leads to unethical behaviour when managers have difficulty meeting target profits.

Managerial Accounting

Problem 2-11 (30 minutes)

	1	2	3	4
Direct materials.........................	$ 7,000	$ 9,000	$ 6,000	$ 8,000
Direct labour	2,000	4,000	5,000*	3,000
Manufacturing overhead...........	10,000	12,000*	7,000	21,000
Total manufacturing costs	19,000*	25,000	18,000	32,000*
Beginning work in process inventory...............................	3,000*	1,000	2,000	1,500*
Ending work in process inventory...............................	(4,000)	(3,500)	(4,000)*	(2,000)
Cost of goods manufactured	$18,000	$22,500*	$16,000	$31,500
Sales...	$25,000	$40,000	$30,000	$50,000
Beginning finished goods inventory...............................	6,000	8,000*	7,000	9,000
Cost of goods manufactured	18,000*	22,500*	16,000*	31,500
Goods available for sale...........	24,000*	30,500*	23,000*	40,500*
Ending finished goods inventory...............................	9,000	4,000	5,000*	7,000
Cost of goods sold....................	15,000*	26,500	18,000	33,500*
Gross margin............................	10,000*	13,500*	12,000*	16,500*
Operating expenses	6,000	8,000*	9,000*	10,000
Net income	$ 4,000*	$ 5,500	$ 3,000	$ 6,500*

*Missing data in the problem.

Problem 2-13 (50 minutes)

1. Schedule of cost of goods manufactured:

MEDCO, INC.
Schedule of Cost of Goods Manufactured
For the Year Ended December 31

Direct materials:		
Raw materials inventory, January 1	$ 10,000	
Add: Purchases of raw materials..............	90,000	
Raw materials available for use	100,000	
Deduct: Raw materials inventory,		
December 31	17,000	
Raw materials used in production		$ 83,000
Direct labour		60,000
Manufacturing overhead:		
Depreciation, factory	42,000	
Insurance, factory	5,000	
Maintenance, factory	30,000	
Utilities, factory	27,000	
Supplies, factory	1,000	
Indirect labour...	65,000	
Total overhead costs		170,000
Total manufacturing costs		313,000
Add: Work in process inventory,		
January 1		7,000
		320,000
Deduct: Work in process inventory,		
December 31		30,000
Cost of goods manufactured		$290,000

Managerial Accounting

Problem 2-13 (continued)

2.

MEDCO, INC.
Income Statement
For the Year Ended December 31

Sales..		$450,000
Less cost of goods sold:		
Finsihed goods inventory, January 1.......	$ 10,000	
Add: Cost of goods manufactured	290,000	
Goods available for sale	300,000	
Deduct: Finished goods inventory,		
December 31.....................................	40,000	260,000
Gross margin		190,000
Less operating expenses:		
Selling expenses	80,000	
Administrative expenses	70,000	150,000
Net income		$ 40,000

3. Direct materials: $83,000 \div 10,000$ units = $8.30 per unit.
   Depreciation: $42,000 \div 10,000$ units = $4.20 per unit.

4. Direct materials:
    Unit cost: $8.30 (unchanged)
    Total cost: 15,000 units x $8.30 = $124,500.
   Depreciation:
    Unit cost: $42,000 \div 15,000$ units = $2.80 per unit.
    Total cost: $42,000 (unchanged)

Problem 2-13 (continued)

5. Unit cost for depreciation dropped from $4.20 to $2.80, because of the increase in production between the two years. Since fixed costs do not change *in total* as the activity level changes, they will decrease on a unit basis as the activity level rises, and increase on a unit basis as the activity level falls.

Managerial Accounting

Problem 2-15 (15 minutes)

1. The controller is correct in his viewpoint that the salary cost should be classified as a selling (marketing) cost. The duties described in the problem have nothing to do with the manufacture of a product, but rather deal with order-taking and shipping finished goods to customers. As stated in the text, selling costs would include all costs necessary to secure customer orders and get the finished product into the hands of customers.

2. No, the president is not correct; from the point of view of the reported net income for the year, it does make a difference how the salary cost is classified. If the salary cost is classified as a selling expense all $35,000 will appear on the income statement as a period cost. However, if the salary cost is classified as a manufacturing (product) cost, then it will be added into Work in Process Inventory along with other manufacturing costs for the period. To the extent that goods are still in process at the end of the period, part of the $35,000 salary cost will remain with these goods in the Work in Process Inventory account. Only that portion of the $35,000 salary cost which is attached to finished units will leave the Work in Process Inventory account and be transferred into the Finished Goods Inventory account. In like manner, to the extent that goods are unsold at the end of the period, part of the $35,000 salary cost will remain with these goods in the Finished Goods Inventory account. Only that portion of the $35,000 salary which is attached to finished units *which are sold during the period* will appear on the income statement as an expense (part of Cost of Goods Sold) for the period.

The problem shows clearly why the distinction between a product (inventoriable) cost and a period (selling and administrative) cost is so important in a manufacturing company.

Problem 2-17 (25 minutes)

1.

Name of the Cost	Variable Cost	Fixed Cost	Product Cost — Direct Materials	Direct Labour	Mfg. Overhead	Period (Selling and Admin.) Cost	Opportunity Cost	Sunk Cost
Frieda's present salary of $3,000 per month							X	
Rent on the garage, $150 per month		X			X			
Rent of production equipment, $500 per month		X			X			
Materials for producing flyswatters, at $0.30 each	X		X					
Labour cost of producing flyswatters, at $0.50 each	X			X				
Rent of room for a sales office, $75 per month		X				X		
Answering device attachment, $20 per month		X				X		
Answering device attachment, at $0.50 per call	X					X		
Interest lost on savings account, $1,000 per year							X	
Adv. cost, $400 per month		X				X		
Sales commission, at $0.10 per flyswatter	X					X		
Cost of Frieda's house								X

Managerial Accounting

Problem 2-17 (continued)

2. The $150,000 cost of Frieda's house is not a differential cost. The reason is that the house has already been purchased; thus, the cost will not differ depending on whether Frieda decides to produce flyswatters or to stay with the computer firm. All other costs listed above are differential costs since they will be sustained only if Frieda leaves the computer firm and produces the flyswatters.

Problem 2-19 (40 minutes)

1.

VALENKO COMPANY
Schedule of Cost of Goods Manufactured
For the Year Ended December 31

Direct materials:

Raw materials inventory, January 1 ...	$ 50,000	
Add: Purchases of raw materials........	260,000	
Raw materials available for use	310,000	
Deduct: Raw materials inventory, December 31	40,000	
Raw materals used in production		$270,000
Direct labour		65,000* ✓
Manufacturing overhead:		
Insurance, factory	8,000	
Rent, factory building	90,000	
Utilities, factory	52,000	
Cleaning supplies, factory	6,000	
Depreciation, factory equipment	110,000	
Maintenance, factory	74,000	
Total overhead costs		340,000
Total manufacturing costs		675,000 (given)
Add: Work in process inventory, January 1		48,000*
		723,000
Deduct: Work in process inventory, December 31		33,000
Cost of goods manufactured		$690,000

Managerial Accounting

Problem 2-19 (continued)

The cost of goods sold section of the income statement follows:

Finished goods inventory, January 1	$ 30,000	
Add: Cost of goods manufactured	690,000*	
Goods available for sale	720,000	(given)
Deduct: Finished goods inventory,		
December 31	85,000*	
Cost of goods sold	$635,000	(given)

*These items must be computed by working backwards up through the statements. An effective way of doing this is to place the form and known balances on the chalkboard, and then to work toward the unknown figures.

2. Direct materials: $270,000 ÷ 30,000 units = $9.00 per unit.
   Rent, factory building: $90,000 ÷ 30,000 units= $3.00 per unit.

3. Direct materials:
   Per unit: $9.00 (unchanged)
   Total: 50,000 units x $9.00 = $450,000.

   Rent, factory building:
   Per unit: $90,000 ÷ 50,000 units = $1.80.
   Total: $90,000 (unchanged).

4. The unit cost for rent dropped from $3.00 to $1.80, because of the increase in production between the two years. Since fixed costs do not change *in total* as the activity level changes, they will decrease on a unit basis as the activity level rises, and increase on a unit basis as the activity level falls.

Problem 2-21 (40 minutes)

1.

HICKEY COMPANY
Schedule of Cost of Goods Manufactured
For the Year Ended December 31

Direct materials:		
Raw materials inventory, January 1...............	$ 20,000	
Add: Purchases of raw materials....................	160,000	
Raw materials available for use.....................	180,000	
Deduct: Raw materials inventory,		
December 31..	10,000	
Raw materials used in production..................		$170,000
Direct labour		80,000
Manufacturing overhead:		
Indirect labour	60,000	
Building rent (80% x $50,000)	40,000	
Utilities, factory	35,000	
Royalty on patent ($1 x 30,000 units)	30,000	
Maintenance, factory	25,000	
Rent on equipment:		
$6,000 + ($0.10 x 30,000, units)	9,000	
Other factory overhead costs	11,000	
Total overhead costs		210,000
Total manufacturing costs		460,000
Add: Work in process inventory,		
January 1		30,000
		490,000
Deduct: Work in process inventory,		
December 31		40,000
Cost of goods manufactured		$450,000

Problem 2-21 (continued)

2. a. To compute the number of units in the finished goods inventory at December 31, we must first compute the number of units sold during the year.

$$\frac{\text{Total sales,}}{\text{Unit selling price,}} \quad \frac{\$650,000}{\$25} = 26,000 \text{ units sold.}$$

Units in the finished goods inventory, January 1 ....   -0-
Units produced during the year   30,000
Units available for sale   30,000
Units sold during the year (above)...........................   26,000
Units in the finished goods inventory, December 31 .   4,000

b. The average production cost per unit during the year would be:

$$\frac{\text{Cost of goods' manufactured,}}{\text{Number of units produced,}} \quad \frac{\$450,000}{30,000} = \$15 \text{ per unit.}$$

Thus, the cost of the units in the finished goods inventory at December 31 would be: 4,000 units x $15 per unit = $60,000.

Problem 2-21 (continued)

3.

HICKEY COMPANY

Income Statement

For the Year Ended December 31

Sales..		$650,000
Less cost of goods sold:		
Finished goods inventory, June 1	$ -0-	
Add: Cost of goods manufactured	450,000	
Goods available for sale	450,000	
Finished goods, inventory, December 31	60,000	390,000
Gross margin		260,000
Less operating expenses:		
Advertising	50,000	
Building rent (20% x $50,000)	10,000	
Selling and administrative salaries	140,000	
Other selling and administrative expense.....	20,000	220,000
Net income..		$ 40,000

Systems Design: Job-Order Costing 3

Exercise 3-1 (10 minutes)

a. Job-order costing
b. Job-order costing
c. Process costing
d. Job-order costing
e. Process costing*
f. Process costing*
g. Job-order costing
h. Job-order costing
i. Job-order costing
j. Job-order costing
k. Process costing
l. Process costing

*Some of the listed companies might use either a process costing or a job-order costing system, depending on how operations are carried out and how homogeneous the final product is. For example, a plywood manufacturer might use job-order costing if plywoods are constructed of different woods or come in markedly different sizes.

Exercise 3-3 (20 minutes)

1. a.   Raw Materials Inventory 210,000
           Accounts Payable 210,000

    b.   Work in Process 152,000
           Manufacturing Overhead 38,000
           Raw Materials Inventory 190,000

    c.   Work in Process 49,000
           Manufacturing Overhead 21,000
           Salaries and Wages Payable............... 70,000

    d.   Manufacturing Overhead 105,000
           Accumulated Depreciation 105,000

    e.   Manufacturing Overhead 130,000
           Accounts Payable 130,000

    f.   Work in Process 300,000
           Manufacturing Overhead 300,000
         75,000 machine-hours x $4 = $300,000.

    g.   Finished Goods 510,000
           Work in Process................................. 510,000

    h.   Cost of Goods Sold 450,000
           Finished Goods 450,000
         Accounts Receivable 675,000
           Sales... 675,000
         450,000 x 1.5 = $675,000.

2.

Manufacturing Overhead				Work in Process		
(b)	38,000	300,000	(f)	Bal.	35,000	510,000 (g)
(c)	21,000			(b)	152,000	
(d)	105,000			(c)	49,000	
(e)	130,000			(f)	300,000	
		6,000 (Overapplied overhead)		Bal.	26,000	

Managerial Accounting

Exercise 3-5 (15 minutes)

1. $\dfrac{\text{Estimated manufacturing overhead cost,}\quad \$170,000}{\text{Estimated machine-hours,}\qquad\qquad\qquad 85,000} = \dfrac{\$2.00\ \text{per}}{\text{machine-hour}}$

2. The amount of overhead cost applied to Work in Process for the year would be: 80,000 machine-hours x $2.00 = $160,000. This amount is shown in entry (a) below:

	Manufacturing Overhead	
(Utilities)	14,000	160,000 (a)
(Insurance)	9,000	
(Maintenance)	33,000	
(Indirect materials)	7,000	
(Indirect labour)	65,000	
(Depreciation)	40,000	
Balance	8,000	

		Work in Process	
(Direct materials)		530,000	
(Direct labour)		85,000	
(Overhead)	(a)	160,000	

3. Overhead is underapplied by $8,000 for the year, as shown in the Manufacturing Overhead account above. Most companies close any balance in the Manufacturing Overhead account to Cost of Goods Sold. The entry to close out this balance would be:

Cost of Goods Sold	8,000	
Manufacturing Overhead		8,000

Exercise 3-7 (15 minutes)

1. Actual manufacturing overhead costs .... $ 48,000
    Manufacturing overhead applied:
        10,000 MH x $5 50,000
        Overapplied overhead cost .... $ 2,000

2. Direct materials:
        Raw materials inventory, January 1.................. $ 8,000
        Add purchases of raw materials........................ 32,000
        Raw materials available for use 40,000
        Deduct raw materials inventory,
            December 31 7,000
        Raw materials used in production....................... $ 33,000
    Direct labour.. 40,000
    Overhead cost applied to work in process............. 50,000
    Total manufacturing costs...................................... 123,000
    Add: Work in process, January 1 6,000
                                                                129,000
    Deduct: Work in process, December 31 7,500
    Cost of goods manufactured................................. $121,000

                                                                121,500

Managerial Accounting

Exercise 3-9 (15 minutes)

1.	a.	Raw Materials..	315,000	
		Accounts Payable		315,000
	b.	Work in Process	216,000	
		Manufacturing Overhead..........................	54,000	
		Raw Materials		270,000
	c.	Work in Process	80,000	
		Manufacturing Overhead..........................	110,000	
		Wages and Salaries Payable................		190,000
	d.	Manufacturing Overhead..........................	63,000	
		Accumulated Depreciation.....................		63,000
	e.	Manufacturing Overhead..........................	85,000	
		Accounts Payable		85,000
	f.	Work in Process	300,000	
		Manufacturing Overhead		300,000

$$\frac{\text{Estimated overhead cost,} \quad \$4,320,000}{\text{Estimated machine-hours,} \quad 576,000} = \$7.50/\text{MH}$$

40,000 MH x $7.50 = $300,000.

2.

Manufacturing Overhead			
(b)	54,000	300,000	(f)
(c)	110,000		
(d)	63,000		
(e)	85,000		

Work in Process		
(b)	216,000	
(c)	80,000	
(f)	300,000	

3. The cost of the completed job would be $596,000 as shown in the Work in Process T-account above. The entry for item (g) would be:

Finished Goods	596,000	
Work in Process......................................		596,000

The cost per unit on the job cost sheet would be:

$596,000 ÷ 8,000 units = $74.50 per unit.

Exercise 3-11 (20 minutes)

1. Since $320,000 of manufacturing overhead cost was applied to Work in Process on the basis of $200,000 of direct materials cost, the apparent predetermined overhead rate is 160%:

    $$\frac{\text{Manufacturing overhead applied, \$320,000}}{\text{Direct materials cost incurred, \quad \$200,000}} = 160\% \text{ rate.}$$

2. Job 15 is the only job remaining in Work in Process at the end of the month; therefore, the entire $40,000 balance in the Work in Process account at that point must apply to it. Recognizing that the predetermined overhead rate is 160% of direct materials cost, the following computation can be made:

Total cost added to job 15		$40,000
Less: Direct materials cost	$13,500	
Manufacturing overhead cost		
(13,500 x 160%)	21,600	35,100
Direct labour cost.......................................		$ 4,900

    With this information, we can now complete the job cost sheet for job 15:

Direct materials	$13,500
Direct labour	4,900
Manufacturing overhead	21,600
Total cost to January 31	$40,000

Managerial Accounting

Problem 3-13 (40 minutes)

1. and 2.

Cash			
Bal.	8,000	190,000	(l)
(k)	197,000		
Bal.	15,000		

Finished Goods			
Bal.	20,000	120,000	(j)
(i)	130,000		
Bal.	30,000		

Salaries & Wages Payable			
(l)	90,000	93,400	(e)
		3,400	Bal.

Capital Stock	
	150,000 Bal.

Accounts Receivable			
Bal.	13,000	197,000	(k)
(j)	200,000		
Bal.	16,000		

Prepaid Insurance			
Bal.	4,000	3,000	(f)
Bal.	1,000		

Retained Earnings	
	78,000 Bal.

Sales		
	200,000	(j)

Raw Materials			
Bal.	7,000	40,000	(b)
(a)	45,000		
Bal.	12,000		

Plant and Equipment	
Bal. 230,000	

Cost of Goods Sold		
(j)	120,000	
(m)	4,000	

Depreciation Expense		
(d)	7,000	

Work in Process			
Bal.	18,000	130,000	(i)
(b)	32,000		
(e)	40,000		
(h)	60,000		
Bal.	20,000		

Accumulated Depreciation		
	42,000	Bal.
	28,000	(d)
	70,000	Bal.

Problem 3-13 (continued)

Sales Commissions Expense	
(e) 10,400	

Administrative Salaries Expense	
(e) 25,000	

Manufacturing Overhead	
(b) 8,000	60,000* (h)
(c) 14,600	
(d) 21,000	
(e) 18,000	
(f) 2,400	
Bal. 4,000	4,000 (m)

Accounts Payable	
(l) 100,000	30,000 Bal.
	45,000 (a)
	14,600 (c)
	18,000 (g)
	7,600 Bal.

Insurance Expense	
(f) 600	

Miscellaneous Expense	
(g) 18,000	

*$40,000 x 150% = $60,000.

3. Overhead is underapplied. Entry (m) above records the closing of this underapplied overhead balance to Cost of Goods Sold.

4.

DURHAM COMPANY
Income Statement
For the Year Ended December 31

Sales		$200,000
Less cost of goods sold ($120,000 + $4,000)		124,000
Gross margin		76,000
Less selling and administrative expenses:		
Depreciation expense	$ 7,000	
Sales commissions expense	10,400	
Administrative salaries expense	25,000	
Insurance expense	600	
Miscellaneous expense	18,000	61,000
Net income		$ 15,000

Managerial Accounting

Problem 3-15 (45 minutes)

1. a. Raw Materials... 160,000
        Accounts Payable   160,000
    b. Work in Process 120,000
        Manufacturing Overhead............................ 20,000
        Raw Materials   140,000
    c. Work in Process 90,000
        Manufacturing Overhead............................ 60,000
        Sales Commissions Expense...................... 20,000
        Salaries Expense....................................... 50,000
        Salaries and Wages Payable.................   220,000
    d. Manufacturing Overhead............................ 13,000
        Insurance Expense....................................   5,000
        Prepaid Insurance................................   18,000
    e. Manufacturing Overhead............................ 10,000
        Accounts Payable   10,000
    f. Advertising Expense.................................. 15,000
        Accounts Payable   15,000
    g. Manufacturing Overhead............................ 20,000
        Depreciation Expense   5,000
        Accumulated Depreciation......................   25,000
    h. Work in Process 110,000
        Manufacturing Overhead   110,000

$$\frac{\text{Estimated overhead cost,} \quad £99,000}{\text{Estimated machine-hours,} \quad 45,000} = £2.20\text{/machine-hour.}$$

50,000 actual machine-hours x £2.20 = £110,000 overhead
applied.

Problem 3-15 (continued)

i.	Finished Goods	310,000	
	Work in Process......................................		310,000
j.	Accounts Receivable................................	498,000	
	Sales..		498,000
	Cost of Goods Sold	308,000	
	Finished Goods......................................		308,000

2.

Raw Materials

Bal.	10,000	140,000	(b)
(a)	160,000		
Bal.	30,000		

Manufacturing Overhead

(b)	20,000	110,000	(h)
(c)	60,000		
(d)	13,000		
(e)	10,000		
(g)	20,000		
Bal.	13,000		

Work in Process

Bal.	4,000	310,000	(i)
(b)	120,000		
(c)	90,000		
(h)	110,000		
Bal.	14,000		

Costs of Goods Sold

(j)	308,000	

Finished Goods

Bal.	8,000	308,000	(j)
(i)	310,000		
Bal.	10,000		

3. Manufacturing overhead is underapplied by £3,000 for the year. The entry to close this balance to Cost of Goods Sold would be:

Cost of Goods Sold	13,000	
Manufacturing Overhead		13,000

Problem 3-15 (continued)

4.

Sovereign Millwork, Ltd.
Income Statement
For the Year Ended June 30

Sales		£498,000
Less cost of goods sold (£308,000 + £13,000) ...		321,000
Gross margin..		177,000
Less selling and administrative expenses:		
Sales commissions	£20,000	
Administrative salaries....................................	50,000	
Insurance expense	5,000	
Advertising expense	15,000	
Depreciation expense	5,000	95,000
Net income		£ 82,000

Problem 3-17 (30 minutes)

1. Department A predetermined overhead rate:

$$\frac{\text{Estimated overhead cost, } \$416,000}{\text{Estimated machine hours, } 80,000} = \$5.20 \text{ per machine-hour.}$$

Department B predetermined overhead rate:

$$\frac{\text{Estimated overhead cost, } \$720,000}{\text{Estimated direct materials cost, } \$400,000} = 180\% \text{ of direct materials cost.}$$

2. Department A overhead applied:
   350 machine-hours x $5.20............................... $1,820
   Department B overhead applied:
   $1,200 direct materials cost x 180% 2,160
   Total overhead cost $3,980

3. Total cost of job 127:

	Dept. A	Dept. B	Total
Direct materials	$ 940	$1,200	$2,140
Direct labour...............................	710	980	1,690
Manufacturing overhead	1,820	2,160	3,980
Total cost....................................	$3,470	$4,340	$7,810

Cost per unit for job 127:

$$\frac{\text{Total cost, } \$7,810}{25 \text{ units}} = \$312.40 \text{ per unit}$$

4.

	Dept. A	Dept. B
Manufacturing overhead cost incurred.....	$390,000	$740,000
Manufacturing overhead cost applied:		
73,000 machine-hours x $5.20.............	379,600	
$420,000 direct materials cost x 180%		756,000
Underapplied (or overapplied) overhead .	$ 10,400	$ (16,000)

Managerial Accounting

Problem 3-19 (60 minutes)

1.
a. Raw Materials.. 820,000
      Accounts Payable   820,000

b. Work in Process 817,000
      Manufacturing Overhead........................... 13,000
         Raw Materials   830,000

c. Work in Process 140,000
      Manufacturing Overhead........................... 60,000
         Salaries and Wages Payable..................   200,000

d. Salaries Expense...................................... 150,000
      Salaries and Wages Payable..................   150,000

e. Prepaid Insurance 38,000
      Cash..   38,000
      Manufacturing Overhead........................... 39,400
      Insurance Expense................................... 600
         Prepaid Insurance...............................   40,000

f. Marketing Expense.................................... 100,000
      Accounts Payable   100,000

g. Manufacturing Overhead........................... 28,000
      Depreciation Expense 12,000
         Accumulated Depreciation......................   40,000

h. Manufacturing Overhead........................... 12,600
      Accounts Payable   12,600

i. Work in Process 156,000
      Manufacturing Overhead   156,000

   $\underline{\$135,000}$ = $7.50/DLH; 20,800 DLH x $7.50 = $156,000.
   18,000 DLH

j. Finished Goods 1,106,000
      Work in Process....................................   1,106,000

k. Accounts Receivable............................... 1,420,000
      Sales..   1,420,000
      Cost of Goods Sold 1,120,000
      Finished Goods....................................   1,120,000

l. Cash 1,415,000
      Accounts Receivable   1,415,000

m. Accounts Payable.................................... 970,000
      Salaries and Wages Payable 348,000
      Cash..   1,318,000

Problem 3-19 (continued)

2.

Cash

Bal.	9,000	38,000	(e)
(l)	1,415,000	1,318,000	(m)
Bal.	68,000		

Finished Goods

Bal.	38,000	1,120,000	(k)
(j)	1,106,000		
Bal.	24,000		

Salaries & Wages Payable

(m)	348,000	3,000	Bal.
		200,000	(c)
		150,000	(d)
		5,000	Bal.

Accounts Receivable

Bal.	30,000	1,415,000	(l)
(k)	1,420,000		
Bal.	35,000		

Prepaid Insurance

Bal.	7,000	40,000	(e)
(e)	38,000		
Bal.	5,000		

Capital Stock

200,000	Bal.

Retained Earnings

30,000	Bal.

Raw Materials

Bal.	16,000	830,000	(b)
(a)	820,000		
Bal.	6,000		

Buildings and Equipment

Bal.	300,000

Sales

1,420,000	(k)

Cost of Goods Sold

(k)	1,120,000

Work in Process

Bal.	21,000	1,106,000	(j)
(b)	817,000		
(c)	140,000		
(i)	156,000		
Bal.	28,000		

Accumulated Depreciation

	128,000	Bal.
	40,000	(g)
	168,000	Bal.

Salaries Expense

(d)	150,000

Managerial Accounting

Problem 3-19 (continued)

Insurance Expense		
(e)	600	

	Manufacturing Overhead			
(b)	13,000	156,000	(i)
(c)	60,000		
(e)	39,400		
(g)	28,000		
(h)	12,600		
		3,000	Bal.

	Accounts Payable		
(m)	970,000	60,000	Bal.
		820,000	(a)
		100,000	(f)
		12,600	(h)
		22,600	Bal.

	Marketing Expense	
(f)	100,000	

	Depreciation Expense	
(g)	12,000	

3. Manufacturing overhead is overapplied by $3,000 for the year. The entry to close this balance to Cost of Goods Sold would be:

Manufacturing Overhead............................	3,000	
Cost of Goods Sold.................................		3,000

4.

Celestial Displays, Inc.
Income Statement
For the Year Ended December 31

Sales		$1,420,000
Less cost of goods sold ($1,120,000 – $3,000) .		1,117,000
Gross margin..		303,000
Less selling and administrative expenses:		
Salaries expense	$150,000	
Insurance expense	600	
Marketing expense	100,000	
Depreciation expense.....................................	12,000	262,600
Net income		$ 40,400

Problem 3-21 (30 minutes)

1.   The cost of raw materials put into production would be:

Raw materials inventory, 1/1............................	$ 30,000
Debits (purchases of materials)	420,000
Materials available for use	450,000
Raw materials inventory, 12/31........................	60,000
Materials requisitioned for production..............	$390,000

2.   Of the $390,000 in materials requisitioned for production, $320,000 was taken into Work in Process as direct materials. Therefore, the difference of $70,000 ($390,000 – $320,000 = $70,000) would have been taken into Manufacturing Overhead as indirect materials.

3.
Total factory wages accrued during the year (credits to the Factory Wages Payable account)....	$175,000
Less direct labour cost (from Work in Process)	110,000
Indirect labour cost..	$ 65,000

4.   The cost of goods manufactured for the year would have been $810,000—the credits to Work in Process.

5.   The Cost of Goods Sold for the year would have been:

Finished goods inventory, 1/1	$ 40,000
Add: Cost of goods manufactured .... (from Work in Process)......................................	810,000
Goods available for sale	850,000
Finished goods inventory, 12/31	130,000
Cost of goods sold	$720,000

Managerial Accounting

Problem 3-21 (continued)

6. The predetermined overhead rate would have been:

$$\frac{\text{Manufacturing overhead cost applied, } \$400,000}{\text{Direct materials cost, } \$320,000} = \begin{array}{l} 125\% \text{ of direct} \\ \text{materials cost} \end{array}$$

7. Manufacturing overhead would have been overapplied by $15,000, computed as follows:

Actual manufacturing overhead cost for the year (debits)	$385,000
Applied manufacturing overhead cost (from Work in Process—this would be the credits to the Manufacturing Overhead account)	400,000
Overapplied overhead...	$ (15,000)

8. The ending balance in Work in Process is $90,000. Direct labour makes up $18,000 of this balance, and manufacturing overhead makes up $40,000. The computations are:

Balance, Work in Process, 12/31	$90,000
Less: Direct materials cost (given)	(32,000)
Manufacturing overhead cost ($32,000 x 125%)...	(40,000)
Direct labour cost (remainder)	$18,000

Problem 3-23 (120 minutes)

1. a. Raw Materials 142,000
            Accounts Payable   142,000
    b. Work in Process 150,000
            Raw Materials....................................   150,000
    c. Manufacturing Overhead 21,000
            Accounts Payable...............................   21,000
    d. Work in Process 216,000
            Manufacturing Overhead 90,000
            Salaries Expense 145,000
                Salaries and Wages Payable   451,000
    e. Manufacturing Overhead 15,000
            Accounts Payable   15,000
    f. Advertising Expense 130,000
            Accounts Payable   130,000
    g. Manufacturing Overhead 45,000
            Depreciation Expense 5,000
                Accumulated Depreciation   50,000
    h. Manufacturing Overhead 72,000
            Rent Expense 18,000
                Accounts Payable   90,000
    i. Miscellaneous Expense 17,000
            Accounts Payable   17,000
    j. Work in Process 240,000
            Manufacturing Overhead   240,000

$$\frac{\text{Estimated overhead cost,} \quad \$248,000}{\text{Estimated direct materials cost,} \quad \$155,000} = \text{160\% of direct materials cost.}$$

$150,000 direct materials cost x 160% = $240,000 applied.

    k. Finished Goods 590,000
            Work in Process..................................   590,000
    l. Accounts Receivable.............................. 1,000,000
            Sales..   1,000,000
            Cost of Goods Sold 600,000
                Finished Goods.................................   600,000

     Managerial Accounting

Problem 3-23 (continued)

2.

Accounts Receivable

(l) 1,000,000	

Finished Goods

Bal.	35,000	600,000	(l)
(k)	590,000		
Bal.	25,000		

Sales

	1,000,000	(l)

Cost of Goods Sold

(l) 600,000	

Raw Materials

Bal.	18,000	150,000	(b)
(a)	142,000		
Bal.	10,000		

Accumulated Depreciation

	50,000 (g)

Salaries Expense

(d) 145,000	

Advertising Expense

(f) 130,000	

Work in Process

Bal.	24,000	590,000	(k)
(b)	150,000		
(d)	216,000		
(j)	240,000		
Bal.	40,000		

Salaries & Wages Payable

	451,000 (d)

Miscellaneous Expense

(i) 17,000	

Depreciation Expense

(g) 5,000	

Rent Expense

(h) 18,000	

Manufacturing Overhead

(c)	21,000	240,000	(j)
(d)	90,000		
(e)	15,000		
(g)	45,000		
(h)	72,000		
Bal.	3,000		

Accounts Payable

	142,000	(a)
	21,000	(c)
	15,000	(e)
	130,000	(f)
	90,000	(h)
	17,000	(i)

Problem 3-23 (continued)

3.

SOUTHWORTH COMPANY
Schedule of Cost of Goods Manufactured
For the Year Ended December 31

Direct materials:

Raw materials inventory, Jan. 1	$ 18,000	
Purchases of raw materials	142,000	
Materials available for use	160,000	
Raw materials inventory, Dec. 31	10,000	
Materials used in production		$150,000
Direct labour..		216,000
Manufacturing overhead:		
Utilities	21,000	
Indirect labour.....................................	90,000	
Maintenance	15,000	
Depreciation	45,000	
Rent on buildings	72,000	
Total actual overhead costs	243,000	
Less underapplied overhead	3,000	
Manufacturing overhead applied to work in process		240,000
Total manufacturing costs		606,000
Add: Work in process, Jan 1.		24,000
		630,000
Deduct: Work in process, Dec. 31		40,000
Cost of goods manufactured		$590,000

4.

Cost of Goods Sold...................................	3,000	
Manufacturing Overhead........................		3,000

Schedule of cost of goods sold:

Finished goods inventory, Jan. 1.............	$ 35,000
Add: Cost of goods manufactured...........	590,000
Goods available for sale.........................	625,000
Finished goods inventory, Dec. 31	25,000
Cost of goods sold..................................	600,000
Add underapplied overhead	3,000
Adjusted cost of goods sold	$603,000

Managerial Accounting

Problem 3-23 (continued)

5.

SOUTHWORTH COMPANY
Income Statement
For the Year Ended December 31

Sales		$1,000,000
Less cost of goods sold		603,000
Gross margin		397,000
Less selling and administrative expenses:		
Salaries expense	$145,000	
Advertising expense............................	130,000	
Depreciation expense	5,000	
Rent expense	18,000	
Miscellaneous expense	17,000	315,000
Net income..		$ 82,000

6.

Direct materals	$ 3,600
Direct labour (400 hrs. x $11)	4,400
Manufacturing overhead cost applied	
(160% x $3,600)...................................	5,760
Total manufacturing cost......................	13,760
Add markup (75% x $13,760)	10,320
Total billed price of job 218......................	$24,080

$24,080 ÷ 500 units = $48.16 per unit.

Problem 3-25 (40 minutes)

1. a. $\dfrac{\text{Estimated manufacturing overhead cost, \$1,440,000}}{\text{Estimated direct labour cost,} \qquad \$900,000} = 160\%$ of direct labour cost.

    b. $21,200 \times 160\% = \$33,920$.

2. a.

	Cutting Department	Machining Department	Assembly Department
Estimated manufacturing overhead cost (a) ...	$540,000	$800,000	$100,000
Estimated direct labour cost (b)	$300,000	$200,000	$400,000
Predetermined overhead rate (a) ÷ (b)	180%	400%	25%

   b. Cutting Department:

$6,500 x 180%	$11,700
Machining Department:	
$1,700 x 400%	6,800
Assembly Department:	
$13,000 x 25%	3,250
Total applied overhead	$21,750

Note that the bulk of the labour cost on the Hastings job is in the Assembly Department, which incurs very little overhead cost. The department has an overhead rate of only 25 percent of direct labour cost as compared to much higher rates in the other two departments. Therefore, as shown above, use of departmental overhead rates results in a relatively small amount of overhead cost being charged to the job.

Managerial Accounting

Problem 3-25 (continued)

Use of a plantwide overhead rate, however, in effect redistributes overhead costs proportionately between the three departments (at 160% of direct labour cost) and results in a large amount of overhead cost being charged to the Hastings job, as shown in Part 1. This very likely is the reason why the company bid too high and lost the job. Too much overhead cost was assigned to the job for the kind of work being done on the job in the plant.

On jobs that require a large amount of labour in the Cutting or Machining Departments the opposite will be true, and the company will tend to charge too little overhead cost to these jobs if a plantwide overhead rate is being used. The reason is that the plantwide overhead rate (160%) is much lower than the rates would be if these departments were considered separately.

3. The company's bid price was:

Direct materials	$ 18,500
Direct labour	21,200
Manufacturing overhead applied (above)	33,920
Total manufacturing cost	73,620
Bidding rate	x 1.5
Total bid price	$110,430

If departmental overhead rates had been used, the bid price would have been:

Direct materials	$ 18,500
Direct labour	21,200
Manufacturing overhead applied (above)	21,750
Total manufacturing cost	61,450
Bidding rate	x 1.5
Total bid price	$ 92,175

Problem 3-25 (continued)

Note that if departmental overhead rates had been used, Lenko Company would have been the low bidder on the Hastings job since the competitor underbid Lenko by only $10,000.

4. a.   Actual overhead cost $1,482,000
         Applied overhead cost ($870,000 x 160%)   1,392,000
         Underapplied overhead cost .... $ 90,000

Problem 3-25 (continued)

b.

	Cutting Department	Machining Department	Assembly Department	Total Plant
Actual overhead cost	$560,000	$830,000	$92,000	$1,482,000
Applied overhead cost:				
$320,000 x 180%	576,000			
$210,000 x 400%		840,000		
$340,000 x 25%			85,000	1,501,000
Underapplied (overapplied) overhead cost	$(16,000)	$(10,000)	$7,000	$ (19,000)

Problem 3-27 (45 minutes)

1. (a) Materials Inventory... 13,000
            Accounts Payable......................................   13,000
    (b) In-Process Inventory..................................... 13,000
            Materials Inventory....................................   13,000
    (c) In-Process Inventory..................................... 3,500
            Cash...   3,500
    (d) Overhead costs.. 18,000
            Various accounts, cash,
            Accumulated depreciation, etc.   18,000
    (e) In-Process Inventory..................................... 20,000
            Overhead costs...   20,000
    (f) Finished Jobs... 35,530
            In-Process Inventory.................................   35,530

    Materials $13,000 - $300 = $12,700
    Labour $3,500 - $180 =   3,320
    Overhead applied
        $20,000 - $490 =   <u>19,510</u>
                                    <u>$35,530</u>

    (g) Cost of Work Done.. 35,530
            Finished Jobs   35,530

	In-Process Inventory	
	13,000	
	3,500	35,530
	20,000	
	36,500	35,530
Balance	970	

         Managerial Accounting

Problem 3-27 (continued)

2. (a) Materials and In-Process Inventory 13,000
   Accounts Payable............................   13,000

 (b) Finished Jobs ($3,500 − $180) 3,320
   Materials and In-Process Inventory 180
   Overhead Costs 18,000
    Cash   3,500
    Various accounts—cash, accumulated
     depreciation, etc.   18,000

 (c) Finished Jobs....................................... 32,210
   Materials and In-Process Inventory 490
   Materials and In-Process Inventory
    ($13,000 − $300)   12,700
    Overhead costs...............................   20,000

Note: Materials and In-Process Inventory contains the cost of the unfinished jobs $180 + $300 + $490 = $970.

 (d) Cost of Work Done............................... 35,530
   Finished Jobs ($3,320 + $32,210).....   35,530

3. (a) Materials Purchased 13,000
   Accounts Payable.............................   13,000

 (b) Labour—mechanics 3,500
   Cash   3,500

 (c) Overhead Costs 18,000
   Various accounts—cash, accumulated
    depreciation, etc.   18,000

 (d) Overhead Applied 20,000
   Overhead Costs   20,000

 (e) In-Process Inventory 970
   Income Summary   970

   Materials $300
   Labour   180
   Overhead <u>490</u>
       <u>$970</u>

Exercise 4-1 (10 minutes)

Weighted-Average Method

Units accounted for as follows:

	Equivalent Units	
	Materials	**Conversion**
Units transferred to Department B	410,000	410,000
Work in process, October 31:		
30,000 units x 70%	21,000	
30,000 units x 50%		15,000
Equivalent units of production	<u>431,000</u>	<u>425,000</u>

Exercise 4-3 (10 minutes)

Weighted-Average Method

1. Work in process, May 1 80,000
    Started into production during May............................... 300,000
      Total kilograms in process 380,000
    Deduct work in process, May 31 50,000
    Completed and transferred out during May 330,000
2. Kilograms to be accounted for:
      Work in process, May 1 (80% complete with
        respect to materials; 20% complete with
        respect to conversion)...................................... 80,000
      Started into production during the month 300,000
        Total kilograms 380,000
    Kilograms accounted for as follows:
      Transferred out during the month.............................. 330,000
      Work in process, May 31 (40% complete with
        respect to materials; 10% complete with
        respect to conversion)....................................... 50,000
        Total kilograms 380,000

Exercise 4-5 (15 minutes)

Weighted-Average Method

	Quantity Schedule
Kilograms to be accounted for:	
Work in process, May 1 (all materials, 55% labour and overhead added last month).....................................	30,000
Started into production during May..	480,000
Total kilograms...........................	510,000

		Equivalent Units	
		Materials	Labour & Overhead
Kilograms accounted for as follows:			
Transferred to department 2....	490,000*	490,000	490,000
Work in process, May 31 (all materials, 90% labour and overhead added this month)	20,000	20,000	18,000
Total kilograms.................	510,000	510,000	508,000

*30,000 + 480,000 − 20,000 = 490,000.

Exercise 4-7 (10 minutes)

Work in Process—Mixing	330,000	
Raw Materials Inventory		330,000
Work in Process—Mixing	260,000	
Work in Process—Baking	120,000	
Wages Payable		380,000
Work in Process—Mixing	190,000	
Work in Process—Baking	90,000	
Manufacturing Overhead		280,000
Work in Process—Baking	760,000	
Work in Process—Mixing		760,000
Finished Goods	980,000	
Work in Process—Baking		980,000

Exercise 4-9 (15 minutes)

FIFO Method

1.

	Quantity Schedule
Litres to be accounted for: Work in process, May 1 (80% materials, 75% labour and overhead added last month).............................	80,000
Started into production..............	760,000
Total litres...........................	840,000

		Equivalent Units		
		Materials	Labour	Overhead
Litres accounted for as follows: Transferred to the next department: From the beginning inventory...............	80,000	16,000*	20,000*	20,000*
Started and completed this month	710,000**	710,000	710,000	710,000
Work in process, May 31 (60% materials, 20% labour and overhead added this month)...............	50,000	30,000	10,000	10,000
Total litres.............	840,000	756,000	740,000	740,000

  *Work required to complete the beginning inventory.
 **790,000 − 80,000 = 710,000.

Managerial Accounting

Exercise 4-9 (continued)

2.

	Total Costs	Materials	Labour	Overhead	Whole Unit
Cost to be accounted for:					
Work in process, May 31	$ 142,300				
Cost added during the month (a)	1,869,200	$907,200	$370,000	$592,000	
	$2,011,500				
	—				
Equivalent units (b)		756,000	740,000	740,000	
Unit cost (a) ÷ (b)		$1.20	+ $0.50	+ $0.80	= $2.50

Exercise 4-11 (10 minutes)

Weighted-Average Method

	Costs	Equivalent Units (EU)	
		Materials	Conversion
Cost accounted for as follows:			
Transferred to the next process:			
300,000 units at			
$2.1248 each	$637,439*	300,000	300,000
Work in process, June 30:			
Materials, at $1.3813			
per EU	27,626	20,000	
Conversion, at $0.7435			
per EU	7,435		10,000
Total work in			
process, June 30	35,061		
Total cost accounted for.............	$672,500		

*Rounded downward to avoid a discrepancy in the column totals.

Managerial Accounting

Exercise 4-13 (15 minutes)

FIFO Method

	Total Costs	Equivalent Units (EU) Materials	Conversion
Cost accounted for as follows:			
Transferred to the next process:			
From the beginning inventory:			
Cost in the beginning inventory	$ 73,000		
Cost to complete these units:			
Materials, at $1.40 per EU ..	21,000	15,000	
Conversion, at $0.75 per EU	27,000		36,000
Total cost	121,000		
Units started and completed this month: 240,000 units x $2.15	516,000	240,000	240,000
Total cost transferred	637,000		
Work in process, June 30:			
Materials, at $1.40 per EU	28,000	20,000	
Conversion, at $0.75 per EU	7,500		10,000
Total work in process, June 30..	35,500		
Total cost accounted for..................	$672,500		

Problem 4-15 (40 minutes)

Weighted-Average Method

1., 2., and 3.

Quantity Schedule and Equivalent Units

	Quantity Schedule
Kilograms to be accounted for:	
Work in process, May 1 (all materials, 90% conversion cost added last month)	70,000
Started into production	350,000
Total kilograms to account for	420,000

	Quantity Schedule	Equivalent Units	
		Materials	**Conversion**
Kilograms accounted for as follows:			
Transferred to molding	380,000*	380,000	380,000
Work in process, May 31 (75% materials, 25% conversion cost added this month)	40,000	30,000	10,000
Total kilograms accounted for	420,000	410,000	390,000

Total and Unit Costs

	Total	Materials	Conversion	Whole Unit
Work in process, May 1	$122,000	$ 86,000	$ 36,000	
Cost added during the month	645,000	447,000	198,000	
Total cost (a)	$767,000	$533,000	$234,000	
Equivalent units (b)	—	410,000	390,000	
Unit cost (a) ÷ (b)		$1.30 +	$0.60 =	$1.90

*70,000 + 350,000 − 40,000 = 380,000.

Managerial Accounting

Problem 4-15 (continued)

Cost Reconciliation

| | Costs | Equivalent Units (EU) | |
		Materials	Conversion
Cost accounted for as follows:			
Transferred to molding: 380,000			
units x $1.90 each	$722,000	380,000	380,000
Work in process, May 31:			
Materials, at $1.30 per EU.........	39,000	30,000	
Conversion, at $0.60 per EU	6,000		10,000
Total work in process	45,000		
Total cost accounted for...................	$767,000		

Problem 4-17 (40 minutes)

Weighted-Average Method

Quantity Schedule and Equivalent Units

	Quantity Schedule
Units to be accounted for:	
Work in process, June 1 (5/7 materials, 3/7 conversion cost added last month)	70,000
Started into production...............	460,000
Total units to be accounted for......	530,000

	Quantity Schedule	Equivalent Units	
		Materials	Conversion
Units accounted for as follows:			
Transferred to bottling...................	450,000	450,000	450,000
Work in process, June 30 (3/4 materials, 5/8 conversion cost added this month)	80,000	60,000	50,000
Total units accounted for..................	530,000	510,000	500,000

Managerial Accounting

Problem 4-17 (continued)

Total and Unit Costs

	Total	Materials	Conversion	Whole Unit
Work in process, June 1	$ 52,000	$ 35,000	$ 17,000	
Cost added during the month	673,000	391,000	282,000	
Total cost (a)	$725,000	$426,000	$299,000	
Equivalent units (b)	—	510,000	500,000	
Unit cost (a) ÷ (b)		$0.835	+ $0.598	= $1.433

Problem 4-17 (continued)

Cost Reconciliation

		Equivalent Units (EU)	
	Costs	Materials	Conversion
Cost accounted for as follows:			
Transferred to bottling:			
450,000 units x $1.433 each	$645,000*	450,000	450,000
Work in process, June 30:			
Materials, at $0.835 per EU.......	50,100	60,000	
Conversion, at $0.598 per EU ...	29,900		50,000
Total work in process,			
June 30	80,000		
Total cost accounted for..................	$725,000		

*The figure is actually $644,850 if a unit cost of $1.433 is used; however, carrying the unit cost to several more decimal places yields a figure of $644,982, which has been rounded upward to avoid the discrepancy.

Managerial Accounting

Problem 4-19 (45 minutes)

Weighted-Average Method

1.
Quantity Schedule and Equivalent Units

	Quantity Schedule
Kilograms to be accounted for:	
Work in process, May 1 (all materials, 4/5 labour and overhead added last month)........	35,000
Started into production....................	280,000
Total kilograms to be accounted for ...	315,000

	Quantity Schedule	Equivalent Units	
Kilograms accounted for as follows:		Materials	Labour & Overhead
Transferred to blending..............	270,000*	270,000	270,000
Work in process, May 31 (all materials, 2/3 labour and overhead added this month)...	45,000	45,000	30,000
Total kilograms accounted for	315,000	315,000	300,000

*35,000 + 280,000 − 45,000 = 270,000.

Problem 4-19 (continued)

Total and Unit Costs

	Total	Materials	Labour & Overhead	Whole Unit
Work in process, May 1	$ 63,700	$ 43,400	$ 20,300	
Cost added during the month	587,300	397,600	189,700	
Total cost (a)	$651,000	$441,000	$210,000	
Equivalent units (b)	—	315,000	300,000	
Unit cost (a) ÷ (b)		$1.40 +	$0.70 =	$2.10

Managerial Accounting

Problem 4-19 (continued)

Cost Reconciliation

	Costs	Equivalent Units (EU)	
		Materials	**Conversion**
Cost accounted for as follows:			
Transferred to blending:			
270,000 kilograms x $2.10			
per kilogram	$567,000	270,000	270,000
Work in process, May 31:			
Materials, at $1.40 per EU	63,000	45,000	
Labour and overhead, at			
$0.70 per EU............................	21,000		30,000
Total work in process,			
May 31	84,000		
Total cost accounted for	$651,000		

2. In computing unit costs, the weighted-average method mixes costs of the prior period in with current period costs. Thus, under the weighted-average method, unit costs are influenced to some extent by what happened in a prior period. This problem becomes particularly significant when attempting to measure performance in the current period. A good job of cost control in the current period might be concealed to some degree by the unit costs which have been brought forward in the beginning inventory. The reverse could also be true in that poor cost control during a period might be concealed somewhat (or entirely) by the costs of the prior period which have been brought forward and added in with current period costs.

Problem 4-21 (35 minutes)

Weighted-Average Method

1. Total units transferred to the next department 30,000
    Less units in the May 1 inventory.............................. <u>5,000</u>
    Units started and completed in May........................... <u>25,000</u>

2. The equivalent units were:

	Quantity Schedule	Equivalent Units	
		Materials	**Conversion**
Units accounted for as follows:			
Transferred to next department	30,000	30,000	30,000
Work in process, May 31*........	<u>4,000</u>	<u>3,000</u>	<u>2,000</u>
Total units............................	<u>34,000</u>	<u>33,000</u>	<u>32,000</u>

*Materials: 4,000 units x 75% = 3,000 equivalent units;
 Conversion: 4,000 units x 50% = 2,000 equivalent units

Managerial Accounting

Problem 4-21 (continued)

3. The unit costs were:

	Total Cost	Materials	Conversion	Whole Unit
Cost to be accounted for:				
Work in process, May 1............	£ 13,400	£ 9,000	£ 4,400	
Cost added in the department.......	87,800	57,000	30,800	
Total cost.........	£101,200	£66,000	£35,200	
Equivalent units (above)........	—	33,000	32,000	
Unit cost........		£2.000	+ £1.100	= £3.100

Problem 4-21 (continued)

4. The ending work in process figure is verified as follows:

Materials, 3,000 equivalent units x £2.00 per unit £6,000
Conversion, 2,000 equivalent units x £1.10 per unit 2,200
   Total work in process £8,200

5. Multiplying the unit cost figure of £3.10 per unit by 1,000 units does *not* provide a valid estimate of the incremental cost of processing an additional 1,000 units through the department. If there is sufficient idle capacity to process an additional 1,000 units, the incremental cost per unit is almost certainly less than £3.10 per unit since there are likely to be substantial fixed costs included in the conversion costs.

Managerial Accounting

Problem 4-23 (50 minutes)

Weighted-Average Method

1. The equivalent units would be:

	Materials	Conversion
Units completed during the year.................	790,000	790,000
Work in process, Dec. 31:		
30,000 units x 100%..............................	30,000	
30,000 units x 50%................................		15,000
Total equivalent units (a)	820,000	805,000

The unit costs would be:

	Total Cost	Materials	Conversion	Whole Unit
Work in process, Jan. 1	$ 70,000	$ 22,000	$ 48,000	
Cost added during the year	3,247,000	880,000	2,367,000	
Total costs (b)	$3,317,000	$902,000	$2,415,000	
Unit cost (b) ÷ (a).......		$1.10 +	$3.00	= $4.10

2. The amount of cost that should be assigned to the ending inventories is:

	Work in Process	Finished Goods	Total
Work in process:			
Materials: 30,000 EU x $1.10	$33,000		$ 33,000
Conversion: 15,000 EU x $3.00........	45,000		45,000
Finished goods: 50,000 EU x $4.10.....		$205,000	205,000
Total cost that should be assigned to inventories	$78,000	$205,000	$283,000

Problem 4-23 (continued)

3. The necessary adjustments would be:

	Work in Process	Finished Goods	Total
Total cost that should be assigned to inventories (see above)	$ 78,000	$205,000	$283,000
Year-end balances in the accounts	95,000	201,000	296,000
Error	$(17,000)	$ 4,000	$ (13,000)

Finished Goods Inventory	4,000	
Cost of Goods Sold	13,000	
Work in Process Inventory		17,000

4. The simplest computation of the cost of goods sold would be:

Beginning finished goods inventory	-0-
Units completed during the year	790,000
Units available for sale	790,000
Less units in ending finished goods inventory	50,000
Units sold during the year	740,000
Cost per unit (from part 1. above)	x $4.10
Cost of goods sold	$3,034,000

Alternative Computation:
Total manufacturing cost incurred:

Materials (part 1. above)	$ 902,000
Conversion (part 1. above)	2,415,000
Total manufacturing cost	3,317,000
Less cost assigned to inventories (part 2. above)	283,000
Cost of goods sold	$3,034,000

Managerial Accounting

Systems Design: Activity-Based Costing and Quality Management

5

Exercise 5-1 (15 minutes)

1. and 2.

	Activity	Activity Level	Possible Cost Driver
a.	Issue of purchase orders	Batch-level activity	Number of orders processed
b.	Design work for new products	Product-level activity	Hours of design time; number of engineering change orders
c.	Management of parts inventories	Product-level activity	Number of part types; number of items in stock
d.	Rough milling work that is done on all products	Unit-level activity	Machine-hours; labour-hours
e.	Hiring new employees through a company personnel office	Facility-level activity*	Number of employees hired; annual turnover
f.	Receipts of material in the company's receiving department	Batch-level activity	Number of items handled; weight of material
g.	Maintenance of general-use equipment by maintenance workers	Unit-level acctivity	Machine-hours; labour hours
h.	Occupancy of the general plant building	Facility-level activity	Space occupied

*As stated in Exhibit 5-4, personnel office costs might be traceable in part to the facility-level and in part to other activity centres at the unit-level, product-level, and batch-level.

Exercise 5-3 (30 minutes)

1. a. When direct labour-hours are used to apply overhead cost to products, other factors affecting the incurrence of overhead cost are ignored. The company's predetermined overhead rate would be:

$$\frac{\text{Manufacturing overhead cost, \$1,480,000}}{\text{Direct labour-hours, \hspace{2em} 20,000}} = \$74 \text{ per DLH}$$

	Product	
	XR7	**ZD5**
b. Direct materials	$35.00	$25.00
Direct labour: $20 x 0.2 DLHs, 0.4 DLHs	4.00	8.00
Manufacturing overhead:		
$74 x 0.2 DLHs, 0.4 DLHs	14.80	29.60
Total unit product cost	$53.80	$62.60

Exercise 5-3 (continued)

2. a. Predetermined overhead rates for the activity centres.

Activity Centre	(1) Estimated Overhead Cost	(2) Expected Activity	(1) ÷ (2) Predetermined Overhead Rate
Machine setups	$ 180,000	250 setups	$720/setup
Special milling	300,000	1,000 MHs	$300/MH
General factory	1,000,000	20,000 DLHs	$50/DLH

The overhead cost that would be applied to each product:

	Product	
	XR7	ZD5
Machine setups: $720 x 150 setups, 100 setups	$108,000	$ 72,000
Special milling: $300 x 1,000 Mhs	300,000	—
General factory: $50 x 4,000 DLHs, 16,000 DLHs	200,000	800,000
Total overhead cost applied...................................	$608,000	$872,000

Exercise 5-3 (continued)

b. Before we can determine the unit product cost of each product under activity-based costing, we must first take the overhead costs applied to each product in part 2(a) above and express them on a per-unit basis:

	Product	
	XR7	**ZD5**
Total overhead cost applied (a)...............	$608,000	$872,000
Number of units produced (b)	20,000	40,000
Overhead cost per unit (a) ÷ (b)	$30.40	$21.80

With this information, the unit product cost of each product under activity-based costing would be:

	Product	
	XR7	**ZD5**
Direct materials...	$35.00	$25.00
Direct labour: $20 x 0.2 DLHs and 0.4 DLHs	4.00	8.00
Manufacturing overhead (above)	30.40	21.80
Total unit product cost...	$69.40	$54.80

Comparing these unit product cost figures with the unit costs in part 1(b), we find that the unit product cost for Product XR7 has increased from $53.80 to $69.40, and the unit product cost for Product ZD5 has decreased from $62.60 to $54.80.

3. It is especially important to note that, even under activity-based costing, 68% of the company's overhead costs continue to be applied to products on the basis of direct labour-hours:

Machine setups (number of setups).................	$ 180,000	12%
Special milling (machine-hours)	300,000	20
General factory (direct labour-hours)	1,000,000	68
Total overhead cost	$1,480,000	100%

Thus, the shift in overhead cost from the high-volume product (Product ZD5) to the low-volume product (Product XR7) occurred as a result of reassigning only 32% of the company's overhead costs.

Managerial Accounting

Exercise 5-3 (continued)

The increase in unit cost for Product XR7 can be explained as follows: First, where possible, overhead costs have been traced to the products rather than being lumped together and spread uniformly over production. Therefore, the special milling costs, which are traceable to Product XR7, have all been assigned to Product XR7 and none assigned to Product ZD5 under the activity-based costing approach. It is common in industry to have some products that require special handling or special processing of some type. This is especially true in modern factories that produce a variety of products. Activity-based costing provides a means for assigning these costs to the appropriate products.

Second, the costs associated with the batch-level activity (machine setups) have also been traced to the specific products to which they relate. These costs have been assigned according to the number of setups completed for each product. However, since a batch-level activity is involved, another factor affecting unit costs comes into play. That factor is batch size. Some products are produced in large batches and some are produced in small batches. The smaller the batch, the higher the per unit cost of the batch activity. In the case at hand, the data can be analyzed as follows:

Product XR7:
    Cost to complete one setup [see 2(b)] .... $720 (a)
    Number of units processed per setup
      (20,000 units ÷ 150 setups = 133 units per setup)   133 units (b)
    Setup cost per unit (a) ÷ (b) $5.41
Product ZD5:
    Cost to complete one setup (above) .... $720 (c)
    Number of units processed per setup
      (40,000 units ÷ 100 setups = 400 units per setup)   400 units (d)
    Setup cost per unit (c) ÷ (d) $1.80

Exercise 5-3 (continued)

Thus, the cost per unit for setups is three times as great for Product XR7, the low-volume product, as it is for Product ZD5, the high-volume product. Such differences in cost are obscured when direct labour-hours (or any other volume measure) is used as a basis for applying overhead cost to products.

In summary, overhead cost has shifted from the high-volume product to the low-volume product as a result of tracing some costs to the products on the basis of the activities involved, rather than on the basis of direct labour-hours.

Managerial Accounting

Exercise 5-5 (10 minutes)

1. Plantwide overhead rate
2. Volume
3. Two stage, stage, stage
4. Process value analysis
5. Unit-level
6. Batch-level
7. Product-level
8. Facility-level
9. High-volume, low-volume, low-volume
10. Activity centres

Exercise 5-7 (10 minutes)

1. Quality
2. Grade
3. Quality of design
4. Quality of design, quality of conformance
5. Prevention costs, appraisal costs
6. Internal failure costs, external failure costs
7. External failure costs
8. Appraisal costs
9. Prevention costs
10. Internal failure costs
11. External failure costs
12. Prevention costs, appraisal costs
13. Quality circles
14. Quality cost report

Exercise 5-9 (15 minutes)

1. The predetermined overhead rates for the activity centres are computed in Exercise 5-8.

This exercise is a good follow-up to Exercise 5-8 since it shows students how the manufacturing overhead cost applied to production is charged to the products.

Activity Centre	Product				
	A	B	C	D	Total
Labour related:					
$6 x 6,000, 10,000, 4,000, and 5,000 DLHs............	$ 36,000	$ 60,000	$ 24,000	$ 30,000	$150,000
Purchase orders:					
$50 x 60, 30, 20, and 90 orders............	3,000	1,500	1,000	4,500	10,000
Parts management:					
$800 x 30, 25, 40, and 15 part types	24,000	20,000	32,000	12,000	88,000
Board etching:					
$45 x 500, 900, 400, and 0 boards	22,500	40,500	18,000	—	81,000
General factory:					
$9 x 3,000, 8,000, 5,000, and 6,000 MHs	27,000	72,000	45,000	54,000	198,000
Total cost assigned	$112,500	$194,000	$120,000	$100,500	$527,000

2. The dollar amounts charged to the products above represent the applied overhead costs from the various activity centres in Exercise 5-8, and the total amount—$527,000—represents the applied overhead cost credited to the Manufacturing Overhead account for the year.

Problem 5-11 (30 minutes)

1. The company's estimated direct labour hours (DLHs) can be computed as follows:

Deluxe model: 15,000 units x 1.6 DLH/unit	24,000
Regular model: 120,000 units x 0.8 DLH/unit...................	96,000
Total direct labour-hours	120,000

Using direct labour-hours as the base, the predetermined overhead rate would be:

$$\frac{\text{Estimated overhead cost,}}{\text{Estimated direct labour-hours,}} \quad \frac{\$6,000,000}{120,000} = \$50 \text{ per DLH}$$

The unit product cost of each model can be computed as follows:

	Deluxe	Regular
Direct materials	$154	$112
Direct labour.......................................	16	8
Manufacturing overhead:		
$50 x 1.6 DLHs..............................	80	
$50 x 0.8 DLHs..............................		40
Total unit product cost.......................	$250	$160

2. Overhead rates by activity centre are computed below:

Activity Centre	(a) Estimated Overhead Cost	(b) Expected Activity	(a) ÷ (b) Predetermined Overhead Rate
Purchase orders	$ 252,000	1,200 orders	$210/order
Scrap/rework orders	648,000	900 orders	$720/order
Product testing	1,350,000	15,000 tests	$90/test
Machine related	3,750,000	50,000 machine-hours	$75/machine-hour

Managerial Accounting

Problem 5-11 (continued)

3. a.

	Deluxe Model		Regular Model	
	Expected Activity	Amount	Expected Activity	Amount
Purchase orders, at $210/order.....	400	$ 84,000	800	$ 168,000
Scrap/rework orders, at $720/order.........	500	360,000	400	288,000
Product testing, at $90/test.........	6,000	540,000	9,000	810,000
Machine related, at $75/machine-hour...................	20,000	1,500,000	30,000	2,250,000
Total overhead cost (a)		$2,484,000		$3,516,000
Number of units produced (b)......		15,000		120,000
Overhead cost per unit (a) ÷ (b)		$165.60		$29.30

Problem 5-11 (continued)

b. Using activity-based costing, the unit product cost of each model would be:

	Deluxe	Regular
Direct materials	$154.00	$112.00
Direct labour	16.00	8.00
Manufacturing overhead (above)	165.60	29.30
Total unit product cost	$335.60	$149.30

Managerial Accounting

Problem 5-11 (continued)

4. Unit costs are distorted as a result of using direct labour-hours as the base for assigning overhead cost to products. Although the deluxe model requires twice as much labour time as the regular model, it still is not being assigned enough overhead cost, as shown in the analysis in part 3(a).

   When the company's overhead costs are analyzed on an activities basis, it becomes obvious that the deluxe model is more expensive to manufacture than the company realizes. Note that the deluxe model accounts for 40% of the machine-hours, although it represents a small part of the company's total production. Also, it consumes a disproportionately large amount of the activities in the other activity centres.

   When activity-based costing is used in place of direct labour as the basis for assigning overhead cost to products, the unit product cost of the deluxe model jumps from $250 to $335.60. If the $250 cost figure is being used as the basis for pricing, then the selling price for the deluxe model is too low. This may be one reason why profits have been declining over the last several years. It may also be the reason why sales of the deluxe model have been increasing rapidly.

5. Given the extensive discussion of activity-based costing and the presence of a *Management Accounting Guideline*, number 17, published in 1993, and *Management Accounting Issues*, paper 3, also published in 1993, it is difficult to believe that the topic is not part of the competence set for management accountants who profess adherence to the ethic of competence. In practice, the ethic of competence is commonly violated in many professions until something happens. Perhaps the accountant could suggest that ABC is too expensive relative to its benefits to implement. Testing of this conclusion would be needed.

Problem 5-13 (30 minutes)

1. The company expects to work 60,000 direct labour-hours during the year, computed as follows:

Mono-circuit: 40,000 units x 1 DLH/unit 40,000
Bi-circuit: 10,000 units x 2 DLH/unit .... <u>20,000</u>
    Total direct labour-hours................................ <u>60,000</u>

Using direct labour-hours as the base, the predetermined overhead rate would be:

$$\frac{\text{Estimated overhead cost,} \quad \$3,000,000}{\text{Estimated direct labour-hours,} \quad 60,000} = \$50 \text{ per DLH}$$

The unit product cost of each product would be:

	Mono-circuit	Bi-circuit
Direct materials (given)	$40	$80
Direct labour (given)......................................	10	20
Manufacturing overhead: $50 x 1 DLH and 2 DLHs...	<u>50</u>	<u>100</u>
Total unit product cost....................................	<u>$100</u>	<u>$200</u>

2. Overhead costs by activity centre are presented below:

Activity Centre	(a) Estimated Overhead Costs	(b) Expected Activity	(a) ÷ (b) Predetermined Overhead Rate
Parts inventory	$ 360,000	900 part orders	$400/part type
Purchase orders	540,000	3,000 orders	$180/order
Quality control	600,000	8,000 tests	$75/test
Machine related	1,500,000	50,000 machine-hours	$30/machine-hour

Problem 5-13 (continued)

3. a.

	Mono-circuit		Bi-circuit	
	Expected Activity	Amount	Expected Activity	Amount
Parts inventory, at $400/part type	300	$ 120,000	600	$ 240,000
Purchase orders, at $180/order.....	2,000	360,000	1,000	180,000
Quality control, at $75/test	2,000	150,000	6,000	450,000
Machine related, at $30/machine-hour...................	20,000	600,000	30,000	900,000
Total overhead cost (a)...........		$1,230,000		$1,770,000
Number of units (b)		40,000		10,000
Overhead cost per unit (a) ÷ (b)		$30.75		$177.00

b. Using activity-based costing, the unit product cost of each product would be:

	Mono-circuit	Bi-circuit
Direct materials	$40.00	$ 80.00
Direct labour..	10.00	20.00
Manufacturing overhead (above)	30.75	177.00
Total unit product cost............................	$80.75	$277.00

Problem 5-13 (continued)

4. Although the bi-circuit accounts for only 20 percent of the company's total production, it is responsible for two-thirds of the part types carried in inventory and 60 percent of the machine-hours. It is also responsible for one-third of the purchase orders and three-fourths of the quality control tests. These factors have been concealed as a result of using direct labour-hours as the base for assigning overhead cost to products. Since the bi-circuit is responsible for a majority of the activity in the company, under activity-based costing it is assigned a larger amount of overhead cost.

    No, the bi-circuit isn't as profitable as the company thinks, and this may be the major reason for the company's declining profits. Note from part (1) that when direct labour is used to assign overhead costs to products, the bi-circuit has a unit product cost of $200. In part (3), however, we have determined that the bi-circuit's unit product cost is $277—a difference of $77 per unit from part (1). If the $200 cost figure is being used as the base for determining a selling price for the bi-circuit, the company may be losing money on this product without knowing it.

Managerial Accounting

Problem 5-15 (45 minutes)

1. Predetermined overhead rates by activity centre:

Activity Centre	(a) Estimated Overhead Costs	(b) Expected Activity	(a) ÷ (b) Predetermined Overhead Rate
Labour related	$ 280,000	40,000 DLHs	$7/DLH
Purchase orders	96,000	1,200 orders	$80/order
Product testing	420,000	3,500 tests	$120/test
Template etching	315,000	10,500 templates	$30/template
General factory	810,000	90,000 MHs	$9/MH

2. a. The journal entry to record actual manufacturing overhead cost:

Manufacturing Overhead............ 1,916,000
   Accounts Payable...................   1,916,000

  b. See the T-accounts on a following page. The above entry is posted as entry (a) in these accounts. Note that the activity centre T-accounts form a subsidiary ledger to the Manufacturing Overhead T-account.

Problem 5-15 (continued)

3. a. The manufacturing overhead cost applied to production is computed as follows:

Activity Centre	(a) Predetermined Overhead Rate	(b) Actual Activity	(a) x (b) Applied Overhead Cost
Labour related	$7/DLH	37,000 DLHs	$ 259,000
Purchase orders	$80/order	1,250 orders	100,000
Product testing	$120/test	3,400 tests	408,000
Template etching	$30/template	11,500 templates	345,000
General factory	$9/MH	87,000 MHs	783,000
Total overhead cost applied			$1,895,000

b. The journal entry to record, applied manufacturing overhead cost is:

Work in Process 1,895,000
    Manufacturing Overhead   1,895,000

This entry is posted as entry (b), in the T-accounts on the following page. Note that the entry is posted to both the activity centre T-accounts and the Manufacturing Overhead control account.

                          Managerial Accounting

Problem 5-15 (continued)

The T-accounts below relate to parts (2)(b), (3)(b), and (4).

Work in Process

DM	2,530,000
DL	410,000
MO (b)	1,895,000

Labour Related Activity Centre

(a) 272,000	(b) 259,000
Bal. 13,000	

Purchase Orders Activity Centre

(a) 98,000	(b) 100,000
	Bal. 2,000

Product Testing Activity Centre

(a) 415,000	(b) 408,000
Bal. 7,000	

Board Etching Activity Centre

(a) 330,000	(b) 345,000
	Bal. 15,000

General Factory Activity Centre

(a) 801,000	(b) 783,000
Bal. 18,000	

Manufacturing Overhead

(a) 1,916,000	(b) 1,895,000
Bal. 21,000	

Problem 5-15 (continued)

4. The underapplied or overapplied overhead cost for each activity centre and for Manufacturing Overhead is computed in the T-accounts on the preceding page. It can also be computed as follows:

	Total	Activity Centre				
		Labour Related	Purchase Orders	Product Testing	Template Etching	General Factory
Actual overhead cost	$1,916,000	$272,000	$ 98,000	$415,000	$330,000	$801,000
Applied overhead cost	1,895,000	259,000	100,000	408,000	345,000	783,000
Underapplied or (overapplied) manufacturing overhead cost	$ 21,000	$ 13,000	$ (2,000)	$ 7,000	$(15,000)	$ 18,000

Managerial Accounting

Problem 5-17 (45 minutes)

1. Predetermined overhead rates by activity centre are:

Activity Centre	(a) Estimated Overhead Costs	(b) Expected Activity	(a) ÷ (b) Predetermined Overhead Rate
Labour related	$220,000	20,000 DLHs	$11.00/DLH
Production orders	40,000	500 orders	80.00/order
Material handling	126,000	1,800 loads	70.00/load
Testing	160,000	4,000 tests	40.00/test
General factory	550,000	25,000 MHs	22.00/MH

2. a. The journal entry to record actual manufacturing overhead cost:

Manufacturing Overhead............	$1,105,000	
Accounts Payable		$1,105,000

   b. See the T-accounts on a following page. The above entry is posted as entry (a) in these accounts. Note that the activity centre T-accounts form a subsidiary ledger to the Manufacturing Overhead T-account.

Problem 5-17 (continued)

3. a. The manufacturing overhead cost applied to production is computed as follows:

Activity Centre	(a) Predetermined Overhead Rate	(b) Actual Activity	(a) x (b) Applied Overhead Cost
Labour related	$11.00/DLH	21,000 DLHs	$ 231,000
Production orders	80.00/order	550 orders	44,000
Material handling	70.00/load	1,850 loads	129,500
Testing	40.00/test	4,100 tests	164,000
General factory	22.00/MH	25,500 MHs	561,000
Total overhead cost applied			$1,129,500

b. The journal entry to record applied manufacturing overhead cost is:

Work in Process	$1,129,500	
Manufacturing Overhead		$1,129,500

This entry is posted as entry (b) in the T-accounts on the following page. Note that the entry is posted to both the activity centre T-accounts and the Manufacturing Overhead Control account.

Managerial Accounting

Problem 5-17 (continued)

The T-accounts below relate to parts (2)(b), (3)(b), and (4).

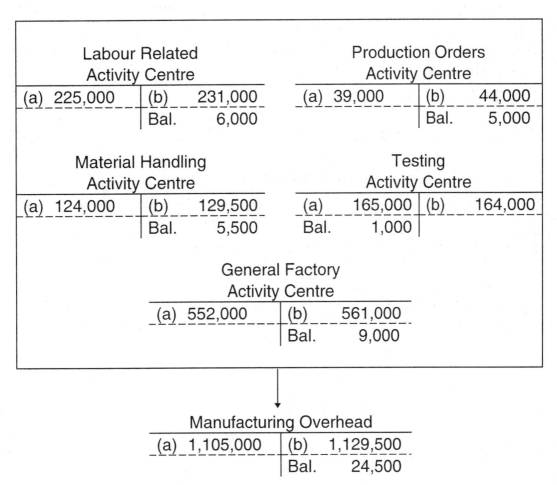

Work in Process

DM	750,000		
DL	230,000		
MO (b)	1,129,000		

Labour Related Activity Centre

(a) 225,000	(b)	231,000	
	Bal.	6,000	

Production Orders Activity Centre

(a) 39,000	(b)	44,000	
	Bal.	5,000	

Material Handling Activity Centre

(a) 124,000	(b)	129,500	
	Bal.	5,500	

Testing Activity Centre

(a) 165,000	(b)	164,000	
Bal. 1,000			

General Factory Activity Centre

(a) 552,000	(b)	561,000	
	Bal.	9,000	

Manufacturing Overhead

(a) 1,105,000	(b)	1,129,500	
	Bal.	24,500	

Problem 5-17 (continued)

4. The underapplied or overapplied overhead cost for each activity centre and for Manufacturing Overhead is computed as follows:

	Total	Labour Related	Production Orders	Material Handling	Testing	General Factory
				Activity Centre		
Actual overhead cost........	$1,105,000	$225,000	$39,000	$124,000	$165,000	$552,000
Applied overhead cost........	1,129,500	231,000	44,000	129,500	164,000	561,000
Underapplied or (overapplied) manufacturing overhead cost........	$ (24,500)	$ (6,000)	$ (5,000)	$ (5,500)	$ 1,000	$ (9,000)

It can also be computed in the T-accounts.

Managerial Accounting

Problem 5-19 (90 minutes)

1. Predetermined overhead rates for the activity centres:

Activity Centre	(1) Estimated Overhead Cost	(2) Expected Activity	(1) ÷ (2) Predetermined Overhead Rate
Machining	$250,000	10,000 computer-hours	$25/computer-hour
Purchase orders	120,000	2,000 orders	$60/order
Parts management	40,000	500 part types	$80/part type
Testing	125,000	5,000 tests	$25/test
General factory	350,000	50,000 machine-hours	$7/machine-hour

2.

			Debit	Credit
a.	Raw Materials		375,000	
	Accounts Payable			375,000
b.	Work in Process		340,000	
	Manufacturing Overhead		50,000	
	Raw Materials			390,000
c.	Work in Process		110,000	
	Manufacturing Overhead		280,000	
	Sales Commissions Expense		90,000	
	Administrative Salaries Expense		240,000	
	Salaries and Wages Payable			720,000
d.	Sales Travel Expense		42,000	
	Accounts Payable			42,000
e.	Manufacturing Overhead		68,000	
	Accounts Payable			68,000
f.	Advertising Expense		165,000	
	Accounts Payable			165,000
g.	Manufacturing Overhead		270,000	
	Depreciation Expense		50,000	
	Accumulated Depreciation			320,000
h.	Manufacturing Overhead		220,000	
	Accounts Payable			220,000

Problem 5-19 (continued)

i.   Computation of the manufacturing overhead cost applied to production:

Activity Centre	(1) Predetermined Overhead Rate	(2) Actual Activity	(1) x (2) Applied Overhead Cost
Machining	$25/computer-hour	10,200 computer-hours	$255,000
Purchase orders	$60/order	2,050 orders issued	123,000
Parts management	$80/part type	475 part types	38,000
Testing	$25/test	4,880 tests completed	122,000
General factory	$7/machine-hour	51,000 machine-hours	357,000
Total			$895,000

Note that the application of overhead cost must be by activity centre, since each activity centre has its own predetermined overhead rate. The journal entry to record this application of overhead to production would be:

Work in Process..	895,000	
Manufacturing Overhead.............................		895,000
j. Finished Goods..	1,365,000	
Work in Process		1,365,000
k. Accounts Receivable	1,975,000	
Sales..		1,975,000
Cost of Goods Sold...	1,360,000	
Finished Goods		1,360,000

Managerial Accounting

Problem 5-19 (continued)

3. See the T-accounts at the end of this solution. Note from these T-accounts that when amounts are posted to Manufacturing Overhead, the amounts must also be posted to the activity centre accounts to which they relate.

4. The underapplied or overapplied overhead cost for each activity centre is computed in the T-accounts. The computations can be summarized as follows:

	Total	Machining	Purchase Orders	Parts Management	Testing	General Factory
Actual overhead cost..........	$888,000	$249,000	$120,000	$43,000	$127,000	$349,000
Applied overhead cost..........	895,000	255,000	123,000	38,000	122,000	357,000
Underapplied or (overapplied) manufacturing overhead cost	$ (7,000)	$ (6,000)	$ (3,000)	$ 5,000	$ 5,000	$ (8,000)

Thus, for the company as a whole, overhead was overapplied by $7,000 for the year. The entry to close this overapplied balance to Cost of Goods Sold would be as follows:

Manufacturing Overhead..........	7,000	
Cost of Goods Sold..........		7,000

Problem 5-19 (continued)

5.

Jarvis Company
Income Statement
For the Year Ended December 31

Sales...		$1,975,000
Less cost of goods sold ($1,360,000 – $7,000)		1,353,000
Gross margin		622,000
Less selling and administrative expenses:		
Commission expense	$ 90,000	
Administrative salaries expense....................	240,000	
Sales travel expense	42,000	
Advertising expense	165,000	
Depreciation expense	50,000	587,000
Net income		$ 35,000

Accounts Receivable		Finished Goods	
(k) 1,975,000		Bal. 45,000	(k) 1,360,000
		(j) 1,365,000	
		Bal. 50,000	

Sales		Cost of Goods Sold	
	(k) 1,975,000	(k) 1,360,000	

Raw Materials		Accumulated Depreciation	
Bal. 25,000	(b) 390,000		(g) 320,000
(a) 375,000			
Bal. 10,000			

Commissions Expense		Administrative Salary Expense	
(c) 90,000		(c) 240,000	

Problem 5-19 (continued)

Work in Process		
Bal. 70,000	(j)	1,365,000
(b) 340,000		
(c) 110,000		
(i) 895,000		
Bal. 50,000		

Accounts Payable	
	(a) 375,000
	(d) 42,000
	(e) 68,000
	(f) 165,000
	(h) 220,000

Sales Travel Expense	
(d) 42,000	

Advertising Expense	
(f) 165,000	

Manufacturing Overhead		
(b) 50,000	(i)	895,000
(c) 280,000		
(e) 68,000		
(g) 270,000		
(h) 220,000		
	Bal.	7,000

Salaries and Wages Payable	
	(c) 720,000

Depreciation Expense	
(g) 50,000	

Problem 5-19 (continued)

Machining Activity Centre			
(b)	30,000	(i)	255,000
(e)	19,000		
(g)	130,000		
(h)	70,000		
		Bal.	6,000

Testing Activity Centre			
(b)	12,000	(i)	122,000
(c)	65,000		
(e)	7,000		
(g)	28,000		
(h)	15,000		
Bal.	5,000		

Purchase Order Activity Centre			
(b)	8,000	(i)	123,000
(c)	80,000		
(e)	11,000		
(h)	21,000		
		Bal.	3,000

General Factory Activity Centre			
(c)	110,000	(i)	357,000
(e)	29,000		
(g)	108,000		
(h)	102,000		
		Bal.	8,000

Parts Management Activity Centre			
(c)	25,000	(i)	38,000
(e)	2,000		
(g)	4,000		
(h)	12,000		
Bal.	5,000		

↓

Various activity centres, which function as manufacturing overhead subsidiary accounts.

Managerial Accounting

Cost Behaviour: Analysis and Use 6

Exercise 6-1 (15 minutes)

1.

	X-rays Taken	X-ray Costs
High activity level (February)	7,000	$29,000
Low activity level (June)	3,000	17,000
Change observed............................	4,000	$12,000

Variable cost element:

$$\frac{\text{Change in X-ray costs, \$12,000}}{\text{Change in X-rays taken, } 4,000} = \$3.00/\text{X-ray}$$

Fixed cost element:

X-ray cost at the high activity level..................................	$29,000
Less variable cost element: 7,000 X-rays x $3.00	21,000
Total fixed cost	$ 8,000

The cost formula is $8,000 per month plus $3.00 per X-ray taken or, in terms of the equation for a straight line:

$$Y = \$8,000 + \$3.00X$$

where X is the number of X-rays taken.

2. Expected X-ray costs when 4,600 X-rays are taken:

Variable cost: 4,600 X-rays x $3.00	$13,800
Fixed cost	8,000
Total cost	$21,800

Exercise 6-3 (25 minutes)

1.

	Units Shipped	Shipping Expense
High activity level	8	$36
Low activity level	2	15
Change observed	6	$21

Variable cost element:

$$\frac{\text{Change in expense, } \$21}{\text{Change in units, } \quad 6} = \$3.50/\text{unit.}$$

Fixed cost element:

Shipping expense at the high activity level	$36
Less variable cost element ($3.50 x 8 units)	28
Total fixed cost	$ 8

The cost formula is $8 per month plus $3.50 per unit shipped or

$$Y = \$8 + \$3.50X$$

where X is the number of units shipped.

2. a. See the graph on the following page.

b. Note: Students' answers will vary, depending on their visual fit of the regression line to the data.

Total cost at 5 units shipped per month [a point falling on the regression line in (a)]	$26
Less fixed cost element (intersection of the Y axis)	11
Variable cost element..	$15

$15 ÷ 5 units = $3 per unit.

The cost formula is $11 per month plus $3 per unit shipped or

$$Y = \$11 + 3X$$

where X is the number of units shipped.

Managerial Accounting

Exercise 6-3 (continued)

2. a. The scattergraph follows:

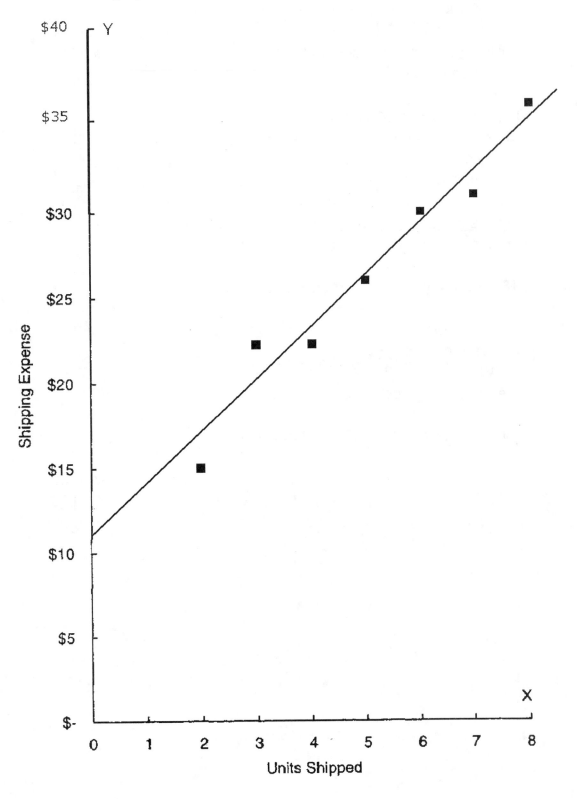

Exercise 6-5 (20 minutes)

1. Monthly operating costs at 70% occupancy:
    2,000 rooms x 70% = 1,400 rooms;

1,400 rooms x $21 x 30 days	$882,000
Monthly operating costs at 45% occupancy (given)...	792,000
Difference in cost	$ 90,000

    Difference in rooms occupied:

70% occupancy (2,000 rooms x 70%)....................	1,400
45% occupancy (2,000 rooms x 45%)....................	900
Difference in rooms...	500

    $$\frac{\text{Change in cost, } \$90,000}{\text{Change in activity, 500 rooms}} = \$180 \text{ per room per month.}$$

    $180 ÷ 30 days = $6 per room per day.

2. | | |
    |---|---:|
    | Monthly operating costs at 70% occupancy (above).. | $882,000 |
    | Less variable costs: | |
    | 1,400 rooms x $6 x 30 days .... | 252,000 |
    | Fixed operating costs per month.............................. | $630,000 |

3. 2,000 rooms x 60% = 1,200 rooms occupied.

Fixed costs	$630,000
Variable costs: 1,200 rooms x $6 x 30 days	216,000
Total expected costs...	$846,000

Exercise 6-7 (20 minutes)

1. The completed scattergraph is presented below:

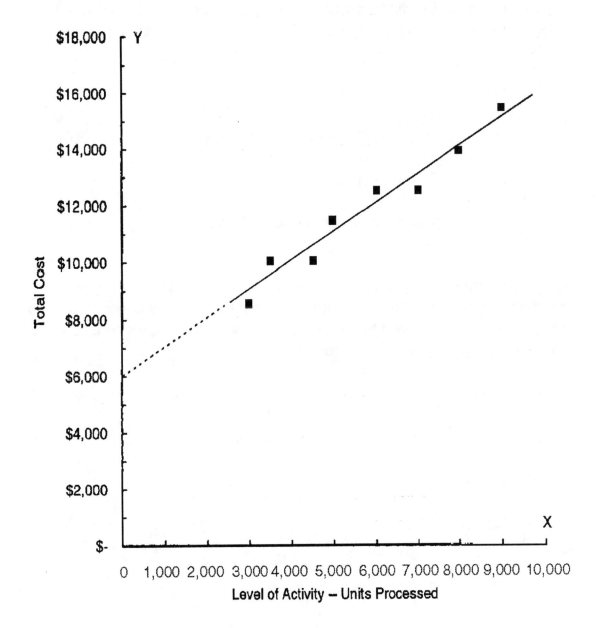

Exercise 6-7 (continued)

2. (Note: Students' answers will vary, depending on their placement of the regression line.) The approximate monthly fixed cost is $6,000—the point where the regression line intersects the cost axis. The variable cost per unit processed is:

Total cost at an 8,000-unit level of activity*.....................	$14,000
Less fixed costs...	6,000
Variable costs at an 8,000-unit level of activity	$ 8,000

$8,000 ÷ 8,000 units $1 per unit.

*Note that total costs at the 8,000-unit level of activity fall on the regression line.

Observe from the scattergraph, that if the company used the high-low method to determine the slope of the regression line, the line would be too steep, causing estimated fixed costs to be lower than they should be, and the variable cost per unit to be too high.

Managerial Accounting

Exercise 6-9 (15 minutes)

1.

	Kilometres Driven	Total Annual Cost*
High level of activity......................................	120,000	$13,920
Low level of activity	80,000	10,880
Difference	40,000	$ 3,040

*120,000 kilometres x $0.116 = $13,920.
  80,000 kilometres x $0.136 = $10,880.

Variable cost per kilometre:

$$\frac{\text{Change in cost,} \quad \$3,040}{\text{Change in activity,} \quad 40,000} = \$0.076 \text{ per kilometre.}$$

Fixed cost per year:

Total cost at 120,000 kilometres.............................	$13,920
Less variable cost element: 120,000 x $.076	9,120
Fixed cost per year	$ 4,800

2. Y = $4,800 + $0.076X

3.

Fixed cost...	$ 4,800
Variable cost: 100,000 kilometres x $0.076	7,600
Total annual cost	$12,400

Problem 6-11 (30 minutes)

1. Cost of goods sold............................ Variable
    Shipping expense............................ Mixed
    Advertising expense......................... Fixed
    Salaries and commissions................ Mixed
    Insurance expense........................... Fixed
    Depreciation expense....................... Fixed

2. Analysis of the mixed expenses:

	Units	Shipping Expense	Salaries and Comm. Expense
High level of activity...................	4,500	£56,000	£143,000
Low level of activity	3,000	44,000	107,000
Difference	1,500	£12,000	£ 36,000

Variable cost element:

$$\frac{\text{Change in cost}}{\text{Change in activity}} = \text{Variable rate}$$

Shipping expense: $\frac{£12,000}{1,500 \text{ units}}$ = £8 per unit.

Salaries and comm. expense: $\frac{£36\,000}{1,500 \text{ units}}$ = £24 per unit.

Fixed cost element:

	Shipping Expense	Salaries and Comm. Expense
Cost at high level of activity	£56,000	£143,000
Less variable cost element:		
4,500 units x £8..................................	36,000	
4,500 units x £24................................		108,000
Fixed cost element................................	£20,000	£ 35,000

Managerial Accounting

Problem 6-11 (continued)

The cost formulas are:

Shipping expense: £20,000 per month plus £8 per unit or
Y = £20,000 + £8X.

Salaries and Comm. expense: £35,000 per month plus £24 per unit
or Y = £35,000 + £24X.

3.

FRANKEL COMPANY
Income Statement
For the Month Ended June 30

Sales in units		4,500
Sales revenue		£630,000
Less variable expenses:		
Cost of goods sold (@ £56)	£252,000	
Shipping expense (@ £8)	36,000	
Salaries and commissions expense		
(@ £24)	108,000	396,000
Contribution margin		234,000
Less fixed expenses:		
Shipping expense	20,000	
Advertising	70,000	
Salaries and commissions	35,000	
Insurance	9,000	
Depreciation..	42,000	176,000
Net income		£58,000

Problem 6-13 (45 minutes)

1.

Year	Number of Leagues(X)	Total Cost (Y)	XY	X^2
19x1	5	$13,000	$65,000	25
19x2	2	7,000	14,000	4
19x3	4	10,500	42,000	16
19x4	6	14,000	84,000	36
19x5	3	10,000	30,000	9
	20	$54,500	$235,000	90

$$b = \frac{n(\sum XY) - (\sum X)(\sum Y)}{n(\sum X^2) - (\sum X)^2}$$

$$= \frac{5(235,000) - (20)(54,500)}{5(90) - (20)^2}$$

$$= \$1,700$$

$$a = \frac{(\sum Y) - b(\sum X)}{n}$$

$$= \frac{(54,500) - 1,700(20)}{5}$$

$$= \$4,100$$

Therefore, the variable cost per league is $1,700 and the fixed cost is $4,100 per year.

2. Y = $4,100 + $1,700X

3. The expected total would be:

Fixed cost	$ 4,100
Variable cost (7 leagues x $1,700)................................	11,900
Total cost	$16,000

Problem 6-13 (continued)

The problem with using the cost formula from (2) to derive this total cost figure is that an activity level of 7 sections lies outside the relevant range from which the cost formula was derived. [The relevant range is represented by a solid line on the graph in part 4 below.]

Although an activity figure may lie outside the relevant range, managers will often use the cost formula anyway to compute expected total cost as we have done above. The reason is that the cost formula frequently is the only basis that the manager has to go on. Using the cost formula as the starting point should not present a problem so long as the manager is alert for any unusual problems that the higher activity level might bring about.

Problem 6-13 (continued)

4.

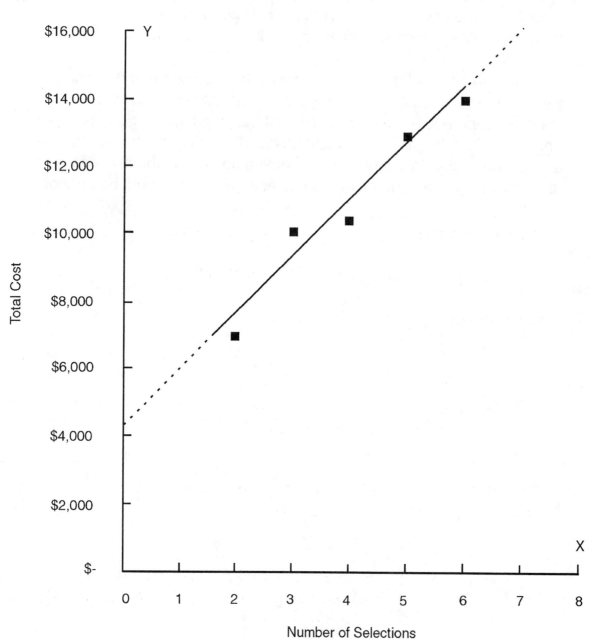

Managerial Accounting

Problem 6-15 (25 minutes)

1. Maintenance cost at the 80,000 machine-hour level of activity can be isolated as follows:

	Level of Activity	
	60,000 MH	80,000 MH
Total factory overhead cost............	274,000 pesos	312,000 pesos
Deduct:		
Indirect materials @ 1.50 pesos/MH*	(90,000)	(120,000)
Rent	(130,000)	(130,000)
Maintenance cost	54,000 pesos	62,000 pesos

*90,000 pesos ÷ 60,000 MH = 1.50 pesos/MH

2. High-low analysis of maintenance cost:

	Maintenance Cost	Machine-Hours
High activity level	62,000 pesos	80,000 MH
Low activity level	54,000	60,000
Change observed	8,000 pesos	20,000 MH

$$\frac{\text{Change in cost,}}{\text{Change in activity,}} \quad \frac{8{,}000 \text{ pesos}}{20{,}000 \text{ MH}} = 0.40 \text{ pesos/MH}$$

Fixed cost element = Total cost – Variable cost element
= 54,000 pesos – (60,000 MHs x 0.40 pesos)
= 30,000 pesos

Therefore, the cost formula is 30,000 pesos per year, plus 0.40 pesos per machine-hour or

$$Y = 30{,}000 \text{ pesos} + 0.40 \text{ pesos}X$$

Problem 6-15 (continued)

3. Indirect materials (65,000 MH x
       1.50 pesos) .... 97,500 pesos
    Rent 130,000
    Maintenance:
       Variable cost element (65,000
          MH x 0.40 pesos) .... 26,000 pesos
       Fixed cost element 30,000   56,000
    Total factory overhead cost .... 283,500 pesos

Managerial Accounting

Problem 6-17 (25 minutes)

1. The scattergraph is presented below.

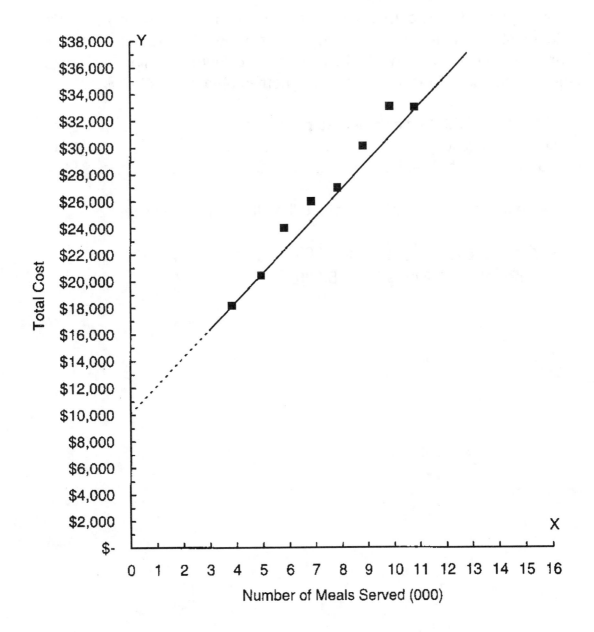

Problem 6-17 (continued)

2. (Note: Students' answers will vary, depending on their placement of the regression line to the plotted points.)

Yes, the president is correct. The cost formula is approximately $10,000 fixed cost per month plus $2.20 per meal served. The fixed cost element can be obtained by noting the point where the regression line intersects the vertical axis. The variable cost element is obtained as follows:

Total cost at 5,000 meals served per month* $21,000
Less fixed cost element 10,000
Variable cost element $11,000

*Note that total costs at this point fall on the regression line.

$$\frac{\text{Variable cost,} \quad \$11,000}{\text{Number of meals served,} \quad 5,000} = \$2.20 \text{ per meal.}$$

Managerial Accounting

Problem 6-19 (25 minutes)

1. High-low method

	Number of Ingots	Power Cost
High activity level	130	$6,000
Low activity level	40	2,400
Change observed	90	$3,600

Variable rate: $\dfrac{\text{Change in cost,} \quad \$3,600}{\text{Change in activity,} \quad 90}$ = $40 per ingot.

Fixed cost: Total power cost at high activity level $6,000
Less variable element:
130 ingots x $40 5,200
Fixed cost element .... $ 800

Therefore, the cost formula is: Y = $800 + $40X.

2. Scattergraph method (see the scattergraph on the following page):

(Note: Students' answers will vary according to their placement of the regression line.)

The regression line intersects the cost axis at $1,200. Therefore, the variable rate would be computed as follows:

Total cost at 100 ingots (a point of activity that falls
on the regression line) $5,000
Less the fixed cost element (intersection of the Y
axis on the graph) 1,200
Variable cost element (total) $3,800

$3,800 ÷ 100 ingots = $38 per ingot.

Therefore, the cost formula is: Y = $1,200 + $38X.

Problem 6-19 (continued)

The completed scattergraph follows:

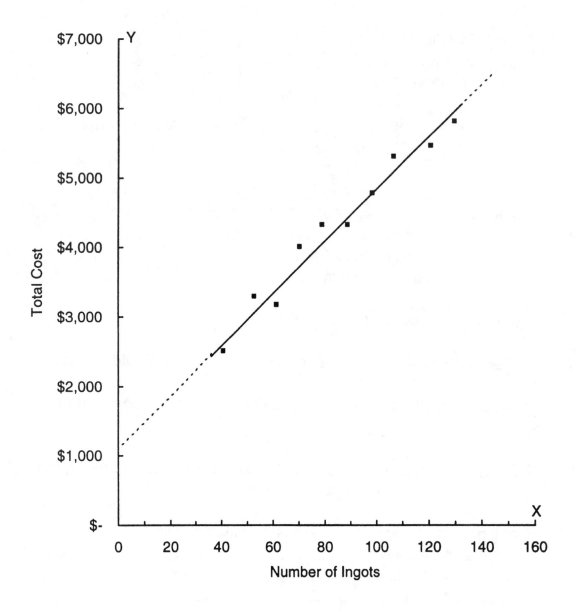

Managerial Accounting

Problem 6-21 (40 minutes)

1.

	July—Low 9,000 Units	October—High 12,000 Units
Direct materials cost @ $15	$135,000	$180,000
Direct labour cost @ $6	54,000	72,000
Manufacturing overhead cost	107,000*	131,000*
Total manufacturing costs	296,000	383,000
Add: Work in process, beginning	14,000	22,000
	310,000	405,000
Deduct: Work in process, ending.........	25,000	15,000
Cost of goods manufactured	$285,000	$390,000

*Computed by working upwards through the statements.

2.

	Units Produced	Cost Observed
October—High level of activity	12,000	$131,000
July—Low level of activity............................	9,000	107,000
Difference	3,000	$ 24,000

$$\frac{\text{Change in cost,} \quad \$24,000}{\text{Change in activity,} \quad 3,000 \text{ units}} = \$8 \text{ per unit}$$

Total cost at the high level of activity	$131,000
Less variable cost element ($8 x 12,000 units)	96,000
Fixed cost element	$ 35,000

Therefore, the cost formula is: $35,000 per month plus $8 per unit produced, or Y = $35,000 + $8X, where X represents the number of units produced.

Problem 6-21 (continued)

3. The cost of goods manufactured if 9,500 units are produced:

Direct materials cost ($15 x 9,500 units)		$142,500
Direct labour cost ($6 x 9,500 units)		57,000
Manufacturing overhead cost:		
Fixed portion	$35,000	
Variable portion ($8 x 9,500 units)	76,000	111,000
Total manufacturing costs		310,500
Add: Work in process, beginning		16,000
		326,500
Deduct: Work in process, ending		19,000
Cost of goods manufactured		$307,500

Managerial Accounting

Cost-Volume-Profit Relationships   7

Exercise 7-1 (20 minutes)

1. Sales = Variable expenses + Fixed expenses + Profits

    $40X = $28X + $150,000 + $0

    $12X = $150,000

    X = $150,000 ÷ $12

    X = 12,500 units, or at $40 per unit, $500,000

    Alternatively:

    $$\frac{\text{Fixed expenses}}{\text{Unit contribution margin}} = \text{Break-even point}$$

    $$\frac{\$150,000}{\$12} = 12,500 \text{ units}$$

    or at $40 per unit, $500,000

2. The contribution margin is $150,000 since it is equal to the fixed expenses at the break-even point.

3. $$\frac{\text{Fixed expenses} + \text{Target net income}}{\text{Unit contribution margin}} = \text{Target sales}$$

    $$\frac{\$150,000 + \$18,000}{\$12} = 14,000 \text{ units}$$

	Total	Unit
Sales (14,000 units x $40)	$560,000	$40
Less variable expenses (14,000 units x $28)	392,000	28
Contribution margin (14,000 units x $12)	168,000	$12
Less fixed expenses	150,000	
Net income	$ 18,000	

Exercise 7-1 (continued)

4.   Margin of safety in dollar terms:

Total sales – Break-even sales = Margin of safety

$600,000 – $500,000 = $100,000

Margin of safety in percentage terms:

$$\frac{\text{Margin of safety in dollars}}{\text{Total sales}} = \frac{\$100,000}{\$600,000} = \underline{16.7\%} \quad \text{(rounded)}$$

5.   The CM ratio is 30%.

Expected total contribution margin: $680,000 x 30%	$204,000
Present total contribution margin: $600,000 x 30%	180,000
Increased contribution margin	$ 24,000

Alternative solution:

$80,000 incremental sales x 30% CM ratio = $24,000.

Since in this case the company's fixed expenses will not change, monthly net income will also increase by $24,000.

Managerial Accounting

Exercise 7-3 (25 minutes)

1. The contribution margin per person would be:

Price per ticket		$30
Less variable expenses:		
Dinner	$ 7	
Favours and program	3	10
Contribution margin per person		$20

The fixed expenses of the Extravaganza total $8,000; therefore, the break-even point would be computed as follows:

Sales = Variable expenses + Fixed expense + Profits

$$\$30X = \$10X + \$8,000 + \$0$$
$$\$20X = \$8,000$$
$$X = \$8,000 \div \$20$$
$$X = 400 \text{ persons; or, at \$30 per person, \$12,000}$$

Alternate solution:

$$\frac{\text{Fixed expenses,} \quad \$8,000}{\text{Unit contribution margin,} \quad \$20} = 400 \text{ persons}$$

or, at $30 per person, $12,000.

2.
Variable cost per person ($7 + $3)		$10
Fixed cost per person ($8,000 ÷ 250)		32
Ticket price per person to break even		$42

Note: Some students will give an answer of $48 per ticket. This answer, which is incorrect, is computed as follows: $12,000 break-even sales from part 1 ÷ 250 persons = $48. The problem with this solution is that the $12,000 figure is no longer the break-even point, since the ticket price is changing.

Exercise 7-3 (continued)

3. The cost-volume-profit graph is presented on the following two pages. It is presented first in the traditional format, and then it is presented in the format that shows the manager the contribution margin at various levels of activity.

Managerial Accounting

Exercise 7-3 (continued)

3. Cost-volume-profit graph:

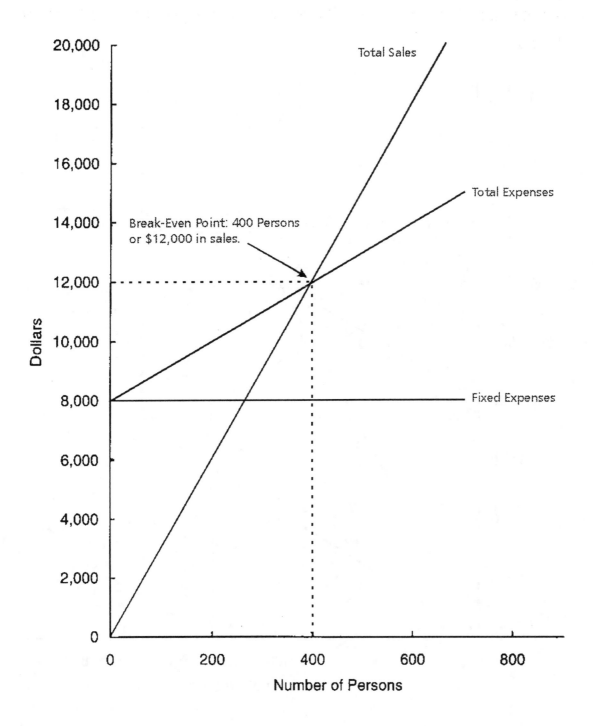

Exercise 7-3 (continued)

Alternate approach to the cost-volume-profit graph:

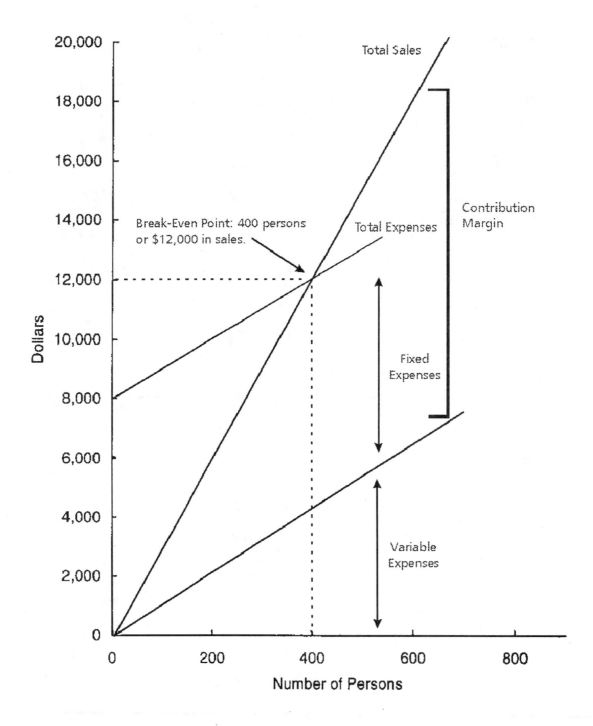

Exercise 7-5 (15 minutes)

1. | Sales (30,000 doors) | $1,800,000 | $60 |
    |---|---|---|
    | Less variable expenses | 1,260,000 | 42 |
    | Contribution margin | 540,000 | $18 |
    | Less fixed expenses | 450,000 | |
    | Net income | $ 90,000 | |

$$\frac{\text{Contribution margin}}{\text{Net Income}} = \text{Degree of operating leverage}$$

$$\frac{\$540,000}{\$90,000} = 6$$

2. a. Sales of 37,500 doors represents an increase of 7,500 doors, or 25%, over present sales of 30,000 doors. Since the operating leverage is 6, net income should increase by 6 times as much, or by 150% (6 x 25%).

   b. Expected total dollar net income for the next year is:

Present net income	$ 90,000
Expected increase in net income next year	
(150% x $90,000)	135,000
Total expected net income	$225,000

Exercise 7-7 (20 minutes)

		Total	Per Unit
1.	Sales (30,000 units x 1.15 = 34,500 units)	$172,500	$5.00
	Less variable expenses	103,500	3.00
	Contribution margin	69,000	$2.00
	Less fixed expenses	50,000	
	Net income	$ 19,000	
2.	Sales (30,000 units x 1.20 = 36,000 units)	$162,000	$4.50
	Less variable expenses	108,000	3.00
	Contribution margin	54,000	$1.50
	Less fixed expenses	50,000	
	Net income	$ 4,000	
3.	Sales (30,000 units x 0.95 = 28,500 units)	$156,750	$5.50
	Less variable expenses	85,500	3.00
	Contribution margin	71,250	$2.50
	Less fixed expenses ($50,000 + $10,000)	60,000	
	Net income	$ 11,250	
4.	Sales (30,000 units x 0.90 = 27,000 units)	$151,200	$5.60
	Less variable expenses	86,400	3.20
	Contribution margin	64,800	$2.40
	Less fixed expenses	50,000	
	Net income	$ 14,800	

Exercise 7-9 (20 minutes)

1.

	Product A		Product B		Total Company	
	Amount	**%**	**Amount**	**%**	**Amount**	**%**
Sales	$700,000	100	$300,000	100	$1,000,000	100
Less variable expenses	280,000	40	90,000	30	370,000	37
Contribution margin..........	$420,000	60	$210,000	70	630,000	63*
Less fixed expenses					598,500	
Net income					$ 31,500	

*$630,000 ÷ $1,000,000 = 63%.

2. The break-even point for the company as a whole would be:

$$\frac{\text{Fixed expenses,} \quad \$598,500}{\text{Overall CM ratio,} \quad 0.63} = \$950,000 \text{ in sales}$$

Problem 7-11 (60 minutes)

1. Sales = Variable expenses + Fixed expenses + Profits
    $40X = $25X + $300,000 + $0
    $15X = $300,000
    X = $300,000 ÷ $15
    X = 20,000 shirts

    20,000 shirts x $40 = $800,000 in sales

    Alternative solution:

    $$\frac{\text{Fixed expenses, } \$300,000}{\text{CM per unit,} \qquad \$15} = 20,000 \text{ shirts}$$

    $$\frac{\text{Fixed expenses, } \$300,000}{\text{CM ratio,} \qquad 0.375} = \$800,000 \text{ in sales}$$

2. See the graphs on the following pages.

3. The simplest approach is:

Break-even sales	20,000 shirts
Actual sales	19,000 shirts
Sales short of break-even	1,000 shirts

    1,000 shirts x $15 contribution margin per shirt = $15,000 loss

    Alternative solution:

Sales (19,000 shirts x $40)	$760,000
Less variable expenses (19,000 shirts x $25)	475,000
Contribution margin	285,000
Less fixed expenses	300,000
Net loss	$ (15,000)

Managerial Accounting

Problem 7-11 (continued)

2. Cost-volume-profit graph:

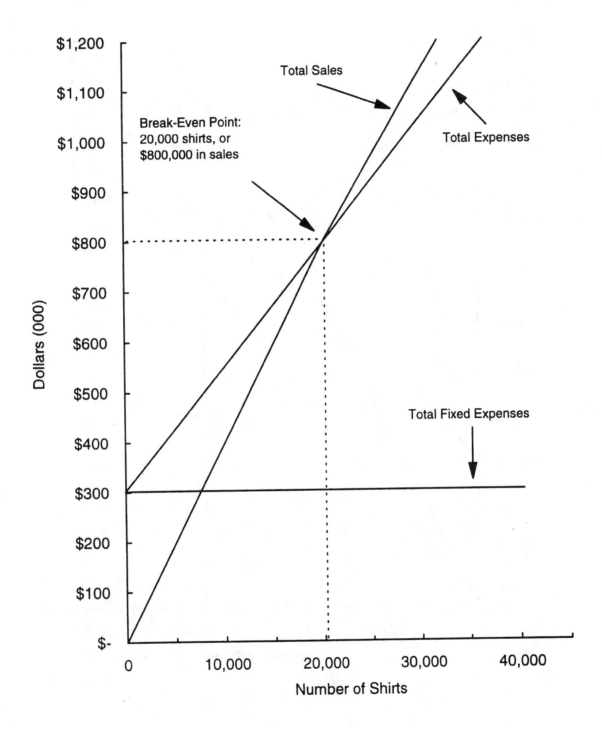

Problem 7-11 (continued)

Alternate approach to the cost-volume-profit graph:

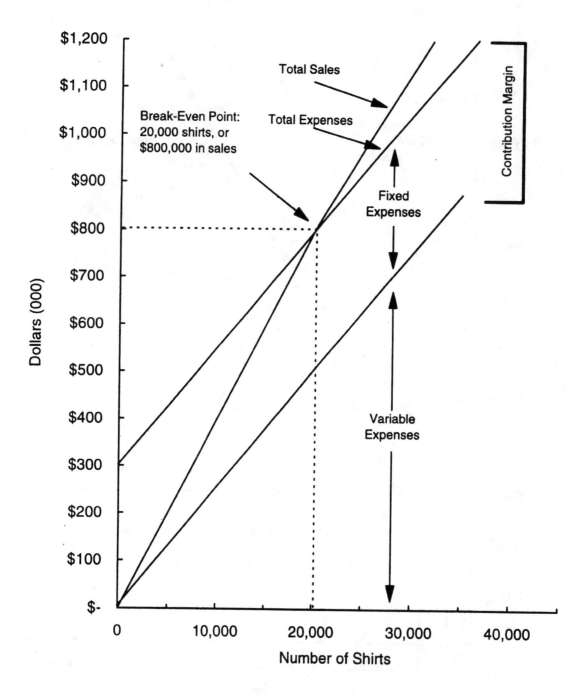

Problem 7-11 (continued)

4. The variable expenses will now be $28 ($25 + $3) per shirt, and the contribution margin will be $12 ($40 − $28) per shirt.

$$
\begin{aligned}
\text{Sales} &= \text{Variable expenses + Fixed expenses + Profits} \\
\$40X &= \$28X + \$300,000 + \$0 \\
\$12X &= \$300,000 \\
X &= \$300,000 \div \$12 \\
X &= 25,000 \text{ shirts}
\end{aligned}
$$

25,000 shirts x $40 = $1,000,000 in sales

Alternative solution:

$$
\frac{\text{Fixed expenses, } \$300,000}{\text{CM per unit, } \quad \$12} = 25,000 \text{ shirts}
$$

$$
\frac{\text{Fixed expenses, } \$300,000}{\text{CM ratio, } \quad 0.30} = \$1,000,000 \text{ in sales}
$$

5. The simplest approach is:

Actual sales	23,500 shirts
Break-even sales	20,000 shirts
Excess over break-even sales	3,500 shirts

3,500 shirts x $12*= $42,000 profit

*$15 present contribution margin − $3 commission = $12

Alternate solution:

Sales (23,500 shirts x $40)	$940,000
Less variable expenses (20,000 shirts @ $25; 3,500 shirts @ $28)	598,000
Contribution margin	342,000
Less fixed expenses	300,000
Net income	$ 42,000

Problem 7-11 (continued)

6. a. The new variable expense will be $18 per shirt (the invoice price).

   Sales = Variable expenses + Fixed expenses + Profits
   $40X = $18X + $407,000 + $0
   $22X = $407,000
   X = $407,000 ÷ $22
   X = 18,500 shirts

   18,500 shirts x $40 = $740,000 in sales

   b. Although the change will lower the break-even point from 20,000 shirts to 18,500 shirts, the company must consider whether this reduction in the break-even point is more than offset by the possible loss in sales arising from having the sales staff on a salaried basis. Under a salary arrangement, the sales staff may have far less incentive to sell than under the present commission arrangement, resulting in a loss of sales and a reduction in profits. Although it generally is desirable to lower the break-even point, management must consider the other effects of a change in the cost structure. The break-even point could be reduced dramatically by doubling the selling price per shirt, but it does not necessarily follow that this would improve the company's overall well-being.

Managerial Accounting

Problem 7-13 (35 minutes)

1.

	Product							
	A		**B**		**C**		**Total**	
Percentage of total sales	32%		40%		28%		100%	
Sales	$160,000	100%	$200,000	100%	$140,000	100%	$500,000	100%
Less variable expenses	48,000	30	160,000	80	77,000	55	285,000	57
Contribution margin	$112,000	70%	$ 40,000	20%	$ 63,000	45%	215,000	43%*
Less fixed expenses							223,600	
Net income (loss)							$ (8,600)	

*$215,000 ÷ $500,000 = 43%.

Problem 7-13 (continued)

2. Break-even sales:

$$\frac{\text{Fixed expenses, \$223,600}}{\text{CM ratio,} \quad\quad\quad .43} = \$520,000 \text{ in sales}$$

3. Memo to the president:

Although the company met its sales budget of $500,000 for the month, the mix of products sold changed substantially from that budgeted. This is the reason the budgeted net income was not met, and the reason the break-even sales were greater than budgeted. The company's sales mix was planned at 48% A, 20% B, and 32% C. The actual sales mix was 32% A, 40% B, and only 28% C.

As shown by these data, sales shifted away from Product A, which provides our greatest contribution per dollar of sales, and shifted strongly toward Product B, which provides our least contribution per dollar of sales. Although the company met its budgeted level of sales, therefore, these sales provided considerably less contribution margin than we had planned, with a resulting decrease in net income. Notice from the attached statements that the company's overall CM ratio was only 43 percent, as compared to a planned CM ratio of 52 percent. This also explains why the break-even point was higher than planned. With less average contribution margin per dollar of sales, a greater level of sales had to be achieved to provide sufficient contribution margin to cover fixed costs.

Managerial Accounting

Problem 7-15 (45 minutes)

1. a.

	Alvaro		Bazan		Total	
	Pesetas	**%**	**Pesetas**	**%**	**Pesetas**	**%**
Sales	80,000	100	48,000	100	128,000	100
Less variable expenses........	48,000	60	9,600	20	57,600	45
Contribution margin............	32,000	40	38,400	80	70,400	55
Less fixed expenses........					66,000	
Net income					4,400	

b. Break-even sales = Fixed expenses ÷ CM ratio
= 66,000 Pesetas ÷ 0.55 = 120,000 pesetas

Margin of safety in pesetas = Actual sales – Break-even sales
= 128,000 pesetas – 120,000 pesetas = 8,000 pesetas

Margin of safety percentage = Margin of safety in pesetas ÷ Actual sales
= 8,000 pesetas ÷ 128,000 pesetas = 6.25%

Problem 7-15 (continued)

2. a.

	Alvaro		Bazan		Cano		Total	
	Pesetas	%	Pesetas	%	Pesetas	%	Pesetas	%
Sales..................	80,000	100	48,000	100	32,000	100	160,000	100
Less variable								
expenses.............	48,000	60	9,600	20	24,000	75	81,600	51
Contribution margin...	32,000	40	38,400	80	8,000	25	78,400	49
Less fixed expenses.....							66,000	
Net income................							12,400	

Problem 7-15 (continued)

    b. Break-even sales = Fixed expenses ÷ CM ratio

                              = 66,000 pesetas ÷ 0.49 = 134,694 pesetas

       Margin of safety in pesetas   = Actual sales – Break-even sales

                              = 160,000 pesetas – 134,694 pesetas

                              = 25,306 pesetas

       Margin of safety percentage = Margin of safety in pesetas ÷ Actual sales

                              = 25,306 pesetas ÷ 160,000 pesetas

                              = 15.82%

3. The reason for the increase in the break-even point can be traced to the decrease in the company's average contribution margin ratio when the third product is added. Note from the income statements above that this ratio drops from 55% to 49% with the addition of the third product. This product, called Cano, has a CM ratio of only 25%, which causes the average contribution margin ratio to fall.

This problem shows the somewhat tenuous nature of break-even analysis when more than one product is involved. The manager must be very careful of his or her assumptions regarding sales mix when making decisions such as adding or deleting products.

It should be pointed out to the president that even though the break-even point is higher with the addition of the third product, the company's margin of safety is also greater. Notice that the margin of safety increases from 8,000 pesetas to 25,306 pesetas or from 6.25% to 15.82%. Thus, the addition of the new product shifts the company much further from its break-even point, even though the break-even point is higher.

Problem 7-17 (50 minutes)

1.   Sales =   Variable expenses + Fixed expenses + Profits

    $2.00X = $0.80X + $60,000 + $0

    $1.20X = $60,000

       X = $60,000 ÷ $1.20

       X =   50,000 pairs

50,000 pairs x $2 = $100,000 in sales.

Alternative solution:

$$\frac{\text{Fixed expenses}}{\text{CM per unit}} = \frac{\$60,000}{\$1.20} = 50,000 \text{ pairs}$$

$$\frac{\text{Fixed expenses}}{\text{CM ratio}} = \frac{\$60,000}{0.60} = \$100,000 \text{ in sales}$$

2. See the graphs which follow.

3.   Sales =   Variable expenses + Fixed expenses + Profits

    $2.00X = $0.80X + $60,000 + $9,000

    $1.20X = $69,000

       X = $69,000 ÷ $1.20

       X =   57,500 pairs

Alternative solution:

$$\frac{\text{Fixed expenses + Target net income}}{\text{CM per unit}} = \frac{\$60,000 + \$9,000}{\$1.20}$$

$$= 57,500 \text{ pairs}$$

                           Managerial Accounting

Problem 7-17 (continued)

4. Incremental contribution margin:

    $20,000 increased sales x 60% CM ratio............................. $12,000
    Less incremental fixed salary cost.. 8,000
    Increased net income .... $ 4,000

    Yes, the position should be converted to a full-time basis.

5. a. Degree of operating leverage:

    $$\frac{\text{Contribution margin, } \$75,000}{\text{Net income, } \qquad \$15,000} = 5$$

    b. 5 x 20% sales increase = 100% increase in net income. Thus, net
    income would double next year, going from $15,000 to $30,000.

Problem 7-17 (continued)

2. Cost-volume-profit graph:

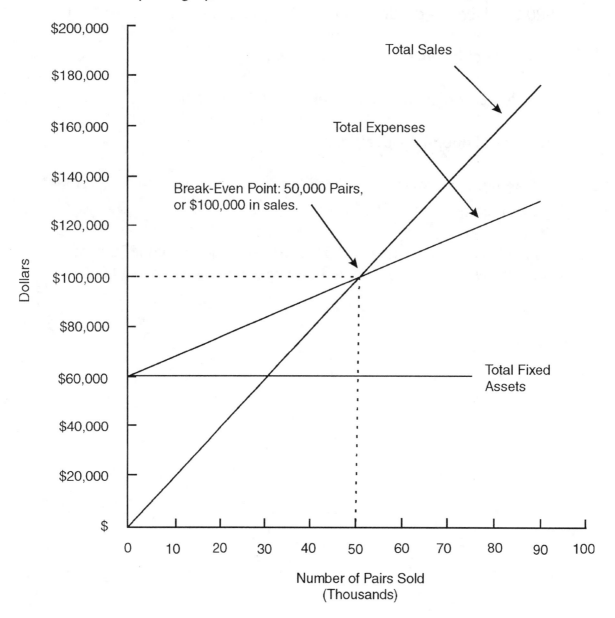

Total Sales

Total Expenses

Break-Even Point: 50,000 Pairs,
or $100,000 in sales.

Total Fixed
Assets

Dollars

$200,000
$180,000
$160,000
$140,000
$120,000
$100,000
$80,000
$60,000
$40,000
$20,000
$

0   10   20   30   40   50   60   70   80   90   100

Number of Pairs Sold
(Thousands)

Problem 7-17 (continued)

Alternate approach to the cost-volume-profit graph:

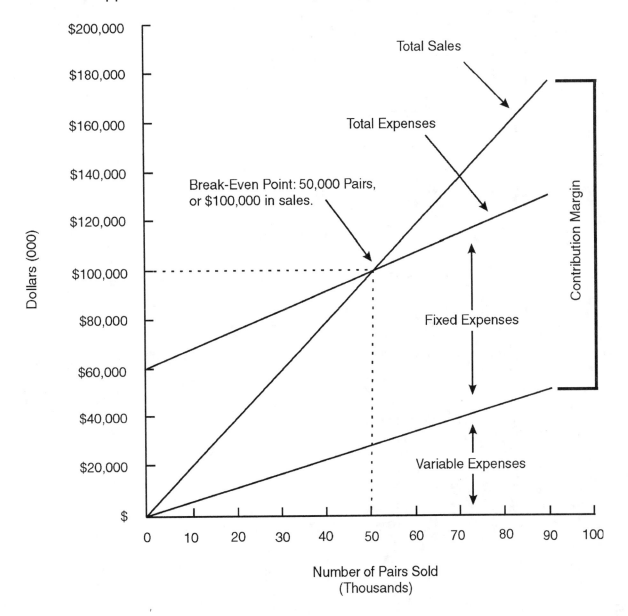

Problem 7-19 (60 minutes)

1. April's Income Statement:

	Standard Amount	%	Deluxe Amount	%	Pro Amount	%	Total Amount	%
Sales	$80,000	100	$60,000	100	$450,000	100	$590,000	100
Less variable expenses:								
Production	44,000	55	27,000	45	157,500	35	228,500	38.7
Selling	4,000	5	3,000	5	22,500	5	29,500	5.0
Total	48,000	60	30,000	50	180,000	40	258,000	43.7
Contribution margin	$32,000	40	$30,000	50	$270,000	60	332,000	56.3
Less fixed expenses:								
Production							120,000	
Advertising							100,000	
Administrative							50,000	
Total							270,000	
Net income							$ 62,000	

Managerial Accounting

Problem 7-19 (continued)

May's Income Statement:

	Standard		Deluxe		Pro		Total	
	Amount	%	Amount	%	Amount	%	Amount	%
Sales	$320,000	100	$60,000	100	$270,000	100	$650,000	100
Less variable expenses:								
Production	176,000	55	27,000	45	94,500	35	297,500	45.8
Selling	16,000	5	3,000	5	13,500	5	32,500	5.0
Total	192,000	60	30,000	50	108,000	40	330,000	50.8
Contribution margin	$128,000	40	$30,000	50	$162,000	60	320,000	49.2
Less fixed expenses:								
Production							120,000	
Advertising							100,000	
Administrative							50,000	
Total							270,000	
Net income							$ 50,000	

Problem 7-19 (continued)

2. The sales mix has shifted over the last month from a greater concentration of Pro rackets to a greater concentration of Standard rackets. This shift has caused a decrease in the company's overall CM ratio from 56.3% in April to only 49.2% in May. For this reason, even though total sales (both in units and in dollars) is greater, net income is lower than last month in the division.

3. $\dfrac{\text{Fixed expenses, } \$270,000}{\text{CM ratio, } \quad 0.563} = \$479,574$ (rounded)

4. May's break-even point has gone up. The reason is that the division's overall CM ratio has declined for May as stated in (2) above. Unchanged fixed expenses divided by a lower overall CM ratio would yield a higher break-even point in sales dollars.

5.

	Standard	Pro
Increase in sales	$20,000	$20,000
Multiply by the CM ratio................................	x 40%	x 60%
Increase in net income*................................	$ 8,000	$12,000

*Assuming that fixed costs do not change.

Managerial Accounting

Problem 7-21 (30 minutes)

1. The contribution margin per unit on the first 30,000 units is:

	Per Unit
Sales price	$2.50
Less variable expenses	1.60
Contribution margin	$0.90

The contribution margin per unit on anything over 30,000 units is:

	Per Unit
Sales price	$2.50
Less variable expenses	1.75
Contribution margin	$0.75

Thus, for the first 30,000 units sold, the total amount of contribution margin generated would be:

30,000 units x $0.90 = $27,000

Since the fixed costs on the first 30,000 units total $40,000, the $27,000 contribution margin above is not enough to permit the company to break even. Therefore, in order to break even, more than 30,000 units will have to be sold. The fixed costs that will have to be covered by the additional sales are:

Fixed costs on the first 30,000 units	$40,000
Less contribution margin from the first 30,000 units	27,000
Remaining unrecovered fixed costs	13,000
Add monthly rental cost of the additional space needed to produce more than 30,000 units	2,000
Total fixed costs to be covered by remaining sales	$15,000

Problem 7-21 (continued)

The additional sales of units required to cover these fixed costs would be:

$$\frac{\text{Total remaining fixed costs,}}{\text{Unit contribution margin on added units,}} \quad \frac{\$15,000}{\$0.75} = 20,000 \text{ units}$$

Therefore, a total of 50,000 units (30,000 + 20,000) must be sold in order for the company to break even. This number of units would equal total sales of:

50,000 units x $2.50 = $125,000 in total sales.

2. $$\frac{\text{Desired profit,}}{\text{Unit contribution margin,}} \quad \frac{\$9,000}{\$0.75} = 12,000 \text{ units}$$

Thus, the company must sell 12,000 units above the break-even point in order to earn a profit of $9,000 each month. These units, added to the 50,000 units required to break even, would equal total sales of 62,000 units each month to reach the target profit figure.

3. If a bonus of $0.15 per unit is paid for each unit sold in excess of the break-even point, then the contribution margin on these units would drop from $0.75 to only $0.60 per unit.

The desired monthly profit would be:,

25% x ($40,000 + $2,000) = $10,500

Thus,

$$\frac{\text{Desired profit,}}{\text{Unit contribution margin,}} \quad \frac{\$10,500}{\$0.60} = 17,500 \text{ units}$$

Therefore, the company must sell 17,500 units above the break-even point in order to earn a profit of $10,500 each month. These units, added to the 50,000 units required to break even, would equal total sales of 67,500 units each month.

Managerial Accounting

Problem 7-23 (90 minutes)

1. a. Before the income statement can be completed, we need to develop the company's revenues and expenses for the month.

   The first step is to compute the sales for the month in both units and dollars. Sales in units would be:

   90,000 units (August sales) ÷ 1.20 = 75,000 units sold in July.

   To determine the sales in dollars, we must integrate the break-even point, the margin of safety in dollars, and the margin of safety percentage. The computations are:

   Total sales – Break-even sales = Margin of safety in dollars

   Total sales – $1,012,500 = Margin of safety in dollars

   $$\frac{\text{Margin of safety in dollars}}{\text{Total sales}} = \text{Margin of safety percentage (25\%)}$$

   If the margin of safety in dollars is 25% of total sales, then the break-even point in dollars must be 75% of total sales. Therefore, total sales would be:

   $$\frac{\$1,012,500}{\text{Total sales}} = 75\%$$

   Total sales = $1,012,500 ÷ 75%

   Total sales = $1,350,000

   The selling price per unit would be:

   $1,350,000 total sales ÷ 75,000 units = $18 per unit.

   The second step is to determine the total contribution margin for the month of June. This can be done by working through the operating leverage concept. Note that a 20% increase in sales has resulted in an 80% increase in net income between July and August:

   $$\frac{\text{August increased net income, (\$243,000} - \$135,000) = \$108,000}{\text{July net income,} \qquad\qquad\qquad \$135,000} = 80\%$$

Problem 7-23 (continued)

Since the net income for August increased by 80% when sales increased by 20%, the degree of operating leverage for July must be 4. Therefore, total contribution margin for July must have been:

4 x $135,000 = $540,000.

With this figure, July's income statement can be completed by simply inserting known data and computing unknown data:

PUTREX COMPANY
Actual Income Statement
For the Month Ended July 31

	Total	Per Unit	Percent
Sales (75,000 units)	$1,350,000	$18.00	100
Less variable expenses	810,000*	10.80*	60*
Contribution margin	540,000	$ 7.20	40*
Less fixed expenses	405,000*		
Net income	$ 135,000		

*Computed by working from known data.

b. The break-even point:

$$\frac{\text{Fixed expenses,} \quad \$405,000}{\text{Unit contribution margin, \$7.20}} = 56,250 \text{ units}$$

In dollars: 56,250 units x $18 = $1,012,500

c. The margin of safety:

Total sales – Break-even sales = Margin of safety in dollars

$1,350,000 – $1,012,500 = $337,500

$$\frac{\text{Margin of safety in dollars,} \quad \$337,500}{\text{Total sales,} \quad \$1,350,000} = 25\%$$

Managerial Accounting

Problem 7-23 (continued)

 d. The degree of operating leverage:

$$\frac{\text{Contribution margin, } \$540,000}{\text{Net income,} \quad\quad \$135,000} = 4$$

2. a. August's income statement can be completed using data given in the problem and data derived for July's income statement above:

PUTREX COMPANY
Projected Income Statement
For the Month Ended August 31

	Total	Per Unit	Percent
Sales (90,000 units)	$1,620,000	$18.00	100
Less variable expenses...................	972,000	10.80	60
Contribution margin.........................	648,000	$ 7.20	40
Less fixed expenses........................	405,000		
Net income	$ 243,000		

 b. The margin of safety:

  Total sales – Break-even sales = Margin of safety in dollars
   $1,620,000 – $1,012,500 = $607,500

$$\frac{\text{Margin of safety in dollars, } \$607,500}{\text{Total sales,} \quad\quad \$1,620,000} = 37.5\%$$

 The degree of operating leverage:

$$\frac{\text{Contribution margin, } \quad \$648,000}{\text{Net income,} \quad\quad\quad \$243,000} = 2.7 \text{ (rounded)}$$

The margin of safety has gone up since the company's sales will be greater in August than they were in July, thus moving the company farther away from its break-even point.

Problem 7-23 (continued)

The degree of operating leverage operates in the opposite manner from the margin of safety. As a company moves farther away from its break-even point, the degree of operating leverage decreases. The reason it decreases is that both contribution margin and net income are increasing at the same *dollar* rate as additional units are sold, and, mathematically, dividing one by the other will yield a progressively smaller figure. In a conceptual sense, we are saying that as sales increase, the sale of an additional unit will have a progressively smaller percentage impact on total net income.

3. The new variable expense will total $11.70 per unit ($10.80 + $0.90), and the new contribution margin ratio will be:

Sales	$18.00	100%
Less variable expenses	11.70	65
Contribution margin	$ 6.30	35%

The target profit per unit will be:

15% x $18 = $2.70.

Therefore,

$$
\begin{aligned}
\text{Sales} &= \text{Variable expenses} + \text{Fixed expenses} + \text{Profits} \\
\$18.00X &= \$11.70X + \$405,000 + \$2.70X \\
\$ 3.60X &= \$405,000 \\
X &= \$405,000 \div \$3.60 \\
X &= 112,500 \text{ units}
\end{aligned}
$$

Alternative solution:

$$
\begin{aligned}
\text{Sales} &= \text{Variable expenses} + \text{Fixed expenses} + \text{Profits} \\
X &= \$0.65X + \$405,000 + \$0.15X \\
\$0.20X &= \$405,000 \\
X &= \$405,000 \div \$0.20 \\
X &= \$2,025,000; \text{ or, at } \$18 \text{ per unit, } 112,500 \text{ units}
\end{aligned}
$$

Managerial Accounting

Problem 7-25 (20 minutes)

1. Construct decision tree:

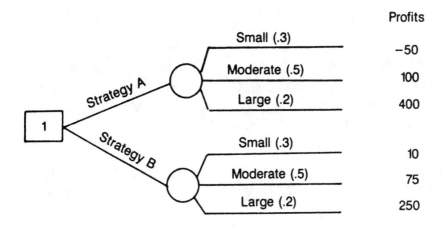

Profits

Small (.3)   −50

Moderate (.5)   100

Large (.2)   400

Small (.3)   10

Moderate (.5)   75

Large (.2)   250

2. Calculate expected profits.

Strategy A:
.3(−50) + .5(100) + .2(400)
−15 + 50 + 80 = 115

Strategy B:
.3(10) + .5(75) + .2(250)
3 + 37.5 + 50 = 90.5

The marketing manager should choose Strategy A.

(CGA-Canada Solution, adapted)

Problem 7-27 (20 minutes)

IF Win

Proposals	Costs	Revenue	Net	Tax 40%	After Tax
A	$60,000	$200,000	$140,000	$56,000	$ 84,000
B	20,000	200,000	180,000	72,000	108,000

IF Lose

A	60,000	-0-	(60,000)	24,000	(36,000)
B	20,000	-0-	(20,000)	8,000	(12,000)

Decision Tree

Win	$ 84,000	×	.50	$ 42,000
Lose	(36,000)	×	.50	(18,000)
				$ 24,000
Win	108,000	×	.30	$ 32,400
Lose	(12,000)	×	.70	(8,400)
				$ 24,000

Decision analysis:

The firm may be indifferent between either alternative. However proposal B may have more risk than proposal A. The actual recommendation will depend on the risk preferences of the decision maker.

Managerial Accounting

Variable Costing: A Tool for Management

8

Exercise 8-1 (20 minutes)

1. Under variable costing, only the variable manufacturing costs are included in product costs.

Direct materials	$60
Direct labour	30
Variable manufacturing overhead	10
Unit product cost	$100

Note that selling and administrative expenses are not treated as product costs; that is, they are not included in the costs that are inventoried. These expenses are always treated as period costs and are charged against the current period's revenue.

2. The variable costing income statement appears below:

Sales		$1,800,000
Less variable expenses:		
Variable cost of goods sold:		
Beginning inventory	$ -0-	
Variable manufacturing costs		
(10,000 units x $100)	1,000,000	
Goods available for sale	1,000,000	
Less ending inventory		
(1,000 units x $100)	100,000	
Variable cost of goods sold*	900,000	
Variable selling and administrative		
(9,000 units x $20)	180,000	1,080,000
Contribution margin		720,000
Less fixed expenses:		
Fixed manufacturing overhead	300,000	
Fixed selling and administrative	450,000	750,000
Net loss		$ (30,000)

*The variable cost of goods sold could be computed more simply as:
9,000 units sold x $100 = $900,000.

Exercise 8-1 (continued)

3. The break-even point in units sold can be computed using the contribution margin per unit as follows:

Selling price per unit	$200
Variable cost per unit	120
Contribution margin per unit	$ 80

$$\text{Break-even unit sales} = \frac{\text{Fixed costs}}{\text{Unit contribution margin}}$$

$$= \frac{\$750,000}{\$80 \text{ / unit}}$$

$$= 9,375 \text{ units}$$

Managerial Accounting

Exercise 8-3 (10 minutes)

1. Under absorption costing, all manufacturing costs (variable and fixed) are included in product costs.

Direct materials	R120
Direct labour..	140
Variable manufacturing overhead	50
Fixed manufacturing overhead	
($600,000 ÷ 10,000 units)..	<u>60</u>
Unit product cost..	<u>R370</u>

2. Under variable costing, only the variable manufacturing costs are included in product costs.

Direct materials	R120
Direct labour..	140
Variable manufacturing overhead	<u>50</u>
Unit product cost..	<u>R310</u>

    Note that selling and administrative expenses are not treated as product costs under either absorption or variable costing; that is, they are not included in the costs that are inventoried. These expenses are always treated as period costs and are charged against the current period's revenue.

Exercise 8-5 (10 minutes)

1. The company is using variable costing. The computations are:

	Variable Costing	Absorption Costing
Direct materials..	$10	$10
Direct labour..	5	5
Variable manufacturing overhead..	2	2
Fixed manufacturing overhead ($90,000/30,000)	—	3
Unit product cost	$17	$20
Total cost, 5,000 units................................	$85,000	$100,000

2. a. Yes, the $85,000 figure is the correct figure to use, because it is the variable costing inventory level. It is correct if the company has used variable costing for external reporting purposes in the past and wishes to remain consistent.

   b. The finished goods inventory account should be stated at $100,000 if management wishes to reflect the absorption cost to manufacture the 5,000 unsold units. The account should be increased by $15,000 for external reporting purposes. This $15,000 consists of the amount of fixed manufacturing overhead cost which is allocable to the 5,000 unsold units under absorption costing:

   5,000 units x $3 fixed manufacturing overhead cost per unit = $15,000

Exercise 8-7 (25 minutes)

1. a. The unit product cost under absorption costing would be:

Direct materials...	$18
Direct labour..	7
Variable manufacturing overhead......................................	2
Total variable manufacturing costs.................................	27
Fixed manufacturing overhead	
($160,000 ÷ 20,000 units)...	8
Unit product cost...	$35

b. The absorption costing income statement:

Sales (16,000 units x $50)		$800,000
Less cost of goods sold:		
Beginning inventory	$ -0-	
Cost of goods manufactured		
(20,000 units x $35).................................	700,000	
Goods available for sale	700,000	
Less ending inventory		
(4,000 units x $35)....................................	140,000	560,000
Gross margin...		240,000
Less selling and administrative expenses.......		190,000*
Net income		$ 50,000

*(16,000 units x $5 = $80,000) + $110,000 = $190,000.

Exercise 8-7 (continued)

2. a. The unit product cost under variable costing would be:

Direct materials..	$18
Direct labour..	7
Variable manufacturing overhead......................................	2
Unit product cost...	$27

b. The variable costing income statement:

Sales (16,000 units x $50)		$800,000
Less variable expenses:		
Variable cost of goods sold:		
Beginning inventory............................	$ -0-	
Variable manufacturing costs		
(20,000 units x $27)	540,000	
Goods available for sale.....................	540,000	
Less ending inventory		
(4,000 units x $27)	108,000	
Variable cost of goods sold	432,000*	
Variable selling expense		
(16,000 units x $5)	80,000	512,000
Contribution margin....................................		288,000
Less fixed expenses:		
Manufacturing overhead.........................	160,000	
Selling and administrative......................	110,000	270,000
Net income...		$ 18,000

*The variable cost of goods sold could be computed more
simply as: 16,000 units x $27 = $432,000.

Problem 8-9 (40 minutes)

1. a. The unit product cost under absorption costing:

Direct materials $15
Direct labour... 7
Variable manufacturing overhead 2
Fixed manufacturing overhead
  (640,000 ÷ 40,000 units) 16
  Unit product cost.. $40

b. The absorption costing income statement follows:

Sales (35,000 units x $60)		$2,100,000
Less cost of goods sold:		
Beginning inventory	$ -0-	
Cost of goods manufactured		
(40,000 units x $40).......................	1,600,000	
Goods available for sale	1,600,000	
Less ending inventory		
(5,000 units x $40).........................	200,000	1,400,000
Gross margin...		700,000
Less selling and administrative		
expenses...		630,000*
Net income		$ 70,000

*(35,000 units x $2) + $560,000 = $630,000.

2. a. The unit product cost under variable costing:

Direct materials $15
Direct labour.. 7
Variable manufacturing overhead 2
  Unit product cost.. $24

Problem 8-9 (continued)

b. The variable costing income statement follows:

Sales (35,000 units x $60)		$2,100,000
Less variable expenses:		
Variable cost of goods sold:		
Beginning inventory	$ -0-	
Variable manufacturing costs		
(40,000 units x $24)	960,000	
Goods available for sale	960,000	
Less ending inventory		
(5,000 units x $24)	120,000	
Variable cost of goods sold	840,000	
Variable selling expense		
(35,000 units x $2)	70,000	910,000
Contribution margin		1,190,000
Less fixed expenses:		
Manufacturing overhead	640,000	
Selling and administrative expense ...	560,000	
		1,200,000
Net loss		$ (10,000)

3. The difference in the ending inventory relates to a difference in the handling of fixed manufacturing overhead costs. Under variable costing, these costs have been expensed in full as period costs. Under absorption costing, these costs have been added to units of product at the rate of $16 per unit ($640,000 ÷ 40,000 units produced = $16 per unit). Thus, under absorption costing a portion of the $640,000 fixed manufacturing overhead cost of the month has been added to the inventory account rather than charged against revenue on the income statement:

Added to the ending inventory (5,000 units x $16)	$ 80,000
Charged against revenue as part of cost of goods	
sold (35,000 units x $16)	560,000
Total fixed manufacturing overhead cost for	
the month	$640,000

Managerial Accounting

Problem 8-9 (continued)

Since $80,000 of fixed manufacturing overhead cost has been deferred in inventory under absorption costing, the net income reported under that costing method is $80,000 higher than the net income under variable costing, as shown in parts (1) and (2) above.

Problem 8-11 (60 minutes)

1. a.

Direct materials...	$1.00
Direct labour	0.80
Variable manufacturing overhead..............................	0.20
Fixed manufacturing overhead	
($75,000/50,000 units)	1.50
Unit product cost......................................	$3.50

b.

Sales (40,000 units)..		$200,000
Less cost of goods sold:		
Beginning inventory......................................	$ -0-	
Add cost of goods manufactured		
(50,000 units x $3.50)	175,000	
Goods available for sale..............................	175,000	
Less ending inventory		
(10,000 units x $3.50)	35,000	140,000
Gross margin..		60,000
Less selling and administrative expenses		50,000*
Net income		$ 10,000

*$30,000 variable plus $20,000 fixed = $50,000.

c.

Variable costing net loss..	$ (5,000)
Add: Fixed manufacturing overhead cost	
deferred in inventory under absorption	
costing (10,000 units x $1.50)	15,000
Absorption costing net income	$ 10,000

Managerial Accounting

Problem 8-11 (continued)

2. Under absorption costing, the company did earn a profit for the month. However, before the question can really be answered, one must first define what is meant by a "profit." The central issue here relates to *timing* of the release of fixed manufacturing overhead costs to expense. Advocates of variable costing would argue that all such costs should be released to expense immediately, and that no profit is earned unless the revenues of a period are sufficient to cover the fixed manufacturing overhead costs in full. From this point of view, then, no profit was earned during the month, because the fixed costs were not fully covered. Advocates of absorption costing would argue, however, that fixed manufacturing overhead costs attach to units of product as they are produced, and that such costs do not become expense until the units are sold. Therefore, if the selling price of a unit is greater than the unit cost (including a proportionate amount of fixed manufacturing overhead), then a profit is earned even if some units produced go unsold and carry some fixed manufacturing overhead with them to the following period.

The purpose of the question is to bring these issues to the attention of the student: no categorical answer as to whether the company earned a profit during the month is possible. It simply depends on the point of view one wishes to take.

Problem 8-11 (continued)

3. a.
Sales (60,000 units x $5).................................		$300,000
Less variable expenses:		
Variable cost of goods sold @ $2	$120,000	
Selling and administrative expenses		
@ $0.75	45,000	165,000
Contribution margin		135,000
Less fixed expense:		
Fixed manufacturing overhead......................	75,000	
Selling and administrative expense...............	20,000	95,000
Net income		$ 40,000

  b. The absorption costing unit product cost will remain at $3.50, the same as in part (1).

Sales (60,000 units x $5).............................		$300,000
Less cost of goods sold:		
Beginning inventory		
(10,000 units x $3.50)	$ 35,000	
Add cost of goods manufactured		
(50,000 units x $3.50)	175,000	
Goods available for sale...........................	210,000	
Less ending inventory	-0-	210,000
Gross margin		90,000
Less selling and administrative expenses		65,000*
Net income		$ 25,000

*$45,000 variable plus $20,000 fixed = $65,000.

  c.
Variable costing net income	$ 40,000
Deduct: fixed manufacturing overhead	
cost released from inventory under	
absorption costing (10,000 units	
x $1.50)	15,000
Absorption costing net income	$ 25,000

                       Managerial Accounting

Problem 8-13 (60 minutes)

1.

	19X1	**19x2**	**19x3**
Sales...	$1,000,000	$ 800,000	$1,000,000
Less variable expenses:			
Variable cost of goods			
sold @ $4.............................	200,000	160,000	200,000
Selling and			
administrative @ $2..............	100,000	80,000	100,000
Total variable expenses........	300,000	240,000	300,000
Contribution margin	700,000	560,000	700,000
Less fixed expenses:			
Manufacturing overhead	600,000	600,000	600,000
Selling and administrative	70,000	70,000	70,000
Total fixed expenses.............	670,000	670,000	670,000
Net income (loss)........................	$ 30,000	$(110,000)	$ 30,000

Problem 8-13 (continued)

2. a.

	19X1	**19x2**	**19x3**
Variable manufacturing cost......................	$ 4	$ 4	$ 4
Fixed manufacturing cost:			
$600,000 ÷ 50,000 units.........................	12		
$600,000 ÷ 60,000 units.........................		10	
$600,000 ÷ 40,000 units.........................	—	—	15
Total cost per unit.....................................	$16	$14	$19

b. Variable costing net income
   (loss) .... $30,000 $(110,000) $ 30,000
   Add (Deduct): Fixed
   manufacturing overhead cost
   deferred in inventory from
   19x2 to 19x3 under
   absorption costing (20,000
   units x $10).............................   200,000   (200,000)
   Add: Fixed manufacturing
   overhead cost deferred in
   inventory from 19x3 to the
   future under absorption
   costing (10,000 units x $15)....   _____   _____   150,000
   Absorption costing net income
   (loss) .... $30,000 $ 90,000 $ (20,000)

3. Production went up sharply in 19x2 thereby reducing the unit product cost, as shown in (2a). This reduction in cost, combined with the large amount of fixed manufacturing overhead cost deferred in inventory for the year, more than offset the loss of revenue. The net result is that the company's net income rose even though sales were down.

Problem 8-13 (continued)

4. The fixed manufacturing overhead cost deferred in inventory from 19x2 was charged against 19x3 operations, as shown in the reconciliation in (2b). This added charge against 19x3 operations was offset somewhat by the fact that part of 19x3's fixed manufacturing overhead costs were deferred in inventory to future years [again see (2b)]. Overall, the added costs charged against 19x3 were greater than the costs deferred to future years, so the company reported less income for the year even though the same number of units was sold as in 19x1.

5. a.   Several things would have been different if the company had been using JIT inventory methods. First, in each year production would have been geared to sales so that little or no inventory of finished goods would have been built up in either 19x2 or 19x3. Second, unit product costs probably would have been the same in all three years, because these costs would have been established on the basis of *expected* sales (50,000 units) for each year. Third, because only 40,000 units were sold in 19x2, the company would have produced only that number of units and therefore would have had some underapplied overhead cost for the year. (See the discussion on underapplied overhead in the following paragraph.)

   b. If JIT had been in use, the net income under absorption costing would have been the same as under variable costing in all three years. The reason is that with production geared to sales, there would have been no ending inventory on hand, and therefore there would have been no fixed manufacturing overhead costs deferred in inventory to other years. Assuming that the company *expected* to sell 50,000 units in each year and that unit product costs were set on the basis of that level of expected activity, the income statements under absorption costing would have appeared as follows:

Problem 8-13 (continued)

	19x1	19x2	19x3
Sales	$1,000,000	$ 800,000	$1,000,000
Less cost of goods sold:			
Cost of goods manufactured (@ $16)	800,000	640,000*	800,000
Add underapplied overhead		120,000**	
Cost of goods sold	800,000	760,000	800,000
Gross margin	200,000	40,000	200,000
Selling and administrative expenses	170,000	150,000	170,000
Net income (loss)	$ 30,000	$(110,000)	$ 30,000

*40,000 units x $16 = $640,000.

**10,000 units *not* produced x $12 fixed overhead cost per unit = $120,000 fixed overhead cost not applied to products.

Managerial Accounting

Profit Planning

9

Exercise 9-1 (20 minutes)

1.

	July	August	September	Total
May sales:				
$430,000 x 10% ...	$ 43,000			$ 43,000
June sales:				
$540,000 x 70%,				
10%.................	378,000	$ 54,000		432,000
July sales:				
$600,000 x 20%,				
70%, 10%............	120,000	420,000	$ 60,000	600,000
August sales:				
$900,000 x 20%,				
70%..................		180,000	630,000	810,000
September sales:				
$500,000 x 20% ...			100,000	100,000
Total cash				
collections	$541,000	$654,000	$790,000	$1,985,000

Notice that even though sales peak in August, cash collections peak in September. This is due to the fact that the bulk of the company's customers pay in the month following sale. The lag in collections which this creates is even more pronounced in some companies. Indeed, it is not unusual for a company to have the least cash available in the months when sales are greatest.

2. Accounts receivable at September 30:

From August sales: $900,000 x 10%	$ 90,000
From September sales: $500,000 x (70% + 10%)	400,000
Total accounts receivable	$490,000

Exercise 9-3 (15 minutes)

		Quarter—19x5			19x6
	First	Second	Third	Fourth	First
Production in calculators..........	60,000	90,000	150,000	100,000	80,000
Number of chips per calculator	× 3	× 3	× 3	× 3	× 3
Total production needs—chips......	180,000	270,000	450,000	300,000	240,000

		19x5			
	First	Second	Third	Fourth	Year
Production needs—chips	180,000	270,000	450,000	300,000	1,200,000
Add: Desired ending inventory—chips.....	54,000	90,000	60,000	48,000	48,000
Total needs—chips	234,000	360,000	510,000	348,000	1,248,000
Deduct: Beginning inventory—chips......	36,000	54,000	90,000	60,000	36,000
Required purchases—chips.........	198,000	306,000	420,000	288,000	1,212,000
Cost of purchases at $2 per chip	$396,000	$612,000	$840,000	$576,000	$2,424,000

Managerial Accounting

Exercise 9-5 (20 minutes)

	Quarter (000 omitted)				
	1	2	3	4	Year
Cash balance, beginning............	$ 9*	$ 5	$ 5	$ 5	$ 9
Add collections from customers .	76	90	125*	100	391*
Total cash available	85*	95	130	105	400
Less disbursements:					
Purchase of inventory	40*	58*	36	32*	166
Operating expenses................	36	42*	54*	48	180*
Equipment purchases	10*	8*	8*	10	36*
Dividends	2*	2*	2*	2*	8
Total disbursements	88	110*	100	92	390
Excess (deficiency) of cash available over disbursements .	(3)*	(15)	30*	13	10
Financing:					
Borrowing...............................	8	20*	—	—	28
Repayments (including interest)	—	—	(25)	(7)*	(32)
Total financing	8	20	(25)	(7)	(4)
Cash balance, ending	$ 5	$ 5	$ 5	$ 6	$ 6

*Given.

Exercise 9-7 (15 minutes)

1. November sales: $40,000 ÷ 10% = $400,000.
    December sales: $180,000 ÷ 40% = $450,000.

2.

	January	February	March	Total
November sales:				
8% x $400,000.....	$ 32,000			$ 32,000
December sales:				
30% x $450,000...	135,000			135,000
8% x $450,000.....		$ 36,000		36,000
January sales:				
60% x $500,000 x				
98%..................	294,000			294,000
30% x $500,000...		150,000		150,000
8% x $500,000.....			$ 40,000	40,000
February sales:				
60% x $700,000 x				
98%..................		411,600		411,600
30% x $700,000...			210,000	210,000
March sales:				
60% x $1,800,000				
x 98%			1,058,400	1,058,400
Total collections......	$461,000	$597,600	$1,308,400	$2,367,000

Managerial Accounting

Problem 9-9 (40 minutes)

1. Production budget:

	July	August	September	October
Budgeted sales (units).......	40,000	50,000	70,000	35,000
Add: Desired ending inventory.........................	20,000	26,000	15,500	11,000
Total needs........................	60,000	76,000	85,500	46,000
Less: Beginning inventory .	17,000	20,000	26,000	15,500
Units to be produced	43,000	56,000	59,500	30,500

2. During July and August the company is building inventories in anticipation of peak sales in September. Therefore, production exceeds sales during these months. In September and October inventories are being reduced in anticipation of a decrease in sales during the last months of the year. Therefore, production is less than sales during these months to cut back on inventory levels.

3. Raw materials purchases budget:

	July	August	September	Third Quarter
Budgeted production (units)..	43,000	56,000	59,500	158,500
Material A production needs per unit....................	x 3 kg	x 3 kg	x 3 kg	x 3 kg
Production needs (kg)...........	129,000	168,000	178,500	475,500
Add: Desired ending inventory (kg).....................	84,000	89,250	45,750*	45,750
Total Material A needs..........	213,000	257,250	224,250	521,250
Less: Beginning inventory (kg)......................................	64,500	84,000	89,250	64,500
Material A purchases (kgs) ...	148,500	173,250	135,000	456,750

*30,500 units (October production) x 3 kg = 91,500 kg; 91,500 kg x 0.5 = 45,750 kg.

As shown in part (1), production is greatest in September; however, as shown in the raw material purchases budget, purchases of materials is greatest a month earlier—in August. The reason for the large purchases of materials in August is that the materials must be on hand to support the heavy production scheduled for September.

Problem 9-11 (60 minutes)

1. Schedule of cash receipts:

Cash sales—June	$ 60,000
Collections on accounts receivable:	
May 31 balance..	72,000
June (50% x $190,000).....................................	95,000
Total cash receipts	$227,000

Schedule of cash payments for purchases:

May 31 accounts payable balance.........................	$ 90,000
June purchases (40% x $200,000)	80,000
Total cash payments..	$170,000

PHOTOTEC, INC.
Cash Budget
For the Month of June

Cash balance, beginning..	$ 8,000
Add receipts from customers (above)	227,000
Total cash available	235,000
Less disbursements:	
Purchase of inventory (above)...........................	170,000
Operating expenses..	51,000
Purchases of equipment	9,000
Total cash disbursements.............................	230,000
Excess of receipts over disbursements...................	5,000
Financing:	
Borrowing—note	18,000
Repayments—note	(15,000)
Interest...	(500)
Total financing	2,500
Cash balance, ending	$ 7,500

Problem 9-11 (continued)

2.

PHOTOTEC, INC.
Budgeted Income Statement
For the Month of June

Sales		$250,000
Cost of goods sold:		
Beginning inventory	$ 30,000	
Add purchases	200,000	
Goods available for sale	230,000	
Ending inventory	40,000	
Cost of goods sold		190,000
Gross margin		60,000
Operating expenses ($51,000 + $2,000)		53,000
Net operating income		7,000
Interest expense		500
Net income		$ 6,500

3.

PHOTOTEC, INC.
Budgeted Balance Sheet
June 30

Assets

Cash	$ 7,500
Accounts receivable (50% x $190,000)	95,000
Inventory	40,000
Plant and equipment, net of depreciation ($500,000 + $9,000 − $2,000)	507,000
Total assets	$649,500

Liabilities and Shareholders' Equity

Accounts payable (60% x $200,000)	$120,000
Note payable	18,000
Capital stock	420,000
Retained earnings ($85,000 + $6,500)	91,500
Total liabilities and Shareholders' equity	$649,500

Problem 9-13 (15 minutes)

1. Cadence and Cross used a top-down approach to prepare the budget. That is, they prepared the budget with little or no input from the individuals who would have to implement the budget. In contrast, the recommended approach is a participative budget in which the individuals who have cost control responsibility initiate and fully participate in the budgeting process. There are a number of advantages of participatory budgets including: 1) those who are closest to the action are likely to have better information; 2) managers are likely to be more committed to and understand a budget they participated in preparing than a budget that is imposed from above; and 3) participative budgets help to foster a sense that everyone's input is valued.

2. While Cadence and Cross are undoubtedly pleased with their work, the dissatisfaction expressed by some employees with the budget process is a sign that there may be storm clouds ahead. If employees feel that the budget is unrealistic, the fact that it was imposed can lead to resentment, anger, and a sense of helplessness. Employees may, as a consequence, spend their time and energy complaining about the budget rather than creatively solving problems. And if the budget is indeed unrealistic and managers are held responsible for meeting the budget, unproductive finger-pointing is likely to result as reality fails to live up to expectations.

Managerial Accounting

Problem 9-15 (60 minutes)

1. The sales budget for the third quarter:

	July	Aug.	Sept.	Quarter
Expected sales in units ..	6,000	7,000	5,000	18,000
Selling price per unit.......	x $50	x $50	x $50	x $50
Budgeted sales	$300,000	$350,000	$250,000	$900,000

The schedule of expected cash collections from sales:

	July	Aug.	Sept.	Quarter
Accounts receivable, beginning balance.......	$130,000			$130,000
July sales: $300,000 x 40%, 50%	120,000	$150,000		270,000
August sales: $350,000 x 40%, 50%.................		140,000	$175,000	315,000
September sales: $250,000 x 40%..........			100,000	100,000
Total cash collections.....	$250,000	$290,000	$275,000	$815,000

2. The production budget for July through October:

	July	Aug.	Sept.	Oct.
Budgeted sales in units	6,000	7,000	5,000	4,000
Add: Desired ending inventory	700	500	400	300
Total needs	6,700	7,500	5,400	4,300
Deduct: Beginning inventory	600	700	500	400
Units to be produced	6,100	6,800	4,900	3,900

Problem 9-15 (continued)

3. The materials purchases budget for the third quarter:

	July	Aug.	Sept.	Quarter
Units to be produced (above)	6,100	6,800	4,900	17,800
Raw materials needs per unit	x 2 kg	x 2 kg	x 2 kg	x 2 kg
Production needs (kg)	12,200	13,600	9,800	35,600
Add: Desired ending inventory	2,720	1,960	1,560*	1,560*
Total needs	14,920	15,560	11,360	37,160
Deduct: Beginning inventory	2,440	2,720	1,960	2,440
Required purchases	12,480	12,840	9,400	34,720
Cost of purchases at $2.50 per kg	$31,200	$32,100	$23,500	$86,800

*3,900 units (October) x 2 kg = 7,800 kg; 7,800 kg x 20% = 1,560 kg.

The schedule of expected cash payments:

	July	Aug.	Sept.	Quarter
Accounts payable, beginning balance	$11,400			$11,400
July purchases: $31,200 x 60%, 40%	18,720	$12,480		31,200
August purchases: $32,100 x 60%, 40%		19,260	$12,840	32,100
September purchases: $23,500 x 60%			14,100	14,100
Total cash payments	$30,120	$31,740	$26,940	$88,800

Managerial Accounting

Problem 9-17 (60 minutes)

1. Collections on sales:

	July	August	Sept.	Quarter
Cash sales.............................	$ 8,000	$14,000	$10,000	$ 32,000
Credit sales:				
May: $30,000 x 80% x 20%.	4,800			4,800
June: $36,000 x 80% x 70%, 20%	20,160	5,760		25,920
July: $40,000 x 80% x 10%, 70%, 20%	3,200	22,400	6,400	32,000
Aug.: $70,000 x 80% x 10%, 70%		5,600	39,200	44,800
Sept.: $50,000 x 80% x 10%			4,000	4,000
Total cash collections	$36,160	$47,760	$59,600	$143,520

2. a. Inventory purchases budget:

	July	August	Sept.	Oct.
Budgeted cost of goods sold	$24,000	$42,000	$30,000	$27,000
Add: Desired ending inventory*	31,500	22,500	20,250	
Total needs.....................	55,500	64,500	50,250	
Less beginning inventory ...	18,000	31,500	22,500	
Required inventory purchases	$37,500	$33,000	$27,750	

*75% of the next month's budgeted cost of goods sold.

b. Schedule of expected cash disbursements for inventory:

	July	August	Sept.	Quarter
Accounts payable June 30...........................	$11,700			$11,700
July purchases	18,750	$18,750		37,500
August purchases		16,500	$16,500	33,000
September purchases........			13,875	13,875
Total cash disbursements.............	$30,450	$35,250	$30,375	$96,075

Problem 9-17 (continued)

3.

JANUS PRODUCTS, INC.
Cash Budget
For the Quarter Ended September 30

	July	August	Sept.	Quarter
Cash balance, beginning......	$ 8,000	$ 8,410	$ 8,020	$ 8,000
Add, collections from sales ..	36,160	47,760	59,600	143,520
Total cash available	44,160	56,170	67,620	151,520
Less disbursements:				
For inventory purchases ...	30,450	35,250	30,375	96,075
For selling expenses.........	7,200	11,700	8,500	27,400
For administrative				
expenses	3,600	5,200	4,100	12,900
For equipment..................	4,500	-0-	-0-	4,500
For dividends	-0-	-0-	1,000	1,000
Total disbursements	45,750	52,150	43,975	141,875
Excess (deficiency) of				
cash available over				
disbursements.................	(1,590)	4,020	23,645	9,645
Financing:				
Borrowing.........................	10,000	4,000		14,000
Repayment.......................	-0-	-0-	(14,000)	(14,000)
Interest at 12 percent........	-0-	-0-	(380)*	(380)
Total financing	10,000	4,000	(14,380)	(380)
Cash balance, ending	$ 8,410	$ 8,020	$ 9,265	$ 9,265

*$10,000 x 12% x 3/12 = $300
$ 4,000 x 12% x 2/12 =   80
$380

Managerial Accounting

Problem 9-19 (45 minutes)

CHEN COMPANY
Budgeted Income Statement
For the year 19y

Sales	$100,000
Cost of goods sold (46/95) x $100,000	48,421
Gross margin..	51,579
Expenses [(33,000 – 18,000 – 3,000)/95,000] x $100,000 = $12,632	
+ 20,000	
+ 3,000	35,632
Pretax income	15,947
Income tax (22%)	3,508
Net income	$ 12,439

CHEN COMPANY
Budgeted Balance Sheet
At year end 19y

Assets

Cash (cal)..	$ 39,887
Accounts receivable [30/(95/2)] x 50,000......................	31,579
Inventory [(40/46) x 48,421]	42,105
Capital assets (100,000 – 20,000 + 10,000)	90,000
Total assets...	$203,571

Liabilities

Accounts payable [[50/46 x 48,421]..................................	$ 52,632
Income taxes payable	1,500
Notes payable, long-term..	25,000
	79,132

Shareholders' Equity

Capital stock (8,000 no par shares)	80,000
Retained earnings (34,000 + 12,439 – 12,000)	34,439
	124,439
Total liabilities and shareholders' equity	$203,571

Note: Careful attention is needed to review the percentage for the calculations.

Problem 9-19 (continued)

Calculation of Cash:

Receipts

Sales cash 1/2..	$50,000	
Collections (50,000 + 30,000 – 31,579)	48,421	$98,421
Payments		
Purchases (48,421 – 40,000 + 42,105)....................	50,526	
+ Accounts payable..	50,000	
– Accounts payable..	(52,632)	47,894
Expenses except dep. (35,632 – 20,000)		15,632
Income taxes (3,508 + 1,000 – 1,500)		3,008
Total payments..		66,534
		31,887
Dividend		12,000
		19,887
Beginning balance..		20,000
Ending balance		$39,887

Problem 9-21 (50 minutes)

1. Collection pattern:

	Percentage of Sales Uncollected at April 30*	Percentage to Be Collected in May
a. January	2½%	2½%
b. February	6%	(b) – (a) = 3½%
c. March	10%	(c) – (b) = 4%
d. April	100%	(d) – (c) = 90%

*Given.

Schedule of expected cash collections:

From January sales (2½% x $340,000)	$ 8,500
From February sales (3½% x $530,000)	18,550
From March sales (4% x $470,000)...............................	18,800
From April sales (90% x $550,000)................................	495,000
Total...	540,850
Less cash discount ($495,000 x 50% x 2%)	4,950
Net collections..	$535,900

Problem 9-21 (continued)

2.

HOUSEHALL COMPANY, LTD.
Cash Budget
May

Cash balance, beginning...		$ 5,750
Add collections from customers		535,900
Total cash available.......................................		541,650
Less disbursements:		
Raw material purchases (April)		320,000
Direct labour (May)		85,000
Accrued wages (April).....................................		11,000
Shipping (May)...		1,000
Indirect labour		34,000
Utilities		1,500
Wage benefits:		
Employment insurance................................	$1,350	
Canada pension	820	
May holiday pay	2,040	
Company pension ($5,000 – $900)	4,100	
Group insurance ($730 x 3 months).............	2,190	10,500
Sales and administrative salaries		60,000
Total disbursements.................................		523,000
Excess of cash...		$ 18,650

3. The treasurer's statement is incorrect. Even though the cash budget shows that cash will be available at the end of a month, there is no assurance that shortages will not develop on a day-to-day basis *during* the month. Cash receipts may come late in a month, for example, whereas cash payments may be made early in the month causing temporary cash shortages to occur. Unless receipts and payments occur smoothly over time, cash budgeting may be needed on a daily or weekly basis for operational purposes.

Managerial Accounting

Problem 9-23 (25 minutes)

(a)   A18 = TOTAL CASH COLLECTIONS
      D13 = 70,000 * .4 * .5
      D16 = + D8 * .5
      D18 = + D10 + D13 + D16
      E8 = + E7 * .4
      E10 = + E7 − E8
      E13 = + D8 * .5
      E16 = + E8 * .5
      E18 = + E10 + E13 + E16
      F8 = + F7 * .4
      F10 = + F7 − F8
      F13 = + E8 * .5
      F16 = + F8 * .5
      F18 = + F10 + F13 + F16
      G7 = + D7 + E7 + F7 or @ Sum (D7.F7)
      G8 = + D8 + E8 + F8 or @ Sum (D8.F8)
      G10 = + G7 − G8
      G13 = + D13 + E13 + F13 or @ Sum (D13.F13)
      G16 = + D16 + E16 + F16 or @ Sum (D16.F16)
      G18 = + G10 + G13 + G16 or (D18 + E18 + F18) or @ Sum (D18.F18)

The completed budget is shown below. (Note that students are not required to do this.)

RAY COMPANY
Budgeted Cash Collections from Sales
For First Quarter, 19x8

	January	February	March	Quarter
Total sales......................	$40,000	$50,000	$60,000	$150,000
Less credit sales	16,000	20,000	24,000	60,000
Cash sales	24,000	30,000	36,000	90,000
Add collections on credit sales from previous month	14,000	8,000	10,000	32,000
Add collections on credit sales from current month	8,000	10,000	12,000	30,000
Total cash collections.....	$46,000	$48,000	$58,000	$152,000

(b)   The value of cell D18 is (80,000 − 32,000) + 14,000 + 16,000 = $78,000.
                                    (CGA-Canada Solution, adapted)

Standard Costs and Operating Performance Measures

10

Exercise 10-1 (15 minutes)

1.

Actual Quantity of Inputs, at Actual Price (AQ x AP)	Actual Quantity of Inputs, at Standard Price (AQ x SP)	Standard Quantity Allowed for Output, at Standard Price (SQ x SP)
20,000 ml x $2.40 = $48,000	20,000 ml x $2.50 = $50,000	18,000 ml* x $2.50 = $45,000

↑ Price Variance, $2,000 F	↑ Quantity Variance, $5,000 U ↑
Total Variance, $3,000 U	

*2,500 units x 7.2 ml = 18,000 ml

Alternatively:

AQ (AP − SP) = Materials Price Variance
20,000 ml ($2.40 − $2.50) = $2,000 F

SP (AQ − SQ) = Materials Quantity Variance
$2.50 (20,000 ml − 18,000 ml) = $5,000 U

Exercise 10-1 (continued)

2.

Actual Hours of Inputs, at the Actual Rate (AH x AR)	Actual Hours of Input, at the Standard Rate (AH x SR)	Standard Hours Allowed for Output, at the Standard Rate (SH x SR)
$10,800	900 hrs. x $10 = $9,000	1,000 hrs.* x $10 = $10,000

Price Variance, $1,800 U	Efficiency Variance, $1,000 F

Total Variance, $800 U

*2,500 units x 0.4 hrs. = 1,000 hrs.

Alternatively:

AH (AR − SR) = Labour Rate Variance
900 hrs. ($12* − $10) = $1,800 U

*10,800 ÷ 900 hrs. = $12/hr.

SR (AH − SH) = Labour Efficiency Variance
$10 (900 hrs. − 1,000 hrs.) = 1,000 F

Exercise 10-3 (20 minutes)

1. a. Notice in the solution below that the materials price variance is computed on the entire amount of materials purchased, whereas the materials quantity variance is computed only on the amount of materials used in production.

Actual Quantity of Inputs, at Actual Price (AQ x AP)	Actual Quantity of Inputs, at Standard Price (AQ x SP)	Standard Quantity Allowed for Output, at Standard Price (SQ x SP)
70,000 diodes x $0.28 = $19,600	70,000 diodes x $0.30 = $21,000	40,000 diodes* x $0.30 = $12,000

Price Variance,
$1,400 F

50,000 diodes x $0.30
= $15,000

Quantity Variance,
$3,000 U

*5,000 toys x 8 diodes per toy = 40,000 diodes.

Alternate Solution:

AQ (AP – SP) = Materials Price Variance
70,000 diodes ($0.28 – $0.30) = $1,400 F

SP (AQ – SQ) = Materials Quantity Variance
$0.30 (50,000 diodes – 40,000 diodes) = $3,000 U

Managerial Accounting

Exercise 10-3 (continued)

b. Direct labour variances:

Actual Hours of Input, at the Actual Rate (AH x AR)	Actual Hours of Input, at the Standard Rate (AH x SR)	Standard Hours Allowed for Output, at the Standard Rate (SH x SR)
$48,000	6,400 hrs. x $7 = $44,800	6,000 hrs.* x $7 = $42,000

Rate Variance, $3,200 U	Efficiency Variance, $2,800 U
Total Variance, $6,000 U	

*5,000 toys x 1.2 hrs. per toy = 6,000 hrs.

Alternate Solution:

AH (AR − SR) = Labour Rate Variance
6,400 hrs. ($7.50* − $7.00) = $3,200 U

*$48,000 ÷ 6,400 hrs. = $7.50/hr.

SR (AH − SH) = Labour Efficiency Variance
$7(6,400 hrs. − 6,000 hrs.) = $2,800 U

Exercise 10-3 (continued)

2. There are usually many possible explanations for a variance. In particular, we should always keep in mind that the standards themselves may be incorrect. Some of the other possible explanations for the variances observed at Topper Toys appear below:

    Materials Price Variance   Since this variance is favourable, the actual price paid per unit for the material was less than the standard price. This could occur for a variety of reasons including the purchase of a lower grade material at a discount, buying in an unusually large quantity to take advantage of quantity discounts, a change in the market price of the material, and particularly sharp bargaining by the purchasing department.

    Materials Quantity Variance   Since this variance is unfavourable, more materials were used to produce the actual output than were called for by the standard. This could also occur for a variety of reasons. Some of the possibilities include poorly trained or supervised workers, improperly adjusted machines, and defective materials.

    Labour Rate Variance   Since this variance is unfavourable, the actual average wage rate was higher than the standard wage rate. Some of the possible explanations include an increase in wages that has not been reflected in the standards, unanticipated overtime, and a shift toward more highly paid workers.

    Labour Efficiency Variance   Since this variance is unfavourable, the actual number of labour hours was greater than the standard labour hours allowed for the actual output. As with the other variances, this variance could have been caused by any of a number of factors. Some of the possible explanations include poor supervision, poorly trained workers, low quality materials requiring more labour time to process, and machine breakdowns. In addition, if the direct labour force is essentially fixed, an unfavourable labour efficiency variance could be caused by a reduction in output due to decreased demand for the company's products.

Managerial Accounting

Exercise 10-5 (15 minutes)

1.
Number of chopping blocks	4,000
Number of board feet per chopping block	x 2.5
Standard board feet allowed	10,000
Standard cost per board foot	x $1.80
Total standard cost	$18,000
Actual cost incurred	$18,700
Standard cost above	18,000
Total variance—unfavourable	$ 700

2.

Actual Quantity of Inputs, at Actual Price (AQ x AP)	Actual Quantity of Inputs, at Standard Price (AQ x SP)	Standard Quantity Allowed for Output, at Standard Price (SQ x SP)
$18,700	11,000 bd. ft. x $1.80 = $19,800	10,000 bd. ft. x $1.80 = $18,000

Price Variance, $1,100 F	Quantity Variance, $1,800 U

Total Variance, $700 U

Alternatively:

Materials price variance:

AQ(AP − SP) = Materials Price Variance
11,000 bd. ft. ($1.70* − $1.80) = $1,100 F

*$18,700 ÷ 11,000 bd. ft. = $1.70.

Materials quantity variance:

SP(AQ − SQ) = Materials Quantity Variance
$1.80(11,000 bd. ft. − 10,000 bd. ft.) = $1,800 U

Exercise 10-7 (20 minutes)

1. Cost per 2 kilogram container .... 6,000.00 Kr
    Less: 2% cash discount 120.00
       Net cost 5,880.00
    Add freight cost per 2 kilogram
       container (1,000 Kr ÷ 10) 100.00
    Total cost per 2 kilogram container .... 5,980.00 Kr   (a)

    Number of grams per container
       (2 kilograms x 1000) 2,000   (b)

    Standard cost per gram purchased
       (a) ÷ (b) .... 2.99 Kr

2. Alpha SR40 required per capsule as per
       bill of materials .... 6.00 grams
    Add allowance for material rejected as
       unsuitable (6 grams ÷ 0.96 = 6.25
       grams; 6.25 grams – 6.00 grams =
       0.25 grams) .... 0.25 grams
         Total .... 6.25 grams
    Add allowance for rejected capsules
       (6.25 grams ÷ 25 capsules) .... 0.25 grams
    Standard quantity of Alpha SR40 per
       salable capsule .... 6.50 grams

3.

Item	Standard Quantity per Capsule	Standard Price per Gram	Standard Cost per Capsule
Alpha SR40	6.50 grams	2.99 Kr	19.435 Kr

                        Managerial Accounting

Exercise 10-9 (20 minutes)

1. Throughput time = Process time + Inspection time + Move time + Queue time
   = 2.8 days + 0.5 days + 0.7 days + 4.0 days
   = 8.0 days

2. Only process time is value-added time; therefore the manufacturing cycle efficiency (MCE) is:

$$MCE = \frac{\text{Value-added time, 2.8 days}}{\text{Throughput time, 8.0 days}}$$

$$= 0.35$$

The MCE puts the throughput time into perspective by showing the percentage of time that units are actually being worked on. In this case, the percentage is only 35%.

3. If the MCE is 35%, then the complement of this figure, or 65% of the time, was spent in non-value-added activities.

4. Delivery cycle time = Wait time + Throughput time
   = 16.0 days + 8.0 days
   = 24.0 days

5. If all queue time in production is eliminated, then the throughput time drops to only 4 days (0.5 + 2.8 + 0.7). The MCE becomes:

$$MCE = \frac{\text{Value-added time, 2.8 days}}{\text{Throughput time, 4.0 days}}$$

$$= 0.70$$

Thus, the MCE increases to 70%. This exercise shows quite dramatically how the JIT approach can improve operations and reduce throughput time.

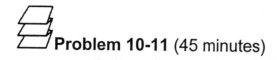

Problem 10-11 (45 minutes)

1. a. Notice in the solution below that the materials price variance is computed on the entire amount of materials purchased, whereas the materials quantity variance is computed only on the amount of materials used in production:

Actual Quantity of Inputs, at Actual Price (AQ x AP)	Actual Quantity of Inputs, at Standard Price (AQ x SP)	Standard Quantity Allowed for Output, at Standard Price (SQ x SP)
$46,000	8,000 kg x $6 = $48,000	4,500 kg* x $6 = $27,000

Price Variance, $2,000 F

6,000 kg x $6 = $36,000

Quantity Variance, $9,000 U

*3,000 units x 1.5 kg per unit = 4,500 kg.

Alternatively:

AQ (AP – SP) = Materials Price Variance
8,000 kg ($5.75* – $6) = $2,000 F

*$46,000 ÷ 8,000 kg = $5.75 per kg

SP (AQ – SQ) = Materials Quantity Variance
$6 (6,000 kg – 4,500 kg) = $9,000 U

b.   No, the contract should probably not be signed. Although the new supplier is offering the materials at only $5.75 per kilogram, the materials do not seem to hold up well in production as shown by the large materials quantity variance. Moreover, the company still has 2,000 kilograms of the material in the warehouse unused; if these materials do as poorly in production as the 6,000 kilograms already used, the total quantity variance on the 8,000 kilograms of materials purchased will be very large indeed.

Problem 10-11 (continued)

2. a.

Actual Hours of Input, at the Actual Rate (AH x AR)	Actual Hours of Input, at the Standard Rate (AH x SR)	Standard Hours Allowed for Output, at the Standard Rate (SH x SR)
1,600 hrs* x $12.50 = $20,000	1,600 hrs. x $12.00 = $19,200	1,800 hrs.** x $12.00 = $21,600

Rate Variance, $800 U	Efficiency Variance, $2,400 F

Total Variance, $1,600 F

*10 workers x 160 hrs. per worker = 1,600 hrs.
**3,000 units x 0.6 hrs. per unit   = 1,800 hrs.

Alternatively:

AH(AR − SR) = Labour Rate Variance
1,600 hrs. ($12.50 − $12.00) = $800 U

SR(AH − SH) = Labour Efficiency Variance
$12.00(1,600 hrs. − 1,800 hrs.) = $2,400 F

b. Yes, the new labour mix should probably be continued. Although it increases the average hourly labour cost from $12.00 to $12.50, thereby causing an $800 unfavourable labour rate variance, this is more than offset by greater efficiency of labour time. Notice that the labour efficiency variance is $2,400 favourable. Thus, the new labour mix reduces overall labour costs.

Problem 10-11 (continued)

3.

Actual Hours of Input, at the Actual Rate (AH x AR)	Actual Hours of Input, at the Standard Rate (AH x SR)	Standard Hours Allowed for Output, at the Standard Rate (SH x SR)
$3,600	1,600 hrs. x $2.50 = $4,000	1,800 hrs. x $2.50 = $4,500

Spending Variance, $400 F ↑   Efficiency Variance, $500 F ↑

Total Variance, $900 F

Alternatively:

AH(AR – SR) = Variable Overhead Spending Variance
1,600 hrs. ($2.25* – $2.50) = $400 F

*$3,600 ÷ 1,600 hrs. = $2.25/hr.

SR(AH – SH) = Variable Overhead Efficiency Variance
$2.50(1,600 hrs. – 1,800 hrs.) = $500 F

Both the labour efficiency variance and the variable overhead efficiency variance are computed by comparing actual labour-hours to standard labour-hours. Thus, if the labour efficiency variance is favourable, then the variable overhead efficiency variance will be favourable as well.

Managerial Accounting

Problem 10-13 (40 minutes)

1. a.

Actual Quantity of Inputs, at Actual Price (AQ × AP)	Actual Quantity of Inputs, at Standard Price (AQ × SP)	Standard Quantity Allowed for Output, at Standard Price (SQ × SP)
25,000 kg × $2.95 = 73,750	25,000 kg × $2.50 = $62,500	20,000 kg × $2.50 = $50,000

Price Variance,
$11,250 U

19,800 kg × $2.50
= $49,500

Quantity Variance,
$500 F

*5,000 ingots x 4.0 kg per ingot = 20,000 kg.

Alternatively:

AQ (AP − SP) = Materials Price Variance
25,000 kg ($2.95 − $2.50) = $11,250 U

SP (AQ − SQ) = Materials Quantity Variance
$2.50(19,800 kg − 20,000 kg) = $500 F

Problem 10-13 (continued)

Actual Hours of Input, at the Actual Rate (AH x AR)	Actual Hours of Input, at the Standard Rate (AH x SR)	Standard Hours Allowed for Output, at the Standard Rate (SH x SR)
3,600 hrs. x $8.70 = $31,320	3,600 hrs. x $9.00 = $32,400	3,000 hrs.* x $9.00 = $27,000

Rate Variance, $1,080 F   Efficiency Variance, $5,400 U

Total Variance, $4,320 U

*5,000 ingots x 0.6 hrs. per ingot = 3,000 hrs.

Alternatively:

AH (AR – SR) = Labour Rate Variance
3,600 hrs. ($8.70 – $9.00) = $1,080 F

SR (AH – SH) = Labour Efficiency Variance
$9.00(3,600 hrs. – 3,000 hrs.) = $5,400 U

Managerial Accounting

Problem 10-13 (continued)

Actual Hours of Input, at the Actual Rate (AH x AR)	Actual Hours of Input, at the Standard Rate (AH x SR)	Standard Hours Allowed for Output, at the Standard Rate (SH x SR)
$4,320	1,800 hrs. x $2.00 = $3,600	1,500 hrs.* x $2.00 = $3,000

Spending Variance, $720 U   Efficiency Variance, $600 U

Total Variance, $1,320 U

*5,000 ingots x 0.3 hrs. per ingot = 1,500 hrs.

Alternatively:

AH (AR − SR) = Variable Overhead Spending Variance
1,800 hrs. ($2.40* − $2.00) = $720 U

*$4,320 ÷ 1,800 hrs. = $2.40/hr.

SR (AH − SH) = Variable Overhead Efficiency Variance
$2.00(1,800 hrs. − 1,500 hrs.) = $600 U

Problem 10-13 (continued)

2. Summary of variances:

Material price variance	$11,250 U
Material quantity variance	500 F
Labour rate variance	1,080 F
Labour efficiency variance	5,400 U
Variable overhead spending variance	720 U
Variable overhead efficiency variance	600 U
Net variance	$16,390 U

The net unfavourable variance of $16,390 for the month caused the plant's variable cost of goods sold to increase from the budgeted level of $80,000 to $96,390:

Budgeted cost of goods sold at $16 per ingot	$80,000
Add the net unfavourable variance (as above)	16,390
Actual cost of goods sold	$96,390

This $16,390 net unfavourable variance also accounts for the difference between the budgeted net income and the actual net loss for the month.

Budgeted net income	$15,000
Deduct the net unfavourable variance added to cost of goods sold for the month	16,390
Net loss	$ (1,390)

3. The two most significant variances are the materials price variance and the labour efficiency variance. Possible causes of the variances include:

Materials Price Variance: Outdated standards, uneconomical quantity purchased, higher-quality materials, wrong method of transport.

Labour Efficiency Variance: Poorly trained workers, poor quality materials, faulty equipment, work interruptions, inaccurate standards.

Managerial Accounting

Problem 10-15 (25 minutes)

1. a., b., and c.

	Month			
	1	**2**	**3**	**4**
Throughput time in days				
Process time	0.6	0.5	0.5	0.4
Inspection time...............................	0.7	0.7	0.4	0.3
Move time	0.5	0.5	0.4	0.5
Queue time	3.6	3.6	2.6	1.7
Total throughput time	5.4	5.3	3.9	2.9
Manufacturing cycle efficiency (MCE):				
Process time ÷ Throughput time........	11.1%	9.4%	12.8%	13.8%
Delivery cycle time in days:				
Wait time..	9.6	8.7	5.3	4.7
Total throughput time.........................	5.4	5.3	3.9	2.9
Total delivery cycle time	15.0	14.0	9.2	7.6

Problem 10-15 (continued)

2. Quality control measures:

Customer complaints as a percentage of units sold	Favourable
Warranty claims as a percentage of units sold	Favourable
Defects as percentage of units produced	Favourable

    Material control measures:

Purchase order lead time (days)	Favourable
Scrap as a percentage of total cost	Favourable

    Inventory control measures:

Raw materials turnover (times)	Favourable
Finished goods turnover (times)	Mixed

    Machine performance measures:

Percentage of machine downtime	Favourable
Use as a percentage of availability	Unfavourable
Average setup time (hours)	Favourable

    Delivery performance measures:

Throughput time, or velocity	Favourable
Manufacturing cycle efficiency	Favourable or Mixed
Delivery cycle time	Favourable
Percentage of on-time deliveries	Favourable
Total throughput (units)	Mixed

The general trend is favourable in all of the operating performance measures except for finished goods turnover, use as a percentage of availability, and total throughput. These may be an indication that the company has not been able to increase its sales as it has improved its operations in the factory. This is not particularly surprising since management attention has undoubtedly been focused on the factory and the changes that have been taking place there. However, it may be time now to exploit the improved quality of the product and the improvement in delivery service to go after more sales—perhaps by increased product promotion and better marketing strategies. Increasing sales will ultimately be necessary in order to translate the operational improvements into more profits.

Managerial Accounting

Problem 10-15 (continued)

3. a. and b.

| | Month | |
	5	6
Throughput time in days		
Process time	0.4	0.4
Inspection time	0.3	—
Move time	0.5	0.5
Queue time	=	=
Total throughput time	1.2	0.9
Manufacturing cycle efficiency (MCE):		
Process time ÷ Throughput time	33.3%	44.4%

As a company pares away non-value-added activities, the manufacturing cycle efficiency improves. The goal, of course, is to have an efficiency of 100%. This will be achieved when all non-value added activities have been eliminated and process time equals throughput time.

Problem 10-17 (45 minutes)

1. Total standard cost for units produced during August:

500 kits x $42	$21,000
Less standard cost of labour and overhead:	
Direct labour	(8,000)
Variable manufacturing overhead	(1,600)
Standard cost of materials used during August	$11,400

2.

Standard cost of materials used during August	$11,400	(a)
Number of units produced	500	(b)
Standard materials cost per kit (a) ÷ (b)	$22.80	

$$\frac{\text{Standard materials cost per kit, } \$22.80}{\text{Standard materials cost per metre}\quad \$6} = 3.8 \text{ m per kit}$$

Actual cost of material used	$10,000	
Standard cost of material used	11,400	
Total variance	$ 1,400	F

The price and quantity variances together equal the total variance. If the quantity variance is $600 U, then the price variance must be $2,000 F:

Price variance	$ 2,000	F
Quantity variance	600	U
Total variance	$ 1,400	F

Managerial Accounting

Problem 10-17 (continued)

Alternate Solution:

Actual Quantity of Inputs, at Actual Price (AQ x AP)	Actual Quantity of Inputs, at Standard Price (AQ x SP)	Standard Quantity Allowed for Output, at Standard Price (SQ x SP)
2,000 m x $5 = $10,000*	2,000 m x $6* = $12,000	1,900 m** x $6* = $11,400

Price Variance, $2,000 F   Quantity Variance, $600 U*

Total Variance, $1,400 F

*Given.
**500 kits x 3.8 m = 1,900 m.

Problem 10-17 (continued)

4. The first step in computing the standard direct labour rate is to determine the standard direct labour-hours allowed for the month's production. The standard direct labour-hours can be computed by working with the variable manufacturing overhead cost figures, since they are based on direct labour-hours worked:

Standard manufacturing variable overhead cost
  for August .... $1,600 (a)
Standard manufacturing variable overhead rate
  per direct labour-hour .... $2 (b)
Standard direct labour-hours for the month (a) ÷ (b) 800

$$\frac{\text{Total standard labour cost for the month,} \quad \$8,000}{\text{Total standard labour-hours for the month,} \quad 800} = \$10/DLH$$

5. Before the labour variances can be computed, it is necessary first to compute the actual direct labour cost for the month:

Actual cost per kit produced ($42.00 + $0.14) .... $ 42.14
Number of kits produced .... x 500
Total actual cost of production $21,070
Less: Actual cost of materials $10,000
  Actual cost of manufacturing variable
    overhead.. 1,620   11,620
Actual cost of direct labour................................... $ 9,450

Problem 10-17 (continued)

With this information, the variances can be computed:

Actual Hours of Input, at the Actual Rate (AH x AR)	Actual Hours of Input, at the Standard Rate (AH x SR)	Standard Hours Allowed for Output, at the Standard Rate (SH x SR)
$9,450	900 hrs.* x $10 = $9,000	$8,000*

Rate Variance, $450 U   Efficiency Variance, $1,000 U

Total Variance, $1,450 U

*Given.

Problem 10-17 (continued)

6.

Actual Hours of Input, at the Actual Rate (AH x AR)	Actual Hours of Input, at the Standard Rate (AH x SR)	Standard Hours Allowed for Output, at the Standard Rate (SH x SR)
$1,620*	900 hrs.* x $2* = $1,800	$1,600*

Spending Variance, $180 F	Efficiency Variance, $200 U
Total Variance, $20 U	

*Given.

7.

	Standard Quantity or Hours	Standard Price or Rate	Standard Cost
Direct materials..................	3.8 metres[1]	$ 6 per metre	$22.80
Direct labour	1.6 hours[2]	$10 per hour[3]	16.00
Variable overhead	1.6 hours	$ 2 per hour	3.20
Total standard cost per kit			$42.00

[1]From part 2.
[2]800 standard hours (from part 4) ÷ 500 kits = 1.6 hours per kit.
[3]From part 4.

Problem 10-19 (35 minutes)

1. a., b., and c.

	Month			
	1	**2**	**3**	**4**
Throughput time in days				
Process time.......................................	0.6	0.6	0.6	0.6
Inspection time.................................	0.1	0.3	0.6	0.8
Move time	1.4	1.3	1.3	1.4
Queue time	<u>5.6</u>	<u>5.7</u>	<u>5.6</u>	<u>5.7</u>
Total throughput time	<u>7.7</u>	<u>7.9</u>	<u>8.1</u>	<u>8.5</u>
Manufacturing cycle efficiency (MCE):				
Process time ÷ Throughput time........	<u>7.8%</u>	<u>7.6%</u>	<u>7.4%</u>	<u>7.1%</u>
Delivery cycle time in days:				
Wait time...	16.7	15.2	12.3	9.6
Total throughput time.......................	<u>7.7</u>	<u>7.9</u>	<u>8.1</u>	<u>8.5</u>
Total delivery cycle time	<u>24.4</u>	<u>23.1</u>	<u>20.4</u>	<u>18.1</u>

2. a. The company seems to be improving mainly in the areas of quality control, material control, on-time delivery, and total delivery cycle time. Customer complaints, warranty claims, defects, and scrap are all down somewhat, which suggests that the company has been paying attention to quality in its improvement campaign. The fact that on-time delivery and delivery cycle time have both improved also suggests that the company is seeking to please the customer with improved service.

   b. The finished goods turnover has gotten worse and inspection time has increased dramatically. Use as percentage of availability has deteriorated, and throughput time as well as MCE show negative trends.

Problem 10-19 (continued)

c. While it is difficult to draw any definitive conclusions, it appears that the company has concentrated first on those areas of performance that are of most immediate concern to the customer—quality and delivery performance. The lower scrap and defect statistics suggest that the company has been able to improve its processes to reduce the rate of defects; although, some of the improvement in quality apparently was due simply to increased inspections of the products before they were shipped to customers. The increase in on-time delivery performance may have been achieved by building more finished goods inventories to act as reserves. This is probably not a good idea in the long run, but it may work temporarily.

When the company embarks on its JIT program, we would expect to see dramatic improvements in most of the operating performance measures that were stagnant or deteriorating in the first four months.

3. a. and b.

	Month	
	5	**6**
Throughput time in days		
Process time	0.6	0.6
Inspection time..	0.8	—
Move time	1.4	1.4
Queue time	—	—
Total throughput time..	2.8	2.0

Manufacturing cycle efficiency (MCE):
Process time ÷ Throughput time 21.4% 30.0%

As a company pares out non-value-added activities, the manufacturing cycle efficiency improves. The goal, of course, is to have an efficiency of 100%. This will be achieved when all non-value-added activities have been eliminated and process time equals throughput time.

Managerial Accounting

Problem 10-21 (45 minutes)

1. Actual cost of materials $66,500
    Standard cost of materials (AQ x SP):
       95,000 m x $.65 .... <u>61,750</u>
       Price variance, unfavourable .... <u>$ 4,750</u>

2. a. and b.

	Lot Number			
	30	**31**	**32**	**Total**
Standard metres:				
Units in lot (doz.)	1,000	1,700	1,200	3,900
Standard metres per doz.	<u>x 24</u>	<u>x 24</u>	<u>x 24</u>	<u>x 24</u>
Total standard metres	24,000	40,800	28,800	93,600
Actual metres used	<u>24,100</u>	<u>40,440</u>	<u>28,825</u>	<u>93,365</u>
Quantity variance in metres	<u>100</u>	<u>(360)</u>	<u>25</u>	<u>(235)</u>
Quantity variance in dollars				
@ $.65	<u>$ 65</u>	<u>$ (234)</u>	<u>$16.25</u>	<u>$(152.75)</u>

( ) Denotes favourable variance.

3. Actual cost of direct labour $80,740
    Standard cost of labour (AH x SR):
       11,000 hrs.* x $7.25 .... <u>79,750</u>
       Labour rate variance, unfavourable.................. <u>$ 990</u>

*2,980 hrs. + 5,130 hrs. + 2,890 hrs. = 11,000 hrs.

Problem 10-21 (continued)

4. a. and b.

	Lot Number			
	30	**31**	**32**	**Total**
Standard hours:				
Units in lot (doz.)	1,000	1,700	1,200	3,900
Standard hours per doz.	x 3	x 3	x 3	x 3
Total..	3,000	5,100	3,600	11,700
Percentage completed.................	x 100	x 100	x 80	—
Total standard hours....................	3,000	5,100	2,880	10,980
Actual hours worked......................	2,980	5,130	2,890	11,000
Labour efficiency variance				
in hours	(20)	30	10	20
Labour efficiency variance				
in dollars @ $7.25........................	$ (145)	$217.50	$72.50	$ 145

( ) Denotes favourable variance.

5. It is often better to express quantity variances in units (hours, metres, etc.) rather than in dollars when those variances are to be used by managers whose day-to-day work deals with activity expressed in units. That is, some middle-level managers rarely deal with anything on a dollar basis; all of their work may be in terms of unit (hours, metres, etc.) activity. For such persons, variances expressed in dollars may not be as useful as variances expressed in terms of what they work with from day to day.

On the other hand, price variances expressed in units (hours, metres) would make little sense. Such variances should always be expressed in dollars to be most useful to the manager. In addition, quantity variances expressed in both dollar and unit terms should be prepared for top management.

Managerial Accounting

Problem 10-23 (30 minutes)

1. Each kilogram of fresh mushrooms yields 150 grams of dried mushrooms suitable for packing:

One kilogram of fresh mushrooms	1,000	grams
Less: unacceptable mushrooms (1/4 of total)	250	
Acceptable mushrooms..	750	
Less 80% shrinkage during drying	600	
Acceptable dried mushrooms.......................................	150	grams

Since 1,000 grams of fresh mushrooms yield 150 grams of dried mushrooms, 100 grams (or, 0.1 kilogram) of fresh mushrooms should yield the 15 grams of acceptable dried mushrooms that are packed in each jar.

The direct labour standards are determined as follows:

	Sorting and Inspecting
Direct labour time per kilogram of fresh mushrooms	15 minutes
Grams of dried mushrooms per kilogram of fresh mushrooms	÷ 150 grams
Direct labour time per gram of dried mushrooms...........	0.10 minute/ gram
Grams of dried mushrooms per jar	x 15 grams
Direct labour time per jar...	1.5 minutes

	Drying
Direct labour time per kilogram of acceptable sorted fresh mushrooms..........................	10 minutes
Grams of dried mushrooms per kilogram of acceptable sorted fresh mushrooms..........................	÷ 200 grams
Direct labour time per gram of dried mushrooms...........	0.05 minute/ gram
Grams of dried mushrooms per jar	x 15 grams
Direct labour time per jar...	0.75 minute

Problem 10-23 (continued)

Standard cost per jar of dried chantrelle mushrooms:

Direct material:
    Fresh mushrooms
        (0.1 kilogram x 300 FF per kilogram)...............   30.00 FF
    Jars, lids and labels (50 FF ÷ 100 jars)..............   <u>0.50 FF</u>   30.50 FF
Direct labour:
    Sorting and inspecting
        (1.5 minutes x I FF per minute*)......................   1.50 FF
    Drying (0.75 minute x 1 FF per minute*).............   0.75 FF
    Packing (0.10 minutes** x 1 FF per minute*)......   <u>0.10 FF</u>   <u>2.35 FF</u>
    Standard cost per jar..   <u>32.85 FF</u>

   *60 FF per hour is 1 FF per minute.
  **10 minutes per 100 jars is 0.10 minute per jar.

2. a. Ordinarily, the purchasing manager has more influence over the prices of purchased materials than anyone else in the organization. Therefore, the purchasing manager is usually held responsible for material price variances.

                    Managerial Accounting

Problem 10-23 (continued)

b. Ordinarily, the production manager is held responsible for materials quantity variances. However, this situation is a bit unusual. The quantity variance will be heavily influenced by the quality of the mushrooms acquired from gatherers by the purchasing manager. If the mushrooms have an unusually large proportion of unacceptable mushrooms, the quantity variance will be unfavourable. The production process itself is likely to have less effect on the amount of wastage and spoilage. On the other hand, if the production manager is not held responsible for the quantity variance, the production workers may not take sufficient care in their handling of the mushrooms. A partial solution to this problem would be to make the sorting and inspection process part of the purchasing manager's responsibility. The purchasing manager would then be held responsible for any wastage in excess of the 100 grams expected for each 300 grams of acceptable fresh mushrooms. The production manager would be held responsible for any wastage after that point. This is only a partial solution, however, because the purchasing manager may pass on at least 300 grams of every 400 grams of fresh mushrooms, whether they are acceptable or not.

Problem 10-25 (40 minutes)

Production Cost Variances Common to Both Approaches
Direct Material Variances:

Price Variance =   (Actual quantity) (Standard price – Actual price)
                     Amak   7,500($2.40 – $2.40) = $-0-
                     Brill   4,050($4.20 – $4.20) =   -0-
                     Comad   1,100($5.15 – $5.15) =   -0-
                     Total material price variance $-0-

Usage Variance = (Standard price) (Flexible budget quantity – Actual quantity)

                     Amak $2.40(6,840* – 7,500) = $2.40 x –660 = –$1,584 U
                     Brill $4.20(4,560* – 4,050) = $4.20 x   510 =   2,142 F
                     Comad $5.15(1,140* – 1,100) = $5.15 x   40 =   206 F
                     Total material usage variance $ 764 F

_____

*Flexible budget quantity = Standard quantity allowed for actual output = (output quantity) (standard quantity per unit of output):
                     Amak   11,400 kg x .6 = 6,840
                     Brill   11,400 kg x .4 = 4,560
                     Comad   11,400 kg x .1 = 1,140

Mix variance =   (Standard price)(Actual input at standard mix – Actual input at actual mix)
                     Amak $2.40(6,900* – 7,500) = $2.40 x –600 =–$1,440 U
                     Brill $4.20(4,600* – 4,050) = $4.20 x   550 =   2,310 F
                     Comad $5.15(1,150* – 1,100) = $5.15 x   50 =   258 F
                     Total material mix variance $1,128 F

_____

*Actual input at standard mix is calculated as follows:
                     Amak   12,650 kg x 6/11 = 6,900
                     Brill   12,650 kg x 4/11 = 4,600
                     Comad   12,650 kg x 1/11 = 1,150

Managerial Accounting

Problem 10-25 (continued)

Yield Variance = (Standard price) (Flexible budget quantity – Actual input at standard mix)

Amak $2.40(6,840 – 6,900) = $2.40 x –60 = –$144 U
Brill $4.20(4,560 – 4,600) = $4.20 x –40 = – 168 U
Comad $5.15(1,140 – 1,150) = $5.15 x –10 = – 52 U
Total material yield variance –$364 U

Direct Labour Variances:

Rate Variance = (Actual quantity) (Standard rate – Actual rate)
= 12,650 x ($5.60 – $5.60)
= -0-

Usage Variance = (Standard price)(Flexible budget quantity – Actual quantity)
= $5.60 x (12,540* – 12,650)
= $5.60 x –110
= –$616 U

_____

*Flexible budget quantity = standard quantity allowed for actual output = output quantity x standard quantity per unit of output = 11,400 kg x 1.1 kg = 12,540 kg.

The production process operated efficiently in April, except for labour. Sticky Division used more labour than the standard allowed to achieve the actual production volume.

(SMAC Solution, adapted)

Problem 10-27 (30 minutes)

a.

	Physical Flow	Materials	Conversion Costs
Beginning inventory	10,000		
Started	32,300		
	42,300		
Finished:			
Beginning inventory..............	10,000	-0-	4,000
Current	15,000	15,000	15,000
Normal spoilage......................	2,000	2,000	1,800
Abnormal spoilage..................	300	300	270
Ending inventory.....................	15,000	15,000	14,250
	42,300	32,300	35,320

b.   Abnormal spoilage:

300 x $3.00...........................	$ 900	
270 x $12.00.........................	3,240	$ 4,140

c.   Normal spoilage:

2,000 x $ 3.00.......................	$ 6,000	
1,800 x $12.00.......................	21,600	$ 27,600

Ending inventory:

15,000 x $ 3.00......................	$ 45,000	
14,250 x $12.00......................	171,000	

$\left(\dfrac{15,000}{40,000} \right)$ x $\dfrac{\$27,600}{\text{(defective assigned)...}}$ 10,350 $226,350

d.   Materials price:

200,000 (.48 − .50) ....   −$4,000 F

Materials quantity:

.50 (195,000 − 193,800) .... $ 600 U

e.   Variable overhead spending:

140,000 − 144,000 (36,000 x 1 x $4)...   −$4,000 F

Variable overhead efficiency:

144,000 − 141,280 (35,320 x $4) .... $2,720 U

(CGA-Canada Solution, adapted)

Problem 10-29 (30 minutes)

1. Cost of subassembly:

Set-up...	$ 50.00
Material 8 x $20.00..	160.00
Labour 29.16 x $9.00	262.44
Variable overhead 1.40 x $262.44	367.42
Total for 8 units	$839.86

Per unit $105.00 (rounded)

Labour Time				**Total Time**
1	x	5 hours	=	5 hours
2	x	4.5 hours	=	9 hours
4	x	4.05 hours	=	16.2 hours
8	x	3.645 hours	=	29.16 hours

2. Lot size to equal $120/unit:

Set-up...	$ 50.00
Material 4 x $20.00..	80.00
Labour 16.2 x $9.00	145.80
Variable overhead 1.40 x $145.80	204.12
Total for 4 units	$479.92

Per unit $120.00 (rounded)

The break-even is 4 units. Less than 4, the unit cost would exceed $120.00.

Problem 10-31 (20 minutes)

Part 1:   Total nursing care hours = 1,025 + 1.179 (Level 1) + 2.059 (Level 2)

Part 2:   Level 1

Base		55 x 365	= 20,075	
Admission	1	(1 x 340)	340	Note: 340 = 365 – 25
	2	(1 x 315)	315	
	3	(_1 x 290)	_290	
		58	21,020	

Level 2
  26 x 365 = 9,490

Therefore,

   predicted nursing care hours are:

   H =   1,025 + 1.179(21,020) + 2.059(9,490)
      = 45,347

Part 3:   Accounting: variable overhead

   Real World
         Reasons: • charting
                   • rounds
                   • training
                   • changing linen
                   • age of residents
                   • staff meetings
                   • physical layout of building, etc.

SMA comments on problem

The question required students to apply, manipulate, and interpret statistical results which were attained from a provided regression analysis performed by a government analyst. The results were intended to estimate the amount of direct medical care required for two classes of residents in a newly constructed municipally and provincially funded home for the aged based on actual data available for eight existing homes.

Problem 10-31 (continued)

Part 2 comments

(a) The question requirements, while very directed, required a basic conceptual understanding of statistical regression analysis which unfortunately seemed to be almost completely absent. Many students stopped after supplying only the prediction equation.

(b) This part, which was handled well by many students, was intended to demonstrate that even the independent variables used for input into a regression equation are rarely as straightforward in real life as they are in a textbook calculation. The most common error in this part was failing to calculate the value of level 1 resident-days correctly. Many students attempted to use a fractional year calculation.

Part 3 comments

While specific knowledge of a home setting may have been useful in answering this question, common sense also could have been sufficient for full marks to a student with understanding of the model. Variations between real world and the model can only be caused by variation, discrepancy or change in things or parameters not included in the model. That, of course, assumes that the model is valid and fundamentally accurate.

(SMAC Solution, adapted)

Flexible Budgets and Overhead Analysis

11

Exercise 11-1 (10 minutes)

Overhead Costs	Cost Formula	Machine-Hours 6,000	8,000	10,000	12,000
Variable Costs:					
Indirect materials	$0.75/MH	$ 4,500	$ 6,000	$ 7,500	$ 9,000
Maintenance	0.60/MH	3,600	4,800	6,000	7,200
Utilities	0.15/MH	900	1,200	1,500	1,800
Total	$1.50/MH	9,000	12,000	15,000	18,000
Fixed Costs:					
Rent		10,000	10,000	10,000	10,000
Supervisory salaries		20,000	20,000	20,000	20,000
Insurance		8,000	8,000	8,000	8,000
Total		38,000	38,000	38,000	38,000
Total overhead costs...		$47,000	$50,000	$53,000	$56,000

Exercise 11-3 (15 minutes)

1.

WHALEY COMPANY
Variable Manufacturing Overhead Performance Report

Budgeted machine-hours 18,000
Actual machine-hours worked 16,000

	Actual 16,000 hours	Budget 16,000 hours	Spending Variance
Variable overhead costs:			
Utilities	$20,000	$19,200	$ 800 U
Supplies	4,700	4,800	100 F
Maintenance	35,100	38,400	3,300 F
Rework time	12,300	9,600	2,700 U
Total costs	$72,100	$72,000	$ 100 U

2. Favourable variances can be as much a matter of managerial concern as unfavourable variances. In this case, the favourable maintenance variance undoubtedly would require investigation. Efforts should be made to determine why maintenance is not being carried out. In terms of percentage deviation from budgeted allowances, the rework time variance is even more significant (equal to 28% of the budget allowance). It may be that this unfavourable variance in rework time is a result of poor maintenance of machines. Some students may say that if the two variances are related, then the trade-off is a good one, since the savings in maintenance cost is greater than the added cost of rework time. But this is short-sighted reasoning. Poor maintenance can reduce the life of equipment, as well as decrease overall output, thereby costing far more in the long run than any short-run savings.

Exercise 11-5 (10 minutes)

Company X: This company has an unfavourable volume variance since the standard direct labour-hours allowed for the actual output are less than the denominator activity.

Company Y: This company has an unfavourable volume variance since the standard direct labour-hours allowed for the actual output are less than the denominator activity.

Company Z: This company has a favourable volume variance since the standard direct labour-hours allowed for the actual output are greater than the denominator activity.

Exercise 11-7 (20 minutes)

1.

Overall rate: $\dfrac{\$33,200}{8,000 \text{ MH}}$ = $4.15/MH

Variable rate: $\dfrac{\$8,400}{8,000 \text{ MH}}$ = $1.05/MH

Fixed rate: $\dfrac{\$24,800}{8,000 \text{ MH}}$ = $3.10/MH

2. The standard hours per unit of product are:
   8,000 hrs. ÷ 3,200 units = 2.5 hours per unit

   The standard hours for the period would be:
   3,500 units x 2.5 hrs. = 8,750 hrs.

3. Variable overhead spending variance:

Actual variable overhead	$9,860
Actual hours x Standard rate: 8,500 hrs. x $1.05.......	8,925
Spending variance	$ 935 U

   Variable overhead efficiency variance:
   $1.05 (8,500 hrs. − 8,750 hrs.) = $262.50 F

   Fixed overhead budget and volume variances:

Actual Fixed Overhead Cost	Flexible Budget Fixed Overhead Cost	Fixed Overhead Cost Applied to Work in Process
$25,100	$24,800*	8,750 standard hrs. x $3.10 = $27,125

Budget Variance, $300 U	Volume Variance, $2,325 F
Total Variance, $2,025 F	

   *Can be expressed as: 8,000 denominator hours x $3.10 = $24,800.

Exercise 11-7 (continued)

Alternate approach to the budget variance:

$$\text{Actual Fixed Overhead Cost} - \text{Flexible Budget Fixed Overhead Cost} = \text{Budget Variance}$$

$$\$25,100 - \$24,800 = \$300 \text{ U}$$

Alternate approach to the volume variance:

$$\text{Fixed Portion of the Predetermined Overhead Rate} \left[\text{Denominator Hours} - \text{Standard Hours Allowed} \right] = \text{Volume Variance}$$

$$\$3.10 \ (8,000 \text{ hrs.} - 8,750 \text{ hrs.}) = \$2,325 \text{ F}$$

Managerial Accounting

Exercise 11-9 (15 minutes)

1. 10,000 units x 0.8 hrs./unit = 8,000 hours.

2. and 3.

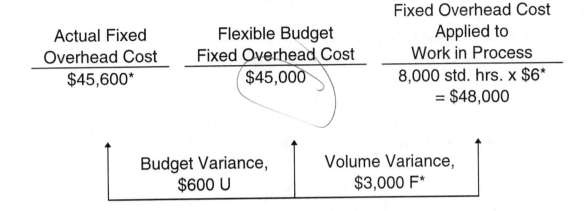

Actual Fixed Overhead Cost	Flexible Budget Fixed Overhead Cost	Fixed Overhead Cost Applied to Work in Process
$45,600*	$45,000	8,000 std. hrs. x $6* = $48,000

Budget Variance, $600 U   Volume Variance, $3,000 F*

*Given.

4.   Flexible Budget
$$\frac{\text{Fixed Overhead Cost}}{\text{Denominator Activity}} = \begin{array}{l}\text{Fixed Cost Element of the}\\ \text{Predetermined Overhead Rate}\end{array}$$

$$\frac{\$45,000}{\text{Denominator Activity}} = \$6$$

Therefore, the denominator activity was 7,500 direct labour-hours.

Problem 11-11 (45 minutes)

1. Direct materials price and quantity variances:

    AQ (AP – SP) = Direct Materials Price Variance
    78,000 yds. ($3.75 – $3.50) = $19,500 U

    SP (AQ – SQ) = Direct Materials Quantity Variance
    $3.50 (78,000 m – 80,000 m*) = $7,000 F

      *20,000 units x 4 m/unit = 80,000 m

2. Direct labour rate and efficiency variances:

    AH (AR – SR) = Direct Labour Rate Variance
    32,500 hrs. ($7.80 – $8.00) = $6,500 F

    SR (AH – SH) = Direct Labour Efficiency Variance
    $8 (32,500 hrs. – 30,000 hrs.*) = $20,000 U

      *20,000 units x 1.5 hrs./unit = 30,000 hrs.

3. a. Variable overhead spending and efficiency variances:

Actual Hours of Input, at the Actual Rate (AH x AR)	Actual Hours of Input, at the Standard Rate (AH x SR)	Standard Hours Allowed for Output, at the Standard Rate (SH x SR)
$68,250	32.500 hrs. x $2 = $65,000	30,000 hrs. x $2 = $60,000

         Spending Variance,   Efficiency Variance,
            $3,250 U $5,000 U

Problem 11-11 (continued)

Alternate Solution:

$$(AH \times AR) - (AH \times SR) = \text{Variable Overhead Spending Variance}$$
$$(\$68,250) - (32,500 \text{ hrs.} \times \$2) = \$3,250 \text{ U}$$

$$SR (AH - SH) = \text{Variable overhead efficiency variance}$$
$$\$2 (32,500 \text{ hrs.} - 30,000 \text{ hrs.}) = \$5,000 \text{ U}$$

b. Fixed overhead budget and volume variances:

Actual Fixed Overhead Cost	Flexible Budget Fixed Overhead Cost	Fixed Overhead Cost Applied to Work in Process
$148,000	$150,000	30,000 hrs. x $6 = $180,000

Budget Variance, $2,000 F	Volume Variance, $30,000 F

Alternate approach to the budget variance:

Actual Fixed Overhead Cost	–	Flexible Budget Fixed Overhead Cost	=	Budget Variance

$$\$148,000 - \$150,000 = \$2,000 \text{ F}$$

Alternate approach to the volume variance:

Fixed Portion of the Predetermined Overhead Rate	[Denominator Hours	–	Standard Hours Allowed]	=	Volume Variance

$$\$6 (25,000 \text{ hrs.} - 30,000 \text{ hrs.}) = \$30,000 \text{ F}$$

Problem 11-11 (continued)

4. The total of the variances would be:

Direct materials variances:	
Price variance	$19,500 U
Quantity variance	7,000 F
Direct labour variances:	
Rate variance	6,500 F
Efficiency variance	20,000 U
Variable manufacturing overhead variances:	
Spending variance	3,250 U
Efficiency variance	5,000 U
Fixed manufacturing overhead variances:	
Budget variance	2,000 F
Volume variance	30,000 F
Total of variances..	$ 2,250 U

Notice that the total of the variances agrees with the $2,250 unfavourable variance on the income statement.

It appears that not everyone should be given a bonus for good cost control. The materials price variance and the labour efficiency variance are 7.1 % and 8.3%, respectively, of the standard cost allowed and thus would warrant investigation. In addition, the variable overhead spending variance is 5% of the standard cost allowed.

The reason the company's large unfavourable variances (for materials price and labour efficiency) do not show up more clearly is that they are offset for the most part by the company's favourable volume variance for the year. This favourable volume variance is the result of the company operating at an activity level that is well above the denominator activity level used to set predetermined overhead rates. (The company operated at an activity level of 30,000 standard hours; the denominator activity level set at the beginning of the year was 25,000 hours.) As a result of the large favourable volume variance, the unfavourable quantity and efficiency variances have been concealed in a small "net" figure on the income statement. Although an income statement showing the net effect of the year's variances on income is important for management to have, such a statement must be accompanied by detailed performance reports from the various areas in the company.

Managerial Accounting

Problem 11-13 (25 minutes)

1. The reports as presently being prepared are of little usefulness to the company. The problem is that the company is using a static budget approach, and is measuring budgeted performance at one level of activity against actual performance at another level of activity. Although the reports do a good job of showing whether or not the budgeted level of activity was attained, they do not tell whether costs were controlled for the period.

2. The company should employ a flexible budget approach in evaluating control over costs. Under the flexible budget approach, the actual costs incurred during the quarter in working 25,000 hours should be compared against budgeted costs at that activity level.

3.

SHIPLEY COMPANY
Overhead Performance Report—Milling Department
For the Quarter Ended June 30

Budgeted machine-hours .... 30,000 hours
Actual machine-hours .... 25,000 hours

Overhead Costs	Cost Formula (per MH)	Actual 25,000 hours	Budget 25,000 hours	Spending or Budget Variance
Variable overhead costs:				
Indirect labour				
Supplies	$0.75	$ 20,000	$ 18,750	$1,250 U
Utilities	0.20	5,400	5,000	400 U
Rework time......................	1.00	27,000	25,000	2,000 U
Total variable costs	0.50	14,000	12,500	1,500 U
	$2.45	66,400	61,250	5,150 U
Fixed overhead costs:				
Maintenance		61,900	60,000	1,900 U
Inspection		90,000	90,000	—
Total fixed costs		151,900	150,000	1,900 U
Total overhead costs...........		$218,300	$211,250	$7,050 U

Problem 11-15 (45 minutes)

1.

THE ROWE COMPANY
Flexible Budget—Finishing Department

Budgeted direct labour-hours 50,000

Item	Cost Formula	Direct Labour-Hours		
		40,000	50,000	60,000
Variable overhead costs:				
Indirect labour	$0.60/DLH	$ 24,000	$ 30,000	$ 36,000
Utilities	1.00/DLH	40,000	50,000	60,000
Maintenance	0.40/DLH	16,000	20,000	24,000
Total....................	$2.00/DLH	80,000	100,000	120,000
Fixed overhead costs:				
Supervisory salaries		60,000	60,000	60,000
Insurance		5,000	5,000	5,000
Depreciation		190,000	190,000	190,000
Equipment rental		45,000	45,000	45,000
Total....................		300,000	300,000	300,000
Total overhead costs ..		$380,000	$400,000	$420,000

2. Total: $\dfrac{\$400,000}{50,000 \text{ DLH}}$ = $8 / DLH

Variable: $\dfrac{\$100,000}{50,000 \text{ DLH}}$ = $2 / DLH

Fixed: $\dfrac{\$300,000}{50,000 \text{ DLH}}$ = $6 / DLH

3. a.

Manufacturing Overhead

Actual costs	385,700	360,000*	Applied costs
	25,700		

*45,000 std. hrs. x $8 = $360,000.

Problem 11-15 (continued)

b. Variable overhead variances:

Actual Hours of Input, at the Actual Rate (AH x AR)	Actual Hours of Input, at the Standard Rate (AH x SR)	Standard Hours Allowed for Output, at the Standard Rate (SH x SR)
$89,700	46,000 hrs. x $2 = $92,000	45,000 hrs. x $2 = $90,000

Spending Variance, $2,300 F	Efficiency Variance, $2,000 U

Alternate Solution:

(AH x AR) − (AH x SR) = Variable Overhead Spending Variance
($89,700) − (46,000 hrs. x $2) = $2,300 F

SR (AH − SH) = Variable Overhead Efficiency Variance
$2 (46,000 hrs. − 45,000 hrs.) = $2,000 U

Fixed overhead variances:

Actual Fixed Overhead Cost	Flexible Budget Fixed Overhead Cost	Fixed Overhead Cost Applied to Work in Process
$296,000	$300,000	45,000 hrs. x $6 = $270,000

Budget Variance, $4,000 F	Volume Variance, $30,000 U

Problem 11-15 (continued)

Alternate approach to the budget variance:

Actual Fixed — Flexible Budget Fixed = Budget
Overhead Cost   Overhead Cost   Variance

$296,000 − $300,000 = $4,000 F

Alternate approach to the volume variance:

$$\text{Fixed Portion of the Predetermined Overhead Rate} \left[\text{Denominator Hours} - \text{Standard Hours Allowed} \right] = \text{Volume Variance}$$

$6 (50,000 hrs. − 45,000 hrs.) = $30,000 U

The overhead variances can be summarized as follows:

Variable overhead:
   Spending variance .... $ 2,300 F
   Efficiency variance .... 2,000 U
Fixed overhead:
   Budget variance .... 4,000 F
   Volume variance .... 30,000 U
Underapplied overhead for the year $25,700

Managerial Accounting

Problem 11-17 (40 minutes)

1. Total: $\dfrac{\$153{,}000}{15{,}000 \text{ DLH}} = \$10.20 \text{ / DLH}$

   Variable: $\dfrac{\$18{,}000}{15{,}000 \text{ DLH}} = \$1.20 \text{ / DLH}$

   Fixed: $\dfrac{\$135{,}000}{15{,}000 \text{ DLH}} = \$9.00 \text{ / DLH}$

2.

Direct materials: 4 kilograms at $8.00	$32.00
Direct labour: 2.5 hours at $7.00	17.50
Variable overhead: 2.5 hours at $1.20	3.00
Fixed overhead: 2.5 hours at $9.00..................................	22.50
Total standard cost per unit...	$75.00

3. See the graph at the end of this solution.

4. a. Fixed overhead variances:

Actual Fixed Overhead Cost	Flexible Budget Fixed Overhead Cost	Fixed Overhead Cost Applied to Work in Process
$137,400	$135,000	14,000 std. hrs.* x $9 = $126,000

Budget Variance, $2,400 U	Volume Variance, $9,000 U

   *5,600 units x 2.5 hrs. per unit = 14,000 hrs.

Alternate Approach:

Fixed overhead budget variance:

$$\text{Actual Fixed Overhead Cost} - \text{Flexible Budget Fixed Overhead Cost} = \text{Budget Variance}$$

$137,400 − $135,000 = $2,400 U

Problem 11-17 (continued)

Fixed overhead volume variance:

Fixed Portion of the Predetermined Overhead Rate $\left[\text{Denominator Hours} - \text{Standard Hours Allowed}\right]$ = Volume Variance

$9/DLH (15,000 hrs. − 14,000 hrs.) = $9,000 U

b. See the graph on the following page.

5. a. The fixed overhead budget variance will not change. The fixed overhead volume variance will be:

Actual Fixed Overhead Cost	Flexible Budget Fixed Overhead Cost	Fixed Overhead Cost Applied to Work in Process
$137,400	$135,000	15,500 hrs.* x $9 = $139,500

Budget Variance, $2,400 U   Volume Variance, $4,500 U

*6,200 units x 2.5 hours 15,500 hours.

Alternate solution to the volume variance:

Fixed Portion of the Predetermined Overhead Rate $\left[\text{Denominator Hours} - \text{Standard Hours Allowed}\right]$ = Volume Variance

$9 (15,000 hrs. − 15,500 hrs.) = $4,500 F

b. See the graph on the following page.

Managerial Accounting

Problem 11-17 (continued)

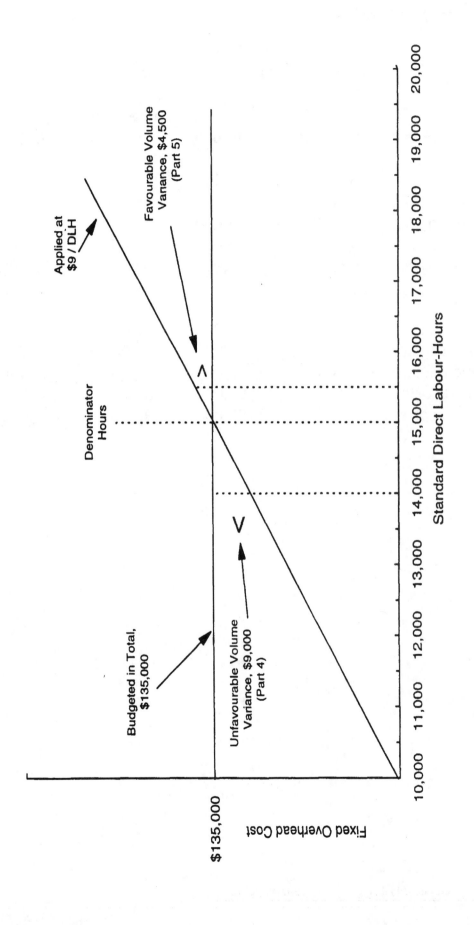

Problem 11-19 (35 minutes)

THE DURRANT COMPANY
Flexible Budget—Machining Department

Overhead Costs	Cost Formula	Machine-Hours		
		10,000	15,000	20,000
Variable:				
Utilities	$0.70/MH	$ 7,000	$ 10,500	$ 14,000
Lubricants	1.00/MH	10,000	15,000	20,000
Machine setup	0.20/MH	2,000	3,000	4,000
Indirect labour	0.60/MH	6,000	9,000	12,000
Total variable cost	$2.50/MH	25,000	37,500	50,000
Fixed:				
Lubricants		8,000	8,000	8,000
Indirect labour		120,000	120,000	120,000
Depreciation............		32,000	32,000	32,000
Total fixed costs ...		160,000	160,000	160,000
Total overhead costs...		$185,000	$197,500	$210,000

Managerial Accounting

Problem 11-19 (continued)

2.

THE DURRANT COMPANY
Performance Report—Machining Department
For the Month of March

Budgeted machine-hours 20,000
Actual machine-hours 18,000

Overhead Costs	Cost Formula	Actual 18,000 MH	Budget 18,000 MH	Spending Variance
Variable:				
Utilities	$0.70/MH	$ 12,000	$ 12,600	$ 600 F
Lubricants	1.00/MH	16,500*	18,000	1,500 F
Machine setup	0.20/MH	4,800	3,600	1,200 U
Indirect labour..........	0.60/MH	12,500	10,800	1,700 U
Total variable cost	$2.50/MH	45,800	45,000	800 U
Fixed:				
Lubricants		8,000	8,000	—
Indirect labour..........		120,000	120,000	—
Depreciation.............		32,000	32,000	—
Total fixed costs ...		160,000	160,000	—
Total overhead costs...		$205,800	$205,000	$ 800 U

*$24,500 total lubricants cost, less $8,000 fixed lubricants cost, equals $16,500 variable lubricants cost. The variable element of other costs is computed in the same way.

3. In order to compute an overhead efficiency variance, it would be necessary to know the standard hours allowed for the 9,000 units produced during March in the machining department.

4. The flexible budget can be used to develop predetermined overhead rates, which are used to apply overhead costs to units of product.

Problem 11-21 (50 minutes)

1. By use of the simple high-low method, the cost formulas below can be developed from the data in the problem. The completed flexible budget over an activity range of 80 to 100% of capacity would be:

ELGIN COMPANY
Flexible Budget

Overhead Costs	Cost Formulas	Percentage of Capacity		
		80%	90%	100%
Machine-hours		40,000	45,000	50,000
Variable overhead costs:				
Utilities	$0.80/MH	$ 32,000	$ 36,000	$ 40,000
Supplies	0.10/MH	4,000	4,500	5,000
Indirect labour	0.20/MH	8,000	9,000	10,000
Maintenance	0.40/MH	16,000	18,000	20,000
Total variable costs .	$1.50/MH	60,000	67,500	75,000
Fixed overhead costs:				
Utilities		9,000	9,000	9,000
Maintenance		21,000	21,000	21,000
Supervision		10,000	10,000	10,000
Total fixed costs		40,000	40,000	40,000
Total overhead costs......		$100,000	$107,500	$115,000

2. The cost formula for all overhead costs would be $40,000 per month plus $1.50 per machine-hour.

Managerial Accounting

Problem 11-21 (continued)

3.

ELGIN COMPANY
Performance Report
For the Month of May

Budgeted machine-hours	40,000
Actual machine-hours allowed.................	41,000
Actual machine-hours.............................	43,000*

Overhead Costs	Cost Formula	Actual Cost 43,000 MH	Budgeted Cost 43,000 MH	Spending Variance
Variable overhead costs:				
Utilities	$0.80/MH	$ 33,540**	$ 34,400	$ 860 F
Supplies......................	0.10/MH	6,450	4,300	2,150 U
Indirect labour	0.20/MH	9,890	8,600	1,290 U
Maintenance	0.40/MH	14,190**	17,200	3,010 F
Total variable costs	$1.50/MH	64,070	64,500	430 F
Fixed overhead costs:				
Utilities		9,000	9,000	—
Maintenance		21,000	21,000	—
Supervision		10,000	10,000	—
Total fixed costs		40,000	40,000	—
Total overhead costs		$104,070	$104,500	$ 430 F

*86% x 50,000 machine-hours = 43,000 machine-hours.
**$42,500 – $9,000 fixed = $33,540.
  $35,190 – $21,000 fixed = $14,190.

4. The unfavourable spending variance could be the result either of price increases or of waste. Unlike the price variance for materials and the rate variance for labour, the spending variance for variable overhead measures both price and waste elements. This is why the variance is called a "spending" variance. Total spending can be affected as much by waste as it can by greater (or lesser) prices paid for items.

Problem 11-21 (continued)

5. SR (AH − SH) = Efficiency Variance
$1.50 (43,000 hrs. − 41,000 hrs.) = $3,000 U

As stated in the text, the overhead efficiency variance is really misnamed, since it does not measure efficiency (waste) in use of variable overhead items. The variance arises solely because of the inefficiency in the *base* underlying the incurrence of variable overhead cost. If the incurrence of variable overhead costs is directly tied to the actual machine-hours worked, then the excessive number of machine-hours worked during May has caused the incurrence of $3,000 in variable overhead costs that would have been avoided had production been completed in the standard time allowed. In short, the overhead efficiency variance is independent of any spillage, waste, or theft of overhead supplies or other variable overhead items that may take place during a month.

Managerial Accounting

Problem 11-23 (50 minutes)

	Correct Budget A	Flexible Budget B		Actual C	Variance B – C
Sales—units	110,000	105,000		105,000	—
	$000's	$000's		$000's	$000's
Sales—dollars ..	2,750	2,625	(Note 1)	2,520	(105)
Variable costs:					
Material	440	420	(Note 2)	421	(1)
Labour	880	840	(Note 3)	845	(5)
Overhead	220	210	(Note 4)	205	5
Selling	220	210	(Note 5)	209	1
	1,760	1,680		1,680	0
Contribution	990	945		840	(105)
Fixed costs					
Factory					
overhead....	300	300		303	(3)
Selling	100	100		102	(2)
Administration	200	200		197	3
	600	600		602	(2)
Profit before tax	390	345		238	(107)
Income tax.....	156	138		95	43
Net earnings	234	207		143	(64)

NOTES:

1. 105,000   x $25 = $2,625,000
2. 105,000   x $ 4 = $ 420,000
3. 105,000   x $ 8 = $ 840,000
4. 105,000   x $ 2 = $ 210,000
5. 105,000   x $ 2 = $ 210,000

                        $16

Contribution/unit $ 9

Problem 11-23 (continued)

2. Note: Various forms are possible here:

		($000's)
Actual contribution		840
Add: Unfavourable variances		
Selling price	105	
Variable costs	-0-	105
Flexible budget contribution		945
Add: Effect sales volume 5 x $9		45
Bank budget contribution		990
Main variances then are		
Selling price		105
Sales volume		45
Fixed-spending		2

3.	Net earnings in 19X8	$143,000
	Add: noncash items—depreciation	200,000
	Cash generation	$343,000

On the assumption that 19X9 net earnings will be the same as 19X8, $343,000 cash will be generated (assuming that all expenses other than depreciation will be cash outlays) from which any dividends and bank loan repayments must be made.

4.   Variable costs per unit
     (Direct material $4 + Direct labour $8 + Variable

overhead $2)	$ 14
Variable cost of order (10,000 x $14)	$140,000

The minimum bid would be above $140,000 and just below the estimate of the best outside bid. The bid would have to be some judgmental amount above $140,000 to warrant the effort. The bid would be made to optimize expected contribution. The variable cost can be $14 if student explains that variable selling is not applicable in this internal sale, otherwise $16.

5. The company should use direct costing, contribution analysis and flexible budgeting. Annual budgets should be prepared and broken down by month for planning and control. Standard costs should be used in reporting with identification of variances.

(CGA-Canada Solution, adapted)

Managerial Accounting

Segment Reporting, Profitability Analysis and Decentralization

12

Exercise 12-1 (15 minutes)

	Total		Product A		Product B	
	Amount	**%**	**Amount**	**%**	**Amount**	**%**
Sales	$750,000	100.0	$300,000*	100	$450,000*	100
Less variable expenses	435,000	58.0	120,000	40	315,000	70
Contribution margin............	315,000	42.0	180,000	60	135,000	30
Less traceable fixed expenses.	183,000	24.4	138,000	46	45,000	10
Product line segment margin.............	132,000	17.6	$ 42,000	14	$ 90,000	20
Less common fixed expenses	105,000	14.0				
Net income.........	$ 27,000	3.6				

*Product A: 37,500 units x $8 = $300,000; Product B: 18,000 units x $25 = $450,000. Variable expenses are computed in the same way.

Exercise 12-3 (10 minutes)

1. The company should focus its campaign on Product B. The computations are:

	Product A	Product B
Increased sales	$70,000	$60,000
Product line CM ratio...	x 35%	x 50%
Incremental contribution margin............................	24,500	30,000
Less cost of the campaign	8,000	8,000
Increased segment margin and net income for the company as a whole..............................	$16,500	$22,000

2. The $90,000 in traceable fixed expenses in Exercise 12-2 is now partly traceable and partly common. When we divide Division Y into product line segments only $72,000 remains a traceable fixed expense. This amount would represent costs such as product line advertising and salaries of product line managers that can be identified with the product lines on a nonarbitrary basis. The remaining $18,000 ($90,000 – $72,000) becomes a common cost when Division Y is divided into product line segments. This amount would include such costs as the salary of the divisional manager or depreciation of a building used jointly to manufacture the two products.

Managerial Accounting

Exercise 12-5 (20 minutes)

	Total Company		A		B		C	
					Product			
Sales	$1,500,000	100.0%	$400,000	100%	$600,000	100%	$500,000	100%
Less variable expenses	588,000	39.2	208,000	52	180,000	30	200,000	40
Contribution margin	912,000	60.8	192,000	48	420,000	70	300,000	60
Less traceable fixed expenses	770,000	51.3	240,000	60	330,000	55	200,000	40
Product line segment margin	142,000	9.5	$(48,000)	(12%)	$ 90,000	15%	$100,000	20%
Less common fixed expenses	175,000*	11.7						
Net income (loss)	$ (33,000)	(2.2%)						

*$945,000 – $770,000 = $175,000.

2.
Incremental sales ($600,000 x 15%)	$90,000
Contribution margin ratio	x 70%
Incremental contribution margin	63,000
Less incremental advertising expense	25,000
Incremental net income	$38,000

Yes, the advertising program should be initiated.

Exercise 12-7 (15 minutes)

	Division A	Division B	Division C
Sales	$800,000*	$650,000	$500,000
Net operating income..................	72 000*	26,000	40,000*
Average operating assets	400,000	130,000*	200,000
Margin	9%	4%*	8%*
Turnover......................................	2	5*	2.5
Return on investment (ROI)	18%*	20%	20%*

*Given.

Note that Divisions B and C employ different strategies to obtain the same 20% return. Division B has a low margin and a high turnover, whereas Division C has just the opposite.

Managerial Accounting

Exercise 12-9 (15 minutes)

	Division A	Division B	Division C
Sales	$400,000*	$750,000*	$600,000*
Net operating income	32,000	45,000*	24,000
Average operating assets	160,000*	250,000	150,000*
ROI	20%*	18%*	16%
Minimum required rate of return:			
Percentage	15%*	20%	12%*
Dollar amount	$ 24,000	$ 50,000*	$ 18,000
Residual income	8,000	(5,000)	6,000*

*Given.

Exercise 12-11 (15 minutes)

1. The recommended transfer price should be between $21 and $38 per unit. The $21 figure is the one we obtain by applying the transfer pricing formula:

> Transfer price = Variable costs per unit + Lost contribution margin per unit on outside sales
>
> Transfer price = $21 + $0
> Transfer price = $21

The $38 figure is what the Audio Division is presently paying for its transformers on the intermediate market:

> $40 − ($40 x .05) = $38

The manager of the Electrical Division undoubtedly will suggest a price of $38 per transformer, since this is the price now being paid by the Audio Division. The manager of the Audio Division may accept this price or haggle for a somewhat lower price. The manager of the Electrical Division does have some room to bargain, since the division has idle capacity and therefore any transfer price over the variable costs of $21 per transformer will increase the division's overall contribution margin (and ROI).

Exercise 12-11 (continued)

2. If the Electrical Division is operating at full capacity, then the recommended transfer price should be $40 per transformer. By taking on the Audio Division's business, the Electrical Division would have to give up outside sales. These outside sales are presently yielding a contribution margin of $19 per transformer which would have to be recovered in any sales to the Audio Division, as shown by the transfer pricing formula:

Transfer price = Variable costs per unit + Lost contribution margin per unit on outside sales

Transfer price = $21 + ($40 − $21 = $19)

Transfer price = $40

Thus, the transfer price should not be less than $40 per transformer. Since the Audio Division can purchase on the outside at a net price of $38 per transformer, no transfers would be made between the two divisions.

Exercise 12-13 (15 minutes)

1. a. Transfer price = Variable costs per unit + Lost contribution margin per
   unit on outside sales

   Transfer price = $28* + ($50 − $30 = $20)
   Transfer price = $48

   *30 − $2 = $28

   b. No transfers will be made between the two divisions since Division Y
   can purchase units from another supplier for only $47 per unit.

2. Since Division X has enough idle capacity to handle all of Division Y's
   needs, there will be no lost contribution margin to consider in the transfer
   pricing formula. Using the formula, we get a transfer price of:

   Transfer price = Variable costs per unit + Lost contribution margin per
   unit on outside sales

   Transfer price = $20 + $0
   Transfer price = $20

   As stated in the text, the formula gives the lower limit for a transfer price;
   the actual price undoubtedly would be more than $20 since Division Y is
   now paying $34 per unit to an outside supplier. Thus, the transfer price
   should fall within a range of $20 to $34 per unit. The final price will have to
   be determined by negotiations between the two divisions.

Managerial Accounting

Problem 12-15 (60 minutes)

1. The disadvantages or weaknesses to the company's format are as follows:

   a. The company should include a column showing the combined results of the three territories taken together.

   b. Additional columns showing percentages would be helpful in assessing performance and pinpointing areas of difficulty.

   c. The territorial expenses should be segregated into variable and fixed categories to permit the computation of both a contribution margin and a territorial segment margin.

   d. The use of the term "margin" at the territorial level is preferred over the terms "income" and "loss."

   e. The corporate expenses are common to the territories and should not be allocated.

2. The corporate advertising has apparently been allocated on the basis of sales dollars; the general administrative expenses have apparently been allocated evenly among the three territories. Such allocations should not be made under the contribution approach, since they can be misleading to management and tend to call attention away from the segment margin. It is the segment margin that should be used in measuring the performance of a segment, not the "net income" or "net loss" after allocating common expenses.

3. See the statement on the following page.

4. The following points should be brought to the attention of management:

   a. Sales in Southern Europe are much lower than in the other two territories. This is not due to lack of salespeople since salaries in Southern Europe are about the same as in Middle Europe, which has the highest sales of the three territories.

Problem 12-15 (continued)

b. Southern Europe is spending less than half as much for advertising as Middle Europe. Perhaps this is the reason for Southern Europe's lower sales.

c. Northern Europe has a poor sales mix in that it apparently is selling a large amount of low margin items. Note that it has a contribution margin ratio of only 49%, as compared to 64% or more for the other two territories.

d. Northern Europe may be overstaffed. Its salaries are about 50% greater than in either of the other two territories.

e. Northern Europe is not covering its own traceable costs. Major attention should be given to changing the sales mix and reducing expenses in this territory.

Managerial Accounting

Problem 12-15 (continued)

3.

	Total		Southern Europe		Middle Europe		Northern Europe	
	Amount GLD	%	Amount GLD	%	Amount GLD	%	Amount GLD	%
Sales	1,800,000	100.0	300,000	100	800,000	100	700,000	100
Less variable expenses:								
Cost of goods sold	648,000	36.0	93,000	31	240,000	30	315,000	45
Shipping expense	89,000	4.9	15,000	5	32,000	4	42,000	6
Total variable expenses	737,000	40.9	108,000	36	272,000	34	357,000	51
Contribution margin	1,063,000	59.1	192,000	64	528,000	66	343,000	49
Less traceable fixed expenses:								
Salaries	222,000	12.3	54,000	18	56,000	7	112,000	16
Insurance	39,000	2.2	9,000	3	16,000	2	14,000	2
Advertising	590,000	32.8	105,000	35	240,000	30	245,000	35
Depreciation	81,000	4.5	21,000	7	32,000	4	28,000	4
Total traceable fixed expenses	932,000	51.8	189,000	63	344,000	43	399,000	57
Territorial segment margin	131,000	7.3	3,000	1	184,000	23	(56,000)	(8)
Less common fixed expenses:								
Advertising (general)	90,000	5.0						
General administration	60,000	3.3						
Total common fixed expense	150,000	8.3						
Net loss	(19,000)	(1.1)*						

*Columns may not total due to rounding.

Problem 12-17 (20 minutes)

1. Breaking the ROI computation into two separate elements helps the manager to see important relationships that might remain hidden if net operating income were simply related to operating assets. First, the importance of turnover of assets as a key element to overall profitability is emphasized. Prior to use of the ROI formula, managers tended to allow operating assets to swell to excessive levels. Second, the importance of sales volume in profit computations is stressed and explicitly recognized. Third, breaking the ROI computation into margin and turnover elements stresses the possibility of trading one off for the other in attempts to improve the overall profit picture. That is, a firm may shave its margins slightly hoping for a great enough increase in turnover to increase the overall rate of return. Fourth, it permits a manager to reduce important profitability elements to ratio form, which enhances comparisons between units (divisions, etc.) of the organization.

2.

	Companies in the Same Industry		
	A	**B**	**C**
Sales...................................	$4,000,000*	$1,500,000*	$6,000,000
Net operating income	560,000*	210,000*	210,000
Average operating assets....	2,000,000*	3,000,000	3,000,000*
Margin..................................	14%	14%	3.5%*
Turnover	2	0.5	2*
Return on investment (ROI)	28%	7%*	7%

*Given.

Because of differences in size between Company A and the other two companies (notice that R and C are equal in income and assets), looking at net operating income and operating assets alone, it is difficult to say much about comparative performance. That is, it is impossible to determine whether Company A's higher ROI is a result of its lower assets or its higher income. This points up the need to specifically include sales as an element in ROI computations. By including sales, light is shed on the comparative performance and possible problems in the three companies above.

Managerial Accounting

Problem 12-17 (continued)

NAA Report No. 35 states (p. 35):

"Introducing sales to measure level of operations helps to disclose specific areas for more intensive investigation. Company B does as well as Company A in terms of profit margin, for both companies earn 14% on sales. But Company B has a much lower turnover of capital than does Company A. Whereas a dollar of investment in Company A supports two dollars in sales each period, a dollar investment in Company B supports only 50 cents in sales each period. This suggests that the analyst should look carefully at Company B's investment. Is the company keeping an inventory larger than necessary for its sales volume? Are receivables being collected promptly? Or did Company A acquire its fixed assets at a price level which was much lower than that at which Company B purchased its plant?"

Thus, by including sales specifically in ROI computations the manager is able to discover possible problems, as well as reasons underlying a strong or a weak performance. Looking at Company A compared to Company C, notice that C's turnover is the same as A's, but C's margin on sales is much lower. Why would C have such a low margin? Is it due to inefficiency, is it due to geographical location (thereby requiring higher salaries or transportation charges), is it due to excessive materials costs, or is it due to still other factors? ROI computations raise questions such as these, which form the basis for managerial action.

To summarize, in order to bring B's ROI into line with A's, it seems obvious that B's management will have to concentrate its efforts on increasing turnover, either by increasing sales or by reducing assets. It seems unlikely that B can appreciably increase its ROI by improving its margin on sales. On the other hand, C's management should concentrate its efforts on the margin element by trying to pare down its operating expenses.

Problem 12-19 (30 minutes)

a) **Budgeted Contribution Margin:**

	Spars	Masts
Selling price	$200	$300
Variable costs:		
Manufacturing	66	108
Selling & administration	18	21
Total variable costs	84	129
Budgeted contribution margin per unit	$116	$171

Budgeted Average Contribution Margin Per Unit:

$$\frac{(4,200)(116) + (17,000)(171)}{(4,200 + 17,000)} = \underline{160.1038}$$

i) **Sales Price Variance:**

Spars	($180 − $200)	6,000 =	$120,000 U
Masts	($300 − $300)	18,000 =	-0-
Total			$120,000 U

ii) **Sales Mix Variance:**

Spars $\left[\; 6,000 - \left(\dfrac{4,200}{21,200} \times 24,000\right)\right]$ $116 = $144,453 F

Masts $\left[\; 18,000 - \left(\dfrac{17,000}{21,200} \times 24,000\right)\right]$ $171 = $212,943 F

Total $\qquad\qquad\qquad\qquad\qquad\qquad\qquad$ $ 68,490 U

An alternative calculation approach not shown in text.

Spars (6,000 − (24,000 x 4,200/21,200)) (116 − 160.1038) = $54,922 (U)
Masts (18,000 − (24,000 x 17,000/21,200)) (171 − 160.1038) = 13,569 (U)
Total sales mix variance = $68,491 (U)

iii) **Sales Quantity Variance:**

Spars $\left[\left(\dfrac{4,200}{21,200} \times 24,000\right) - 4,200\right]$ $116 = $ 64,347 F

Masts $\left[\left(\dfrac{17,000}{21,200} \times 24,000\right) - 17,000\right]$ $171 = 383,943 F

Total $\qquad\qquad\qquad\qquad\qquad\qquad\qquad$ $448,290 F

An alternative calculation approach not shown in text.

Spars (6,000 − 4,200) x 160.1038 = $288,187 (F)
Masts (18,000 − 17,000) x 160.1038 = 160,104 (F)
Total sales quantity variance = $448,291 (F)

Managerial Accounting

Problem 12-19 (continued)

   iv) **Market Share Variance**:

$$\text{Spars} \left[6,000 - \left(\frac{4,200}{48,000} \right) 60,000 \right] \$116 = \$ \ 87,000 \ F$$

$$\text{Masts} \left[18,000 - \left(\frac{17,000}{85,000} \right) 100,000 \right] \$171 = \underline{342,000} \ U$$

Total $\hspace{9cm} \underline{\$255,000} \ U$

   v) **Market Size Variance**:

$$\text{Spars} \ (60,000 - 48,000) \left(\frac{4,200}{48,000} \right) \$116 = \$121,800 \ F$$

$$\text{Masts} \ (100,000 - 85,000) \left(\frac{17,000}{85,000} \right) \$171 = \underline{\$513,000} \ F$$

Total $\hspace{9cm} \underline{\$634,800} \ F$

b) Gallant is wrong in believing that a bonus is warranted due to increased sales, as the increased sales volumes were due largely to the following reasons:

   – A reduction in the selling price of Spars which caused an unfavourable variance of $120,000.

   – A change in the mix of products sold with an increased portion being the less profitable product line (Spars) therefore causing an unfavourable mix variance of $68,490.

   – The increased volume of sales were primarily due to increased demand in the overall industry. The company was not able to maintain their market share ($255,000 unfavourable variance) which is a major item that normally would be controllable by the Marketing and Sales Department.

   Thus, the marketing and sales employees should not receive the bonus.

$\hspace{8cm}$ (SMAC Solution, adapted)

Problem 12-21 (40 minutes)

1. Transfer price = Variable costs per unit + Lost contribution margin per unit on outside sales

   Transfer price = $58* + ($100 − $63 = $37)
   Transfer price = $95

   *$63 − $5 = $58.

   No transfers will be made between the two divisions since Division B can purchase from the outside at $92 per unit.

2. a. Transfer price = Variable costs per unit + Lost contribution margin per unit on outside sales

   Transfer price = $15* + ($40 − $19 = $21)
   Transfer price = $36

   *$19 − $4 = $15.

   In this case there may be disagreement over the transfer price since Division B is now paying $39 per unit on the outside and Division A may expect the same price to be paid on any internal sales. The $36 figure computed above is an appropriate transfer price in that it allows Division A (the selling division) to realize the same amount of contribution margin per unit as it presently is receiving from outside sales. But, as stated in the text, this represents a *lower limit* for a transfer price; the price can be as high as $39 per unit without leading to inappropriate decisions. Thus, we have a transfer price *range* in this case of $36 to $39 per unit. Where the actual price falls within this range will depend on negotiations between the two divisions.

Managerial Accounting

Problem 12-21 (continued)

b. The loss in potential profits to the company as a whole will be:

Division B's outside purchase price	$39
Division A's minimum transfer price............................	36
Potential contribution margin which is lost to the company as a whole	3
Number of units..	x 70,000
Potential contribution margin and company profits forgone	$210,000

Another way to derive the same answer is to look at the loss in potential profits for each division and then total the losses for the impact on the company as a whole. The loss in potential profits in Division A will be:

Suggested selling price per unit..................................	$38
Division A's minimum transfer price............................	36
Potential added contribution margin per unit...........	2
Number of units..	x 70,000
Potential contribution margin and divisional profits forgone	$140,000

The loss in potential profits in Division B will be:

Outside purchase price per unit.................................	$39
Suggested price per unit inside..................................	38
Potential cost avoided per unit	1
Number of units..	x 70,000
Potential contribution margin and divisional profits forgone	$ 70,000

The total of these two amounts ($140,000 + $70,000) equals the $210,000 loss in potential profits for the company as a whole.

Problem 12-21 (continued)

3. a. Since Division A has idle capacity there is no lost contribution margin to consider in computing the lower limit for a transfer price. Using the formula, we get:

Transfer price = Variable costs per unit + Lost contribution margin per unit on outside sales

Transfer price = $35 + $0
Transfer price = $35

The upper limit for a transfer price would be the price now being paid by Division B to its outside supplier:

$60 − (.05 x $60) = $57

Thus, the transfer price should be within a range of $35 to $57 per unit. The final price will again depend on negotiations between the two divisions.

b. Division A's ROI should increase. Since the division has idle capacity, there should be little or no increase needed in the division's operating assets as a result of selling 20,000 units a year to Division B. Therefore, Division A's asset turnover should increase. The division's margin earned on sales should also increase, since its contribution margin will increase by $340,000 as a result of the new sales, with no offsetting increase in fixed costs:

Selling price per unit	$52
Less variable costs	35
Contribution margin per unit...	17
Number of units	x 20,000
Added contribution margin..	$340,000

Thus, with both the margin and the turnover increasing, the division's ROI would also increase.

Managerial Accounting

Problem 12-21 (continued)

4. In order to use the transfer pricing formula, we must first determine the loss in contribution margin to Division A from giving up sales of 30,000 units of its present product to outside customers:

Contribution margin per unit ($45 − $30)	$ 15
Number of units given up	x 30,000
Total lost contribution margin	$450,000

This lost contribution margin must be spread over the 60,000 units of new product which are to be manufactured for Division B:

$$\frac{\text{Total lost contribution margin,} \quad \$450,000}{\text{Number of units of new product,} \quad 60,000} = \$7.50 \text{ per unit}$$

Using this figure in the transfer pricing formula, we get:

Transfer price = Variable costs per unit + Lost contribution margin per unit on outside sales

Transfer price = $25 + $7.50
Transfer price = $32.50

Again, this represents a minimum transfer price; Division A may wish to charge a higher price if it wants to increase its overall profits and ROI.

Problem 12-23 (30 minutes)

1.

$$\frac{\text{NOI}}{\text{Sales}} \quad \times \quad \frac{\text{Sales}}{\text{Average operating assets}} \quad = \text{ROI}$$

$$\frac{\$80,000}{\$1,000,000} \quad \times \quad \frac{\$1,000,000}{\$500,000} \quad = \text{ROI}$$

$$8\% \quad \times \quad 2 \quad = 16\%$$

2.

$$\frac{\$90,000}{\$1,000,000} \quad \times \quad \frac{\$1,000,000}{\$500,000} \quad = \text{ROI}$$

9%	×	2	= 18%
(Increase)		(Unchanged)	(Increase)

3.

$$\frac{\$80,000}{\$1,000,000} \quad \times \quad \frac{\$1,000,000}{\$400,000} \quad = \text{ROI}$$

8%	×	2.5	= 20%
(Unchanged)		(Increase)	(Increase)

4. The company has a contribution margin ratio of 40% ($20 CM per unit, divided by $50 selling price per unit). Therefore, a $100,000 increase in sales would result in a new net operating income of:

Sales	$1,100,000	100%
Less variable expenses.............................	660,000	60
Contribution margin...................................	440,000	40%
Less fixed expenses..................................	320,000	
Net operating income	$ 120,000	

$$\frac{\$120,000}{\$1,100,000} \quad \times \quad \frac{\$1,100,000}{\$500,000} \quad = \text{ROI}$$

10.91%	×	2.2	= 24%
(Increase)		(Increase)	(Increase)

As stated in the text, notice that a change in sales affects *both* the margin and the turnover.

Problem 12-23 (continued)

5. Interest is a financing expense and thus is not used to compute net operating income.

$$\frac{\$85{,}000}{\$1{,}000{,}000} \quad \times \quad \frac{\$1{,}000{,}000}{\$625{,}000} \quad = \quad \text{ROI}$$

8.5%	x	1.6	= 13.6%
(Increase)		(Decrease)	(Decrease)

6. $$\frac{\$80{,}000}{\$1{,}000{,}000} \quad \times \quad \frac{\$1{,}000{,}000}{\$320{,}000} \quad = \quad \text{ROI}$$

8%	x	3.125	= 25%
(Unchanged)		(Increase)	(Increase)

7. $$\frac{\$60{,}000}{\$1{,}000{,}000} \quad \times \quad \frac{\$1{,}000{,}000}{\$480{,}000} \quad = \quad \text{ROI}$$

6%	x	2.08	= 12.5%
(Decrease)		(Increase)	(Decrease)

Problem 12-25 (25 minutes)

1. In order to compute the ROI and the residual income, it is necessary first to compute the average operating assets for the year. The computation is:

Ending balance...	$15,500,000
Beginning balance ($15,500,000 ÷ 1.24).........................	12,500,000
Total	$28,000,000
Average balance. ($28,000,00 ÷ 2)	$14,000,000

a. $\underline{\text{Net operating income}}$ X $\dfrac{\text{Sales}}{\text{Average operating assets}}$ = ROI

$\dfrac{\$2,800,000}{\$35,000,000}$ X $\dfrac{\$35,000,000}{\$14,000,000}$ = ROI

8%   X   2.5   = 20%

b.
Net operating income		$2,800,000
Minimum required net operating income:		
Average operating assets	$14,000,000	
Minimum required return	X 15%	2,100,000
Residual income		$ 700,000

2. Yes, Presser's management probably would have accepted the investment if residual income were used. The investment opportunity would have lowered Presser's ROI because the expected return (18%) was lower than the division's historical returns (19–22%) as well as its most recent ROI (20%). Management rejected the investment because bonuses are based in part on the performance measure of ROI. If residual income were used as a performance measure (and as a basis for bonuses), management would accept investments that would increase residual income (i.e., a dollar amount rather than a percentage) including the investment opportunity with an ROI of 18%.

3. Presser must be free to control all items related to profit (revenues and expenses) and investment if it is to be evaluated fairly as an investment centre by either of the ROI or residual income performance measures.

Managerial Accounting

Problem 12-27 (40 minutes)

1. The division's target net income is $36,000:

$$12\% \times \$300,000 = \$36,000$$

Let x = units sold
$$\$4x = \$2.50x + \$234,000 + \$36,000$$
$$\$1.50x = \$270,000$$
$$x = 180,000 \text{ bearings, or } \$720,000 \text{ in sales}$$

a. Margin = $\dfrac{\text{Net operating income,}}{\text{Sales,}}$ $\dfrac{\$36,000}{\$720,000}$ = 5%

b. Turnover = $\dfrac{\text{Sales,}}{\text{Operating assets,}}$ $\dfrac{\$720,000}{\$300,000}$ = 2.4

2. a. and b.

		Sales Volume		
Units sold		160,000	180,000*	200,000
(1)	Sales @ $4.25, $4.00, and $3.75	$680,000	$720,000	$750,000
	Less variable expense @ $2.50	400,000	450,000	500,000
	Contribution margin	280,000	270,000	250,000
	Less fixed expenses	234,000	234,000	234,000
(2)	Net income	$ 46,000	$ 36,000	$ 16,000
(3)	Total assets	$290,000	$300,000	$310,000
(4)	Margin (2) ÷ (1)	6.76%	5%	2.13%
(5)	Turnover (1) ÷ (3)	2.34	2.4	2.42
	ROI (4) x (5)	15.82%	12%	5.15%

*Column not required.

Problem 12-27 (continued)

3.

		Present Sales	New Sales	Total Sales
	Units sold..	180,000	20,000	200,000
(1)	Sales @ $4.00 and $3.25.........	$720,000	$65,000	$785,000
	Less variable expense @			
	$2.50.....................................	450,000	50,000	500,000
	Contribution margin..................	270,000	15,000	285,000
	Less fixed expenses................	234,000	—	234,000
(2)	Net income	$ 36,000	$15,000	$ 51,000
(3)	Total assets............................	$300,000	$25,000	$325,000
(4)	Margin (2) ÷ (1)........................	5%	23.08%	6.50%
(5)	Turnover (1) ÷ (3)	2.4	2.6	2.42
	ROI (4) x (5)	12%	60%	15.73%

Yes, the manager of the Bearing Division should accept the $3.25 price.

Managerial Accounting

Problem 12-29 (30 minutes)

1. The Consumer Products Division will probably reject the $400 price. This is because the price is below the division's "variable costs" of $420 per CD player. Although these "variable costs" contain a $190 transfer price from the Board Division, which in turn includes $30 per unit in fixed costs, the Consumer Products Division will not be aware of the Board Division's cost breakdown and will simply view the $190 purchase price from the Board Division as a variable cost. Thus, it will reject the $400 price offered.

2. If both the Board Division and the Consumer Products Division have idle capacity, then it would be a disadvantage to the company for the Consumer Products Division to reject the $400 price. By rejecting the $400 price, the company will lose $50 per CD player in potential contribution margin:

Price offered per player...		$400
Less variable costs per player:		
Board Division..	$120	
Consumer Products Division.......................................	230	350
Potential contribution margin per player........................		$ 50

Problem 12-29 (continued)

3. If the Board Division is operating at capacity, then the minimum transfer price between the two divisions should be:

> Transfer price = Variable costs per unit + Lost contribution margin per
> unit on outside sales
>
> Transfer price = $120 + ($190 − $120 = $70)
> Transfer price = $190

Any sales by the Consumer Products Division would have to recover this $190 transfer price, as well as the variable costs that it incurs in the manufacture of the CD players. Therefore, the minimum selling price per player that the Consumer Products Division can accept is $420 ($190 + $230). If the Consumer Products Division accepts the $400 price, the loss to the company as a whole on the 5,000 units will be as follows:

Minimum selling price per player	$420
Price offered per player	400
Potential lost contribution margin	20
Number of players	x 5,000
Total potential lost contribution margin	$100,000

4. The Consumer Products Division needs a breakdown of the unit transfer price being charged by the Board Division. This is true regardless of whether the transfer price is based on full cost, intermediate market price, or something else. By having access to the cost breakdown of the transfer price, the Consumer Products Division would be in a better position to assess the merits of special orders and of other methods of marketing its CD players. Unfortunately, a breakdown of the unit transfer price is rarely provided in actual practice.

Managerial Accounting

Problem 12-31 (30 minutes)

1. a. Employing the transfer pricing formula, we get:

Transfer price = Variable costs + Lost contribution margin per unit on
outside sales

Transfer price = $18* + $0
Transfer price = $18

*$16 + ($4 x 50%) = $18

Thus, the lowest transfer price that can be justified is $18 per unit, which represents Division X's variable costs.

b. The highest transfer price that can be justified is the price now being paid by Division Y to its outside supplier. This would be $27 per unit:

$30 – (10% x $30) = $27

c. No. The selling division must be free to reject intracompany business. The division manager may wish to let his/her idle capacity remain idle and look for other, more profitable business.

Problem 12-31 (continued)

d. If Division Y is forced to purchase internally and pay $35 per unit, rather than buy outside at $27 per unit, it will result in *greater* total corporate profits. The reason is that by purchasing inside rather than outside, Division Y will be providing $9 per unit in contribution margin to the company as a whole that otherwise would not be realized. The computations are:

Benefit to Division X:		
Transfer price paid to Division X per unit................		$35
Less Division X variable costs ($16 + $2)..............		18
Division X increased contribution margin per unit..		17
Less loss in contribution margin to Division Y:		
Outside purchase price per unit............................	$27	
Internal transfer price per unit..............................	35	
Division Y reduced contribution margin per unit		(8)
Net increase in contribution margin to the company as a whole..		$ 9

e. No. Even though suboptimization will result if Division Y goes outside for the units, the buying division must always be free to get the best price it can if it is to be evaluated as an independent, autonomous unit.

2. a.   Employing the transfer pricing formula, we get:

Transfer price = Variable costs per unit + Lost contribution margin per unit on outside sales
Transfer price = $18 + ($30 − $20 = $10)
Transfer price = $28

A transfer price of $28 per unit will provide Division X with the same amount of contribution margin per unit as selling outside at $30 per unit.

Since Division Y can purchase outside for only $27 per unit, no transfers will be made between the two divisions.

Managerial Accounting

Problem 12-31 (continued)

b. Again, the answer is $28 per unit. It can be argued that an upper limit isn't relevant in this situation, since the lower limit ($28) is above the buying division's outside purchase price ($27).

c. No, for the reasons given in (2a) above.

d. If Division Y is forced to buy internally at $35 per unit, rather than buy externally at $27 per unit, it will result in less total corporate profits. The computations are:

Outside sales revenue foregone by Division X		$35
Less: Outside purchase price avoided by Division Y	$27	
Reduction in selling and administrative		
expenses on intracompany business	2	29
Net reduction in contribution margin per unit to the		
company as a whole..		$ 6

e. No, for two reasons. First, the buying division must always be free to go outside and get the best price it can. And second, if Division Y is forced to buy internally, the result will be suboptimization for the company as a whole, as shown in Part (2d) above.

Relevant Costs for Decision Making   13

Exercise 13-1 (15 minutes)

Item	Case 1 Relevant	Case 1 Not Relevant	Case 2 Relevant	Case 2 Not Relevant
a. Sales revenue	X			X
b. Direct materials	X		X	
c. Direct labour	X			X
d. Variable manufacturing overhead	X			X
e. Depreciation—Model B100 machine		X		X
f. Book value—Model B100 machine		X		X
g. Disposal value—Model B100 machine		X	X	
h. Market value—Model B300 machine (cost)	X		X	
i. Depreciation—Model B300 machine	X		X	
j. Fixed manufacturing overhead		X		X
k. Variable selling expense	X			X
l. Fixed selling expense	X			X
m. General administrative overhead	X			X

Exercise 13-3 (10 minutes)

Cost savings if the high-speed lathe is purchased:		
($36,000 – $21,000 = $15,000; $15,000 x		
5 years = $75,000)..		$75,000
Incremental cost:		
Cost of the high-speed lathe...	$60,000	
Less salvage from the standard lathe............................	8,000	52,000
Net advantage of purchasing the high-speed lathe............		$23,000

Exercise 13-5 (20 minutes)

1.

	Per Unit Differential Costs		15,000 units	
	Make	**Buy**	**Make**	**Buy**
Cost of purchasing............................		$20		$300,000
Direct materials................................	$ 6		$ 90,000	
Direct labour	8		120,000	
Variable manufacturing overhead.....	1		15,000	
Fixed manufacturing overhead, traceable[1]	2		30,000	
Fixed manufacturing overhead, common	—	—	—	—
Total costs.....................................	$17	$20	$255,000	$300,000
Difference in favour of continuing to make the parts	$3		$45,000	

[1] Only the supervisory salaries can be avoided if the parts are purchased. The remaining book value of the special equipment is a sunk cost; hence, the $3 per unit depreciation expense is not relevant to this decision. Based on these data, the company should reject the offer and should continue to produce the parts internally.

2.

	Make	**Buy**
Cost of purchasing (part 1)		$300,000
Cost of making (part 1)	$255,000	
Opportunity cost—segment margin foregone on a potential new product line	65,000	—
Total cost...	$320,000	$300,000
Difference in favour of purchasing from the outside supplier		$20,000

Thus, the company should accept the offer and purchase the parts from the outside supplier.

Managerial Accounting

Exercise 13-7 (20 minutes)

1.

		A	B	C
(1)	Contribution margin per unit...	$18	$36	$20
(2)	Direct labour cost per unit...	$12	$32	$16
(3)	Direct labour rate per hour..	8	8	8
(4)	Direct labour-hours required per unit (2) ÷ (3)	1.5	4	2
(5)	Contribution margin per direct labour-hour (1) ÷ (4)	$12	$ 9	$10

2. The company should concentrate its labour time on producing product A:

	A	B	C
Contribution margin per direct labour-hour	$12	$9	$10
Direct labour-hours available.................	x 3,000	x 3,000	x 3,000
Total contribution margin	$36,000	$27,000	$30,000

Although product A has the lowest contribution margin per unit and the second lowest contribution margin ratio, it promises the greatest amount of contribution margin per direct labour-hour. Since labour time seems to be the scarce resource in the company, it is the measure that should guide management in its production decisions when demand outstrips the company's ability to produce.

3. The amount Banner Company should be willing to pay in overtime wages for additional direct labour time depends upon how the time would be used. If there are unfilled orders for all of the products, Banner would presumably use the additional time to make more of product A. Each hour of direct labour time generates $12 of contribution margin over and above the usual direct labour cost. Therefore, Banner should be willing to pay up to $20 per hour (the $8 usual wage plus the contribution margin per hour of $12) for additional labour time, but would of course prefer to pay far less. The upper limit of $20 per direct labour hour signals to managers how valuable additional labour hours are to the company.

Exercise 13-7 (continued)

If all the demand for product A has been satisfied, Banner Company would then use any additional direct labour-hours to manufacture product C. In that case, the company should be willing to pay up to $18 per hour (the $8 usual wage plus the $10 contribution margin per hour for product C) to manufacture more product C.

Likewise, if all the demand for both products A and C has been satisfied, additional labour-hours would be used to make product B. In that case, the company should be willing to pay up to $17 per hour to manufacture more product B.

Managerial Accounting

Exercise 13-9 (5 minutes)

1. b.   3. a.   5. b.   7. b.   9. a
2. a.   4. a   6. b.   8. a.   10. b.

Problem 13-11 (25 minutes)

1. a. and b.

	5 Year Summary		
	Keep Old Press	**Difference**	**Buy New Press**
Sales ($200,000 x 5 years)	$1,000,000	$ -0-	$1,000,000
Selling and administrative expenses ($116,000 x 5 years)	580,000	-0-	580,000
Operating expenses—press..........	200,000	140,000	60,000
Depreciation of the old press, or loss write-off.............................	70,000	-0-	70,000*
Salvage value—old press	—	30,000	(30,000)*
Depreciation—new press..............	—	(110,000)	110,000
Total expenses	850,000		790,000
Net operating income...................	$ 150,000	$ 60,000	$ 210,000

*In a formal income statement, these two items would be shown as a single $40,000 "loss from disposal" figure.

The new press should be purchased. The savings in operating costs over the next five years will exceed the net investment by $60,000.

2. Reduction in annual operating costs
    ($28,000 x 5 years) $140,000
    Investment in the new press:
       Original cost $110,000
       Less salvage value of the old press 30,000   80,000
    Net advantage of purchasing the new press .... $ 60,000

All other costs are either sunk or do not differ between the two alternatives.

Managerial Accounting

Problem 13-13 (60 minutes)

1. Contribution margin lost if Department A is dropped:

Lost from Department A	$700,000
Lost from Department B (10% x $2,400,000)	240,000
Total	940,000
Less fixed costs that can be avoided ($900,000 – $370,000)	530,000
Decrease in profits for the company as a whole	$410,000

2. Product A should be processed further and sold for $60,000:

Sales value after further processing	$60,000
Sales value at the split-off point	40,000
Incremental revenue from further processing	20,000
Cost of further processing	13,000
Profit from further processing	$ 7,000

The $10,000 in allocated common costs (1/3 x $30,000) will be the same regardless of which alternative is selected, and hence is not relevant to the decision.

3. The company should accept orders first for Z, second for X, and third for Y. The computations are:

	X	Y	Z
(1) Direct materials required per unit	$24	$15	$ 9
(2) Cost per kilogram	$ 3	$ 3	$ 3
(3) Kilograms required per unit (1) ÷ (2)	8 kg	5 kg	3 kg
(4) Contribution margin per unit	$32	$14	$21
(5) Contribution margin per kilogram of materials used (4) ÷ (3)	$4/kg	$2.80/kg	$7/kg

Problem 13-13 (continued)

Since Z uses the least amount of material per unit of the three products, and since it is the most profitable of the three in terms of its use of materials, some students will immediately assume that this is an infallible relationship. That is, they will assume that the way to spot the most profitable product is to find the one using the least amount of the scarce resource. The way to dispel this notion is to point out that product X uses more material (the scarce resource) than does product Y, but yet it is preferred over product Y. *The key factor is not how much of a scarce resource a product uses, but rather how much contribution margin the product generates per unit of the scarce resource.*

Managerial Accounting

Problem 13-13 (continued)

4.

| Item | "Cost" per Part | Differential Costs | | Explanation |
		Make	Buy	
Direct materials.....	$4.00	$4.00	—	Differential, because the cost can be avoided by buying the parts.
Direct labour	2.75	2.75	—	Differential, because the cost can be avoided by buying the parts.
Variable manufacturing overhead	.50	.50	—	Differential, because the cost can be avoided by buying the parts.
Fixed manufacturing overhead, traceable	3.00	1.00	—	Only the supervisory salaries and other costs which can be avoided are differential costs. The sunk costs are not differential, since they can't be avoided by buying.
Fixed manufacturing overhead, common	2.25	—	—	Not differential, since these costs can't be avoided by buying.
Outside purchase price	—	—	$10.00	Differential, since the cost can be avoided by continuing to make the parts.
Total cost..............	$12.50	$8.25	$10.00	

The company should continue to make the parts. The dollar disadvantage of accepting the supplier's offer is $1.75 per part ($10.00 – $8.25), or $105,000 per year:

$1.75 x 60,000 parts = $105,000.

Problem 13-13 (continued)

5. Monthly profits will be increased by $9,000:

	Per Unit	2,000 Units
Incremental sales	$12.00	$24,000
Incremental costs:		
Direct materials	2.50	5,000
Direct labour	3.00	6,000
Variable manufacturing overhead	0.50	1,000
Variable selling and administrative	1.50	3,000
Total	7.50	15,000
Incremental profits	$ 4.50	$ 9,000

The fixed costs are not relevant to the decision, since they will not change in total amount regardless of whether the special order is accepted or rejected.

6. The relevant cost figure is $1.50 (the variable selling and administrative costs). All other variable costs are sunk, since the units have already been produced. The fixed costs would not be relevant, since they will not change in total regardless of the price charged for the leftover units.

Problem 13-15 (35 minutes)

1. The fixed overhead costs are common and will not change regardless of whether the cartridges are produced internally or purchased outside. Hence, they are not relevant to the decision at hand. The variable overhead cost per box of pens is $0.30, as shown below:

Total manufacturing overhead cost per box of pens	$0.80
Less fixed manufacturing overhead portion	
($50,000 ÷ 100,000 boxes)	0.50
Variable manufacturing overhead cost per box.........................	$0.30

The total variable costs of producing one box of Zippo pens would be:

Direct materials	$1.50
Direct labour..	1.00
Variable manufacturing overhead	0.30
Total variable costs per box..	$2.80

If the cartridges for the Zippo pens are purchased from the outside supplier, then the variable cost per box of Zippo pens would be:

Direct materials ($1.50 x 80%)...	$1.20
Direct labour ($1.00 x 90%)	0.90
Variable manufacturing overhead ($0.30 x 90%).......................	0.27
Purchase of cartridges	0.48
Total variable costs per box..	$2.85

Therefore, the company should reject the outside suppliers offer. Producing the cartridges internally is less costly by $0.05 per box of pens.

Problem 13-15 (continued)

The solution prepared by most students will be shown as above. *A better approach to the solution would be:*

Cost avoided by purchasing the cartridges:
Direct materials ($1.50 x 20%)... $0.30
Direct labour ($1.00 x 10%) 0.10
Variable manufacturing overhead
   ($0.30 x 10%) 0.03
   Total costs avoided.. $0.43

Cost of purchasing the cartridges.. $0.48

Cost savings per box by making.. $0.05

Notice that the $0.43 above represents *the cost of making one box of cartridges internally,* since this is the overall cost saving realized per box of pens by purchasing the cartridges from the outside.

2. The *maximum* price would be $0.43 per box. The company would not be willing to pay more than this amount, since this represents the cost of producing one box of cartridges internally, as shown in part 1 above. To make the purchasing of cartridges attractive, however, the purchase price should be *less than* $0.43 per box.

3. The company has three alternatives as to how it can obtain the necessary cartridges. It can:

   1—Produce all cartridges internally.
   2—Purchase all cartridges externally.
   3—Produce 100,000 boxes internally and purchase 50,000 boxes externally.

Many students will prepare computations for alternatives 1 and 2, but will overlook the possibility of producing some cartridges and purchasing the rest.

Managerial Accounting

Problem 13-15 (continued)

The costs under the three alternatives are:

Alternative #1—Produce all cartridges internally:
Variable costs (150,000 boxes x $0.43)...................................	$64,500
Fixed costs of adding capacity..	30,000
Total cost	$94,500

Alternative #2—Purchase all cartridges externally:
Variable costs (150,000 boxes x $0.48)................................	$72,000

Alternative #3—Produce 100,000 boxes internally, and
purchase 50,000 boxes externally:

Variable costs:
100,000 boxes x $0.43...	$43,000
50,000 boxes x $0.48	24,000
Total cost..	$67,000

Or, in terms of total cost per box of pens, the answer would be:

Alternative #1—Produce all cartridges internally:
Variable costs (150,000 boxes x $2.80)................................	$420,000
Fixed costs of adding capacity..	30,000
Total cost	$450,000

Alternative #2—Purchase all cartridges externally:
Variable costs (150,000 boxes x $2.85)................................	$427,500

Alternative #3—Produce 100,000 boxes internally, and
purchase 50,000 boxes externally:

Variable costs:
100,000 boxes x $2.80...	$280,000
50,000 boxes x $2.85	142,500
Total cost..	$422,500

Thus, the company should accept the outside supplier's offer for 50,000 boxes of cartridges.

Problem 13-15 (continued)

4. The company should consider at least the following factors before accepting the outside supplier's offer:

a. The ability of the outside supplier to meet required delivery schedules.
b. The quality of the cartridges purchased from the outside supplier.
c. The ability of the outside supplier to supply more cartridges if volume increases In future years.
d. The alternative uses for the capacity which is now being used to produce the cartridges (i.e., the opportunity cost of the space).
e. The problem of alternate sources of supply if the outside supplier proves to be undependable.

Managerial Accounting

Problem 13-17 (30 minutes)

1. Selling price per unit $40
    Less variable expenses per unit 24*
    Contribution margin per unit $16

    *$9.50 + $10 + $2.80 + $1.70 = $24.

    Increased sales in units (80,000 x 25%) 20,000
    Contribution margin per unit .... x $16
    Incremental contribution margin $320,000
    Less added fixed selling expense 150,000
    Incremental net operating income $170,000

    Yes, the increase in fixed selling expense would be justified.

2. Variable production cost per unit $22.30
    Import duties, etc. ($14,000 ÷ 20,000 units) 0.70
    Shipping cost per unit 1.50
    Break-even price per unit $24.50

3. If the plant operates at 25% of normal levels, then only 5,000 units
    will be produced and sold during the three-month period:

    80,000 units per year x 3/12 = 20,000 units.
    20,000 units x 25% = 5,000 units produced and sold.

    Given this information, the simplest approach to the solution is:

    Contribution margin lost if the plant is closed
      (5,000 units x $16*) .... $(80,000)
    Less fixed costs which can be avoided if the
      plant is closed:
        Fixed manufacturing overhead cost
          ($400,000 x 3/12 = $100,000; $100,000
          x 40%) $40,000
        Fixed selling cost ($360,000 x 3/12 =
          $90,000; $90,000 x 1/3) 30,000   70,000
    Net disadvantage of closing the plant .... $(10,000)

    *$40 − ($9.50 + $10 + $2.80 + $1.70) = $16.

Problem 13-17 (continued)

Some students will take a longer approach such as that shown below:

	Keep the Plant Open	Close the Plant
Sales (5,000 units @ $40)................................	$200,000	$ —
Less variable expenses (5,000 units @ $24)....	120,000	—
Contribution margin...	80,000	—
Less fixed expenses:		
Fixed manufacturing overhead cost:		
$400,000 x 3/12...	100,000	
$400,000 x 3/12 x 60%..............................		60,000
Fixed selling expense:		
$360,000 x 3/12...	90,000	
$360,000 x 3/12 x 2/3		60,000
Total fixed expenses	190,000	120,000
Net operating income (loss)	$(110,000)	$(120,000)

4. The relevant cost figure is $1.70 per unit, which is the variable selling expense per Zet. Since the blemished units have already been produced, all production costs (including the variable production costs) are sunk. The fixed selling expenses are not relevant since they will not change regardless of whether or not the blemished units are sold.

5. The costs that are relevant are those which can be avoided by purchasing from the outside supplier. These costs are:

Variable production costs...	$22.30
Fixed manufacturing overhead cost ($400,000 x 70% = $280,000; $280,000 ÷ 80,000 units)	3.50
Variable selling expense ($1.70 x 60%)...................................	1.02
Total costs avoided..	$26.82

To be acceptable, the outside manufacturer's quotation must be less than $26.82 per unit.

Managerial Accounting

Problem 13-19 (45 minutes)

1. Only the avoidable costs are relevant in a decision to drop the Kensington product line. These costs are:

Direct materials	£ 32,000
Direct labour	200,000
Fringe benefits (30% of labour)	60,000
Variable manufacturing overhead	30,000
Royalties (5% of sales)	24,000
Product-line managers' salaries	8,000
Sales commissions (10% of sales)	48,000
Fringe benefits	
(30% of salaries and commissions)	16,800
Shipping	10,000
Advertising	15,000
Total avoidable costs	£443,800

The following costs are not relevant in this decision:

Cost	Reason not relevant
Building rent and maintenance	All products use the same facilities; no space would be freed up if a product were dropped.
Depreciation	All products use the same equipment so no equipment can be sold. Furthermore, the equipment does not wear out through use.
General administrative expenses	Dropping the Kensington product line would have no effect on total general administrative expenses.

Problem 13-19 (continued)

Having determined the costs that can be avoided if the Kensington product line is dropped, we can now make the following computation:

Sales revenue lost if the Kensington line is dropped £480,000
Less costs that can be avoided (see above)....................... 443,800
Decrease in overall company net operating income if
   the Kensington line is dropped... £ 36,200

Thus, the Kensington line should not be dropped unless the company can find more profitable uses for the resources consumed by the Kensington line.

2. To determine the minimum acceptable sales level, we must first classify the avoidable costs into variable and fixed costs as follows:

	Variable	**Fixed**
Direct materials	£ 32,000	
Direct labour..	200,000	
Fringe benefits (30% of labour).....................	60,000	
Variable manufacturing overhead	30,000	
Royalties (5% of sales)	24,000	
Product-line managers' salaries....................		£ 8,000
Sales commissions (10% of sales)	48,000	
Fringe benefits		
(30% of salaries and commissions)	14,400	2,400
Shipping	10,000	
Advertising		15,000
Total costs..	£418,400	£25,400

The Kensington product line should be retained as long as the contribution margin from the product line covers its avoidable fixed costs. We can find the sales volume where the contribution margin just equals the avoidable fixed costs using break-even analysis. We just have to be careful to use the avoidable costs in the formula.

Managerial Accounting

Problem 13-19 (continued)

The contribution margin ratio is computed as follows:

$$\text{CM ratio} = \frac{\text{Contribution margin}}{\text{Sales revenue}}$$

$$= \frac{480,000 - 418,400}{480,000} = 2.83\% \text{ (rounded)}$$

And the break-even sales volume can be found using the break-even formula:

$$\text{Break- even point} = \frac{\text{Fixed costs}}{\text{CM ratio}}$$

$$= \frac{25,400}{0.1283} = £198,000 \text{ (rounded)}$$

Therefore, as long as the sales revenue from the Kensington product line exceeds £198,000, it is covering its own avoidable fixed costs and is contributing toward covering the common fixed costs and toward the profits of the entire company.

Problem 13-21 (20 minutes)

1. Incremental revenue:

    Fixed fee (4 mk x 10,000 pairs)...................................... 40,000 mk

    Reimbursement for costs of production: (Variable
    production cost of 16 mk, plus fixed overhead
    cost of 5 mk = 21 mk per pair. 21 mk x 10,000

    pairs)... 210,000

        Total incremental revenue...................................... 250,000

    Incremental costs:

    Variable production costs (16 mk x 10,000 pairs)......... 160,000

    Increase in net operating income...................................... 90,000 mk

2. Sales revenue through regular channels

    (10,000 pairs x 32 mk).. 320,000 mk

    Sales revenue from the army (above)............................ 250,000 mk

        Decrease in revenue received...................................... 70,000

    Less variable selling expenses avoided if the army's

    offer is accepted (10,000 pairs x 2 mk)....................... 20,000

    Net decrease in net operating income with

    the army's offer... 50,000 mk

Managerial Accounting

Problem 13-23 (60 minutes)

1. Total fixed costs = ($100 + $80) x 2,500 = $450,000
   Contribution margin/unit = $700 − (75 + 125 + 20 + 30) = $450
   Break-even point (units) = 450,000/450 = 1,000 units

   Break-even point ($) = 1,000 x $700 = $700,000

2. Present contribution margin = 450 x 2,500 = $1,125,000
   If price lowered to $630, contribution margin would be $380 per unit.
   Total contribution margin = 380 x 3,200 = $1,216,000

   Based on the above analysis, total contribution margin and income would increase by $91,000 so I would recommend that the price be lowered to $630.

3. If the government's contract is accepted, Humbug will forego contribution from their regular customers of:

   $450 x 600 = $270,000

   Income from government contract:

Fixed fee	$240,000
Share of fixed manufacturing costs (600/4,000 x 250,000)	37,500
	$277,500

   Based on the above analysis, Humbug would be better off by $7,500 in accepting the government contract and should therefore, accept it.

   Note:

   This is one of the shorter ways to do the problem; other methods are equally acceptable.

4. Minimum price = Variable manufacturing costs + shipping costs + order costs
   = $220 + $60 + ($3,000/1,000)
   = $283

5. Since these units have already been made, their manufacturing costs are sunk. Consequently, any price received in excess of the differential costs of selling the motors will increase income. The only differential costs will be the $30 per unit variable marketing costs since the motors are to be sold through regular channels.

   The minimum price is $30 per unit,

6.

Variable manufacturing cost	$220.00
Variable marketing opportunity cost ($30.00 − $22.50)	7.50
Fixed manufacturing opportunity cost ($250,000 − $175,000) ÷ 1,000	75.00
Equivalent in-house cost	$302.50

Problem 13-23 (continued)

A $310 proposal from the outside contractor will not be acceptable since it will reduce income by ($310.00 − $302.50)1,000 = $7,500 (see note at end of part (c)).

7. Alternative I

If status quo maintained — 2,500 regular motors produced in-house.

Revenue ($700 x 2,500)	=	$1,750,000
Variable manufacturing ($220 x 2,500)	=	(550,000)
Variable marketing ($30 x 2,500)	=	(75,000)
Contribution margin		1,125,000
Fixed manufacturing		(250,000)
Fixed marketing		(200,000)
Income		$ 675,000

Alternative II

Contract 1,000 regular motors and produce 750 special motors.

	In-House	Contract	Special	Total
Revenues	$1,050,000	$700,000	$637,500	$2,387,500
Variable manufacturing costs	(330,000)	-0-	(356,250)	(686,250)
Variable marketing costs	(45,000)	(22,500)	(60,000)	(127,500)
Contribution margin	675,000	$677,500	$221,250	1,573,750
Fixed manufacturing costs				(250,000)
Fixed marketing costs				(200,000)
Income				$1,123,750

Ignoring for the time being the costs of $310,000 ($310 x 1,000) to be paid to the outside contractor, as the above analysis shows, Humbug could improve its income by ($1,123,750 − $675,000) = $448,750 if it were to contract out 1,000 motors and produce themselves the 750 special motors. This means that under Alternative II, Humbug could pay the outside contractor up to $448.75 ($448,750 ÷ 1,000) and still be as profitable as under Alternative I. In other words, under Alternative II, Humbug's overall profitability will be greater by $138,750 ($448,750 ÷ $310,000) than under Alternative I. Humbug should, therefore, accept a price of $310 from the outside contractor.

(CGA-Canada, adapted)

Managerial Accounting

Problem 13-25 (40 minutes)

1. Computation of the EOQ:

	Gross Ordered					
	1	2	3	4	5	6
a. Average inventory in units	.5	1.0	1.5	2.0	2.5	3.0
b. Number of purchase orders	36	18	12	9	7.2	6
c. Delivered cost per gross	$ 500	$ 500	$ 500	$ 500	$ 500	$ 500
d. Value of average inventory	$ 250	$ 500	$ 750	$ 1,000	$ 1,250	$ 1,500
Delivered cost of inventory	$18,000	$18,000	$18,000	$18,000	$18,000	$18,000
Annual carrying cost at 20% of line d (above)	50	100	150	200	250	300
Annual storage cost at $24 x line a (above)	12	24	36	48	60	72
Annual ordering cost at $30 x line b (above)	1,08	540	360	270	216	180
Total annual cost	$19,142	$18,664	$18,546	$18,518	$18,526	$18,552

The EOQ would be 4 gross.

Problem 13-25 (continued)

2. Average daily usage = $\dfrac{5{,}184 \text{ annual usage}}{259 \text{ working days}}$ = 20 units per day

Normal lead time = 20 working days		
Average lead-period usage: 20 x 20 =	400	units
Maximum daily usage.............................	28	units per day
Less average daily usage........................	20	units per day
Excess above average	8	units per day
Times normal lead time	20	days
Safety stock required..............................	160	units
Average lead-period usage (above)	400	units
Safety stock required..............................	160	units
Minimum stock order point	560	units

Problem 13-27 (30 minutes)

1. Projected raw material issues:

	Plastic	Brass	Aluminum
AD-5 (8,000 units)	16,000 kg	4,000 kg	—
FX-3 (6,000 units)	6,000 kg	—	9,000 kg
Projected raw material issues	22,000 kg	4,000 kg	9,000 kg

2. and 3. Projected inventory activity and ending balance:

	Plastic	Brass	Aluminum
Average daily usage (issues ÷ working days)	1,100 kg	200 kg	450 kg
Beginning inventory	16,000 kg	9,000 kg	14,000 kg
Orders received:			
Ordered in 7th period	15,000[4] kg	—	10,000[2] kg
Ordered in 8th period	15,000[5] kg	—	—
Subtotal	46,000 kg	9,000 kg	24,000 kg
Issues	22,000[1] kg	4,000[3] kg	9,000[6] kg
Projected ending inventory balance	24,000 kg	5,000 kg	15,000 kg

[1]Ordered 15,000 kilograms of plastic on fourth working day.
[2]Order for 10,000 kilograms of aluminum ordered during seventh period received on fourth working day.
[3]Ordered 5,000 kilograms of brass on eighth working day.
[4]Order for 15,000 kilograms of plastic ordered during seventh period received on tenth working day.
[5]Order for 15,000 kilograms of plastic ordered on fourth working day of eighth period received on fourteenth working day.
[6]No orders for aluminum would be placed during the eighth period.

4. Projected payments for raw material purchases:

Raw Material	Day/Period Ordered	Day/Period Received	Quantity Ordered	Amount Due	Period Due
Plastic	20th/Seventh	10th/Eighth	15,000 kg	$6,000	Eighth
Aluminum	4th/Seventh	4th/Eighth	10,000 kg	5,500	Eighth
Plastic	4th/Eighth	14th/Eighth	15,000 kg	6,000	Eighth
Brass	8th/Eighth	Due Ninth	5,000 kg	4,750	Ninth

Problem 13-29 (50 minutes)

A1	B	C	D	E	F	G	H	I	J	K	L	M	N	O	P	Q

2

3

4 The Daffodil Co. Ltd has obtained the following costs and

5 other data pertaining to one of its raw materials:

6

7 Working days per year .... 250 days

8 Normal use per day .... 400 units

9 Maximum use per day .... 600 units

10 Minimum use per day .... 100 units

11 Lead time .... 8 days

12 Cost of placing one order $20.00

13 Carrying cost per unit per year $0.30

14 Stock out costs $0.05

15

16   DAILY

17   DEMAND   PROBABILITY

18

19   400   0.40

20   450   0.30

21   500   0.20

22   550   0.05

23   600   0.05

24

25 Required: Compute the following

26

27 (a)   Economic order quantity

28 (b)   Safety stock

29 (c)   Reorder point

30 (d)   Normal maximum inventory

31 (e)   Absolute maximum inventory

32 (f)   Average inventory

33 (g)   Assuming use per day can occur at the following levels and

34   their respective probabilities compute the safety stock

35   amount that minimizes the capital costs incurred.

36

37 _____

38

39 SOLUTION AREA:

40

41

42 (a) Economic order quantity:

43

44 $O = ((2 * Q * P)/C)^{0.5}$

45

46 O = order size in units

47 Q = annual quantity used in units

48 P = cost of placing one order

49 C = annual cost of carrying one unit in stock

50

51

52 Q = normal use/day * workdays/year = ? units

53   P = $20

54   C = $0.30

55

Problem 13-29 (continued)

56	Economic order quantity (units), 0, = ? units
57	
58	
59	(b) Safety stock
60	
61	Maximum expected usage per day .... ? units
62	Average use per day .... ? units
63	
64	Excess... ? units
65	Lead time .... ? days
66	?
67	Safety stock... ? units
68	
69	
70	(c) Reorder point:
71	
72	reorder point = (lead time * avg. daily usage) + safety stock
73	
74	reorder point = ? units
75	
76	
77	
78	
79	(d) Normal maximum inventory:
80	
81	Normal maximum inventory = EOQ + safety stock
82	= ? units
83	
84	
85	
86	(e) Absolute maximum inventory:
87	
88	Absolute maximum inventory =
89	= (EOQ + SS) + (normal – minimum use) * lead time)
90	Absolute maximum inventory = ? units
91	
92	
93	
94	(f) Average inventory:
95	
96	Average inventory = Safety stock + (1/2 * EOQ)
97	
98	Average inventory = ? units
99	
100	(g)
101	

	DEMAND (units)	PROBABILITIES	
102	**DEMAND**		
103	(units)	**PROBABILITIES**	
104			
105	3,200	0.40	average demand = 3,200
106	3,600	0.30	
107	4,000	0.20	
108	4,400	0.05	*note that demands have been
109	4,800	0.05	increased to reflect a lead
110			time of 8 days.
111			

Problem 13-29 (continued)

	Safety Stock Level (Units)	Carry Cost Per Year	Stock-out in Units	Stock-out Cost Per Order Time	Number of Orders Placed Per Year	Prob. of Stock-out	Expected Stock-out Cost per Year	Total Cost Per Year
112								
113								
114								
115								
116								
117	-0-	$-0-	-0-	$0.00	28	0.40	$0.00	
118			400	20.00	28	0.30	170.32	
119								
120								
121								
122	400							
123								
124								
125								
126	800							
127								
128								
129	1,200							
130								
131	1,600							
132								
133								

134 It appears that we should maintain a safety stock of ?
135 units in order to minimize the costs associated with carrying
136 excess inventory and the costs associated with stock-outs.

137 ──
138
139
140
141
142
143
144
145
146
147
148
149
150
151
152
153
154
155
156
157 SOLUTION
158
159 (a) Economic order quantity:
160
161 O = ((2 * Q * P)/C/^0.5
162
163 O = order size in units
164 Q = annual quantity used in units
165 P = cost of placing one order
166 C = annual cost of carrying one unit in stock
167
168

Managerial Accounting

Problem 13-29 (continued)

169   Q = normal use/day * workdays/year = 100,000 units

170   P = $20

171   C = $0.30

172

173   Economic order quantity (units), 0, = 3,651 units

174

175

176   (b) Safety stock

177

178   Maximum expected usage per day   600   units

179   Average usage per day........................   <u>400</u>   units

180

181   Excess...   200   units

182   Lead time ....   <u>8</u>   days

183

184   Safety stock.......................................   <u>1,600</u>   units

185

186

187   (c) Reorder point:

188

189   reorder point = (lead time * avg. daily usage) + safety stock

190

191   reorder point = 4,800 units

192

193

194

195

196   (d)   Normal maximum inventory:

197

198   Normal maximum inventory = EOQ + safety stock

199   = 5,251 units

200

201

202

203   (e) Absolute maximum inventory:

204

205   Absolute maximum inventory =

206   = (EOQ + SS) + (normal – minimum use) * lead time)

207   Absolute maximum inventory = 7,651 units

208

209

210

211   (f) Average inventory:

212

213   Average inventory = Safety stock + (1/2 * EOQ)

214

215   Average inventory = 3,426 units

216

217   (g)

218

219   DEMAND

220   (units)   PROBABILITIES

221

222   3,200   0.40   average demand = 3,200

223   3,600   0.30

224   4,000   0.20

225   4,400   0.05   *note that demands have been

226   4,800   0.05   increased to reflect a lead

227   time of 8 days.

Problem 13-29 (continued)

	Safety Stock Level (Units)	Carry Cost Per Year	Stock-out in Units	Stock-out Cost Per Order Time	Number of Orders Placed Per Year	Prob. of Stock-out	Expected Stock-out Cost per Year	Total Cost Per Year
228								
229								
230								
231								
232								
233								
234	-0-	$-0-	-0-	$0.00	28	0.40	$0.00	
235			400	20.00	28	0.30	170.32	
236			800	40.00	28	0.20	227.09	
237			1,200	60.00	28	0.05	85.16	
238			1,600	80.00	28	0.05	113.54	$596.11
239	400	$120	-0-	0.00	28	0.30	0.00	
240			400	20.00	28	0.20	113.54	
241			800	40.00	28	0.05	56.77	
242			1,200	60.00	28	0.05	85.16	$375.48
243	800	$240	-0-	0.00	28	0.20	0.00	
244			400	20.00	28	0.05	28.39	
245			800	40.00	28	0.05	56.77	$325.16
246	1,200	$360	-0-	0.00	28	0.05	0.00	
247			400	20.00	28	0.05	28.39	388.39
248	1,600	$580	-0-	0.00	28	0.05	0.00	$480.00
249								
250								

251 It appears that we should maintain a safety stock of 800
252 units in order to minimize the costs associated with carrying
253 excess inventory and the costs associated with stock-outs.
254
255 Sample calculations:
256
257 Safety stock level in units = possible demand – expected demand
258   = 4,000 units – 3,200 units
259   = 800 units
260
261 Carrying cost per year = Safety stock level in units
262   * unit carrying cost per year
263   = 800 units * $0.30 per unit
264   = $240
265
266
267 Stock-out in units = possible demand
268   – expected demand
269   – safety stock
270
271   = 4,800 units – 3,200 units – 800 units safety stock
272   = 800 units
273
274
275 Stock-out cost per = stock-out in units
276   * stock-out cost per unit order time
277
278   = 800 units * $0.05 per unit
279   = $40
280
281
282 Number orders placed per year = Annual demand in units/EOQ
283
284   = 100,000 units/3,651 units

Managerial Accounting

Problem 13-29 (continued)

285 = 28 orders per year (this has been rounded UP to
286 avoid a shortage in inventory)
287
288
289 Expected stock-out cost per year = Stock-out cost per order time
290 * the number of orders placed per year
291 * probability of stockout each time
292
293 Expected stock-out cost per year = $40 * 28 orders * 0.05
294 = $56.77
295
296
297 Total cost per year = carrying cost of safety stock
298 + the expected stock-out cost/year for the
299 appropriate demand levels
300
301 Total cost per year = $240 + $28.39 + $56.77
302 = $325.16

Problem 13-31 (20 minutes)

State of Nature (demand)

Quantity Produced	20	22	24	26	28
20	20(2) = 40	40	40	40	40
22	20(2) − 2 = 38	22(2) = 44	44	44	44
24	20(2) − 4 = 36	22(2) − 2 = 42	24(2) = 48	48	48
26	20(2) − 6 = 34	22(2) − 4 = 40	24(2) − 2 = 46	26(2) = 52	52
28	20(2) − 8 = 32	22(2) − 6 = 38	24(2) − 4 = 44	26(2) = 2 = 50	28(2) = 56

EV(produce 20) = $40
EV(produce 22) = .1(38) + .9(44) = $43.40
EV(produce 24) = .1(36) + .2(42) + .7(48) = $45.60
EV(produce 26) = .1(34) + .2(40) + .3(46) + .4(52) = $46.00*

EV(produce 28) = .1(32) + .2(38) + .3(44) + .3(50) + .1(56) = $44.60

Bruno's Bakery should produce 26 dozen doughnuts each morning to maximize net income.

(SMAC Solution, adapted)

Managerial Accounting

Capital Budgeting Decisions

14

Exercise 14-1 (20 minutes)

1.

Year(s)	Amount of Cash Flows		20% Factor	Present Value of Cash Flows	
	X	Y		X	Y
1	$1,000	$4,000	$0.833	$ 833	$3,332
2	2,000	3,000	0.694	1,388	2,082
3	3,000	2,000	0.579	1,737	1,158
4	4,000	1,000	0.482	1,928	482
				$5,886	$7,054

Investment opportunity Y is best.

2. a. From Table 14C-3, the factor for 6% for 3 periods is 0.840. Therefore, the present value of the investment required is:
$12,000 x 0.840 = $10,080.

b. From Table 14C-3, the factor for 10% for 3 periods is 0.751. Therefore, the present value of the investment required is:
$12,000 x 0.751 = $9,012.

Exercise 14-1 (continued)

3.

Option	Year(s)	Amount of Cash Flows	10% Factor	Present Value of Cash Flows
A	Now	$50,000	1.000	$50,000
B	1-8	$ 6,000	5.335	$32,010
	8	20,000	0.467	9,340
				$41,350

Mark should accept option A. (The instructor may wish to point out that, on the surface, option B appears to be a better choice since it promises a cash inflow totalling $68,000*, whereas option A promises a cash inflow of only $50,000. However, the cash inflows under option B are spread out over eight years, causing the present value to be much less than the $50,000 which can be received right now, if money can be invested at 10%.)

  *$6,000 x 8 = $48,000; $48,000 + $20,000 = $68,000.

4. You would prefer option a:

  Option a: $50,000 x 1.000 = $50,000.
  Option b: $75,000 x 0.507 = $38,025. (From Table 14C-3)
  Option c: $12,000 x 4.111 = $49,332. (From Table 14C-4)

Exercise 14-3 (15 minutes)

	Year(s)	Amount of Cash Flows	12% Factor	Present Value of Cash Flows
Purchase of the shares	Now	$(18,000)	1.000	$(18,000)
Annual dividends received	1-4	720*	3.037	2,187
Sale of the shares	4	22,500	0.636	14,310
Net present value				$ (1,503)

*900 shares x $0.80 = $720 per year.

No, Mr. Critchfield did not earn a 12% return on the shares.

Exercise 14-5 (15 minutes)

1. Factor of the Internal = Investment in the Project
   Rate of Return   Annual Cash Inflow

$$= \frac{\$136,700}{\$25,000} = 5.468$$

Looking in Table 14C-4 and scanning along the 14-period line, a factor of 5.468 represents an internal rate of return of 16%.

2.

Item	Year(s)	Amount of Cash Flows	16% Factor	Present Value of Cash Flows
Initial investment............	Now	$(136,700)	1.000	$(136,700)
Net annual cash inflows	1-4	25,000	5.468	136,700
Net present value				$ -0-

The reason we have a zero net present value is that 16% (the discount rate we have used) represents the machine's internal rate of return. As stated in the text, the internal rate of return is that rate that causes the present value of a project's cash inflows to just equal the present value of the investment required.

Yes, this would be an acceptable investment since the return promised by the machine is greater than the company's cost of capital.

3. Factor of the Internal = Investment in the Project
   Rate of Return   Annual Cash Inflow

$$= \frac{\$136,700}{\$20,000} = 6.835$$

Exercise 14-5 (continued)

Looking in Table 14C-4 and scanning along the 14-period line, a factor of 6.835 falls between 10% and 12%. Interpolating we get:

	Present Value Factors	
10% factor	7.367	7.367
True factor	6.835	
12% factor		6.628
Difference..................	0.532	0.739

$$\text{Internal rate of return} = 10\% + \left[\frac{0.532}{0.739} \times 2\% \right]$$

Internal rate of return = <u>11.4%</u>

Exercise 14-7 (15 minutes)

Item	Year(s)	Amount of Cash Flows	20% Factor	Present Value of Cash Flows
Project A:				
Cost of the equipment...................	Now	$(300,000)	1.000	$(300,000)
Annual cash inflows.......	1-7	80,000	3.605	288,400
Salvage value of the equipment...................	7	20,000	0.279	5,580
Net present value				$ (6,020)
Project B:				
Working capital investment..................	Now	$(300,000)	1.000	$(300,000)
Annual cash inflows.......	1-7	60,000	3.605	216,300
Working capital released.....................	7	300,000	0.279	83,700
Net present value...........				$ -0-

The $300,000 should be invested in Project B. Note that the project has a zero net present value, which means that it promises exactly a 20% rate of return. Project A is not acceptable at all, since it has a negative net present value.

Managerial Accounting

Exercise 14-9 (15 minutes)

1. Note: All present value factors in the computation below have been taken from Table 14C-3 in Appendix 14C, using a 16% discount rate.

Investment in the equipment.....................................		$134,650
Less present value of Year 1 and Year 2 cash inflows:		
Year 1: $45,000 x 0.862..	$38,790	
Year 2: $60,000 x 0.743..	44,580	83,370
Present value of Year 3 cash inflow.........................		$ 51,280

Therefore, the expected cash inflow for Year 3 would be:

$51,280 ÷ 0.641 = $80,000.

2. The equipment's net present value without considering the intangible benefits would be:

Item	Year(s)	Amount of Cash Flows	20% Factor	Present Value of Cash Flows
Cost of the equipment	Now	$(2,500,000)	1.000	$(2,500,000)
Annual cash savings	1-15	400,000	4.675	1,870,000
Net present value				$ (630,000)

Therefore, the dollar value per year of the intangible benefits would have to be great enough to offset a $630,000 negative present value for the equipment. This dollar value can be computed as follows:

$$\frac{\text{Net Present Value,} \quad \$(630,000)}{\text{Factor for 15 Years,} \quad 4.675} = \$134,759$$

Exercise 14-9 (continued)

3. $\dfrac{\text{Factor of the Internal}}{\text{Rate of Return}} = \dfrac{\text{Investment in the Project}}{\text{Annual Cash Inflow}}$

$$= \frac{\$307{,}100}{\$\ 50{,}000} = 6.142$$

Looking in Table 14C-4, and scanning *down* the 14% column, we find that a factor of 6.142 equals 15 years. Thus, the equipment will have to be used for 15 years in order to yield a return of 14%.

As a follow-up question, the instructor may wish to ask the class how many years (approximately) the equipment would have to be used to yield a return of 10%, 16%, and so forth.

Managerial Accounting

Exercise 14-11 (15 minutes)

1. Computation of the annual cash inflow associated with the new ride:

    Net income $63,000
    Add: Noncash deduction for depreciation 27,000
    Net annual cash inflow $90,000

    The payback computation would be:

    Payback Period $= \dfrac{\text{Investment Required}}{\text{Net Annual Cash Inflow}}$

    $= \dfrac{\$450,000}{\$\ 90,000} = 5$ years

    Yes, the new ride meets the requirement. The payback period is less than the maximum 6 years required by the park.

2. The simple rate of return would be:

    Simple Rate of Return $= \dfrac{\overset{\text{Incremental}}{\text{Revenues}} - \overset{\text{Incremental Expenses,}}{\text{including Depreciation}} = \text{Net Income}}{\text{Initial Investment}}$

    $= \dfrac{\$63,000}{\$450,000} = 14\%$

    Yes, the new ride satisfies the criterion. The 14% return that it promises is greater than the park's requirement of a 12% return.

Problem 14-13 (25 minutes)

1. The annual cash inflows would be:

   Reduction in annual operating costs:
Operating costs, present hand method	$35,000
Operating costs, new machine	14,000
Annual savings in operating costs	21,000

   Increased annual contribution margin:
5,000 packages x $0.60	3,000
Total annual cash inflows...	$24,000

2.

Item	Year(s)	Amount of Cash Flows	16% Factor	Present Value of Cash Flows
Cost of the machine.....................	Now	$(90,000)	1.000	$(90,000)
Overhaul required.........	5	(7,500)	0.476	(3,570)
Annual cash inflows	1-8	24,000	4.344	104,256
Salvage value	8	6,000	0.305	1,830
Net present value				$ 12,516

Problem 14-15 (30 minutes)

1. The net annual cost savings is computed as follows:

Reduction in labour costs	$240,000
Reduction in material costs	96,000
Total cost reductions	336,000
Less increased maintenance costs ($4,250 x 12)	51,000
Net annual cost savings	$285,000

2. Using this cost savings figure, and other data provided in the text, the net present value analysis is:

	Year(s)	Amount of Cash Flows	18% Factor	Present Value of Cash Flows
Cost of the machine	Now	$(900,000)	1.000	$ (900,000)
Installation and software	Now	(650,000)	1.000	(650,000)
Salvage of the old machine	Now	70,000	1.000	70,000
Annual cost savings	1-10	285,000	4.494	1,280,790
Overhaul required	6	(90,000)	0.370	(33,300)
Salvage of the new machine.............	10	210,000	0.191	40,110
Net present value				$ (192,400)

No, the etching machine should not be purchased. It has a negative net present value at an 18% discount rate.

3. The dollar value per year that would be required for the intangible benefits would be:

$$\frac{\text{Net Present Value,} \quad \$(192,400)}{\text{Factor for 10 Years,} \quad 4.494} = \$42,813$$

Thus, if management believes that the intangible benefits are worth at least $42,813 per year to the company, then the new etching machine should be purchased.

Problem 14-17 (35 minutes)

1. A net present value analysis for each investment follows:

	Year(s)	Amount of Cash Flows	16% Factor	Present Value of Cash Flows
Preferred shares:				
Purchase of the shares.............	Now	$ (50,000)	1.000	$ (50,000)
Annual cash dividend (7%)	1-3	3,500	2.246	7,861
Sale of the shares....	3	49,000	0.641	31,409
Net present value.....				$ (10,730)
Common shares:				
Purchase of the shares.............	Now	$ (95,000)	1.000	$ (95,000)
Sale of the shares....	3	160,000	0.641	102,650
Net present value.....				$ 7,560
Bonds:				
Purchase of the bonds..................	Now	$(100,000)	1.000	$(100,000)
Semiannual interest.	1-6*	6,000	4.623**	27,738
Sale of the bonds.....	6*	113,400	0.630**	71,442
Net present value.....				$ (820)

*6 semiannual interest periods.
**Factor for 6 periods at 8%. (As stated in the text, we must halve the discount rate and double the number of periods.)

Mr. Vecci earned a 16% rate of return on the common shares, but not on the preferred shares or the bonds.

Managerial Accounting

Problem 14-17 (continued)

2. Considering all three investments together, Mr. Vecci did not earn a 16% return. The computation is:

	Net Present Value
Preferred shares	$(10,730)
Common shares	7,560
Bonds	(820)
Overall net present value	$ (3,990)

3. Factor of the Internal = Investment in the Project
   Rate of Return   Annual Cash Inflow

Substituting the $322,400 investment and the factor for 18% for 10 periods into this formula, we get:

$$\frac{\$322,400}{\text{Annual Cash Inflow}} = 4.494$$

Therefore, the required net annual cash inflow would be: $322,400 ÷ 4.494 = $71,740.

Problem 14-19 (45 minutes)

1. Factor of the Internal $=$ <u>Investment in the Project</u>
   Rate of Return   Annual Cash Inflow

$$= \frac{\$142{,}950}{\$37{,}500} = 3.812$$

From Table 14C-4 in Appendix 14C, reading along the 7-period line, a factor of 3.812 equals an 18% rate of return.

Verification of the 18% figure:

Item	Year(s)	Amount of Cash Flows	18% Factor	Present Value of Cash Flows
Investment in equipment................	Now	$(142,950)	1.000	$(142,950)
Annual cash inflows.....................	1-7	37,500	3.812	142,950
Net present value........				$ -0-

2. Factor of the Internal $=$ <u>Investment in the Project</u>
   Rate of Return   Annual Cash Inflow

We know that the investment is $142,950, and we can determine the factor for an internal rate of return of 14% by looking in Table 14C-4 along the 7-period line. This factor is 4.288. Using these figures in the formula, we get:

$$\frac{\$142{,}950}{\text{Annual Cash Inflow}} = 4.288$$

Therefore, the annual cash inflow would be: $142,950 ÷ 4.288 = $33,337.

Problem 14-19 (continued)

3. a. 5-year life for the equipment:

The factor for the internal rate of return would still be 3.812 [as computed in (1) above]. From Table 14C-4, reading this time along the 5-period line, a factor of 3.812 falls between 8% and 10%. By interpolating:

8% factor	3.993	3.993
True factor...................	3.812	
10% factor	____	3.791
Difference...................	0.181	0.202

$$\text{Internal Rate of Return} = 8\% + \left[\frac{0.181}{0.202} \times 2\% \right]$$

b. 9-year life for the equipment:

The factor of the internal rate of return would again be 3.812. From Table 14CA reading along the 9-period line, a factor of 3.812 falls between 20% and 22%. By interpolating:

20% factor	4.031	4.031
True factor...................	3.812	
22% factor	____	3.786
Difference...................	0.219	0.245

$$\text{Internal Rate of Return} = 20\% + \left[\frac{0.219}{0.245} \times 2\% \right]$$

Internal Rate of Return = 21.8%

Problem 14-19 (continued)

Most students will want to point out that the 9.8% return in part (a) is less than the 14% minimum return that Dr. Black wants to earn on the project. Of equal or even greater importance, the following diagram should be pointed out to Dr. Black:

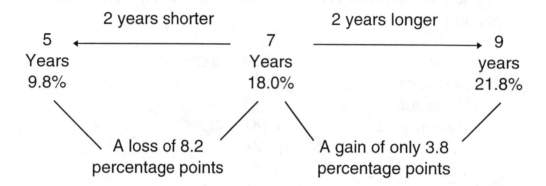

As this illustration shows, a *decrease* in years has a much greater impact on the rate of return than an *increase* in years. This is because of the time value of money; added cash inflows far into the future do little to enhance the rate of return, but loss of cash inflows in the near term can do much to reduce it. Therefore, Dr. Black should be *very* concerned about any potential decrease in the life of the equipment, while at the same time realizing that any increase in the life of the equipment will do little to enhance her rate of return.

Managerial Accounting

Problem 14-19 (continued)

4. a. The expected annual cash inflow would be:

$37,500 x 120% = $45,000.

$$\frac{\$142,950}{\$45,000} = 3.177$$

From Table 14C-4 in Appendix 14C, reading along the 7-period line, a factor of 3.177 falls between 24% and 26%. By interpolating:

24% factor	3.242	3.242
True factor	3.177	
26% factor		3.083
Difference	0.065	0.159

$$\text{Internal Rate of Return} = 24\% + \left[\frac{0.065}{0.159} \times 2\% \right]$$

Internal Rate of Return = 24.8%

b. The expected annual cash inflow would be:

$37,500 x 80% = $30,000.

$$\frac{\$142,950}{\$30,000} = 4.765$$

From Table 14C-4 in Appendix 14C, reading along the 7-period line, a factor of 4.765 falls between 10% and 12%. By interpolating:

Problem 14-19 (continued)

10% factor..................	4.868	4.868
True factor..................	4.765	
12% factor..................		4.564
Difference..................	0.103	0.304

$$\text{Internal Rate of Return} = 10\% + \left[\frac{0.103}{0.304} \times 2\% \right]$$

Internal Rate of Return = 10.7%

Unlike changes in time, increases and decreases in cash flows at a given point in time have basically the same impact on the rate of return, as shown below:

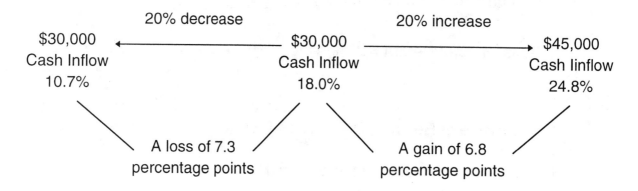

Problem 14-19 (continued)

5. Since the cash flows are not even over the five-year period (there is an extra $61,375 cash inflow from sale of the equipment at the end of the fifth year), it will be necessary to use a trial-and-error approach in computing the internal rate of return. A good way to start is to estimate what the rate of return would be *without* the sale of equipment:

$$\frac{\$142,950 \text{ Investment}}{\$30,000 \text{ Annual Cash Inflow}} = 4.765 \text{ Factor}$$

Looking in Table 14C-4 in Appendix 14C, and scanning along the 5-period line, we can see that a factor of 4.765 would represent an internal rate of return of less than 4%. If we now consider the fact that an additional cash inflow of $61,375 will be realized at the end of the fifth year, it becomes obvious that the true internal rate of return will be greater than 4%. By a trial-and-error process, and moving upward from 4%, we can eventually determine that the actual internal rate of return will be 12% (to the nearest whole percent):

Item	Year(s)	Amount of Cash Flows	12% Factor	Present Value of Cash Flows
Investment in the equipment	Now	$(142,950)	1.000	$(142,950)
Annual cash inflow	1-5	30,000	3.605	108,150
Sale of the equipment	5	61,375	0.567	34,800
Net present value				$ -0-

Problem 14-21 (30 minutes)

1. The present value of cash flows would be:

Item	Year(s)	Amount of Cash Flows	18% Factor	Present Value of Cash Flows
Purchase alternative:				
Purchase cost of the plane..........................	Now	$(850,000)	1.000	$(850,000)
Annual cost of servicing, etc.	1-5	(9,000)	3.127	(28,143)
Repairs:				
First three years	1-3	(3,000)	2.174	(6,522)
Fourth year................	4	(5,000)	0.516	(2,580)
Fifth year	5	(10,000)	0.437	(4,370)
Resale value of the plane..........................	5	425,000	0.437	185,725
Present value of cash flows..................				$(705,890)
Lease alternative:				
Damage deposit.............	Now	$ (50,000)	1.000	$ (50,000)
Annual lease payments...................	1-5	(200,000)	3.127	(625,400)
Refund of deposit...........	5	50,000	0.437	21,850
Present value of cash flows..................				$(653,550)
Net present value in favour of leasing the plane				$ 52,340

2. The company should accept the leasing alternative, since it has the lowest present value of total cost.

Managerial Accounting

Problem 14-23 (40 minutes)

1. a.

Sales revenue...		$500,000
Less variable production expenses (@ 60%)		300,000
Contribution margin		200,000
Less fixed expenses:		
Advertising..	$36,000	
Salaries	90,000	
Insurance..	4,000	
Depreciation	26,250*	
Total fixed expenses		156,250
Net income..		$ 43,750

*$350,000 − (10% x $350,000) = $315,000
$315,000 ÷ 12 years = $26,250.

b. The formula for the simple rate of return is:

$$\text{Simple Rate of Return} = \frac{\text{Incremental Revenue} - \text{Incremental Expenses, including Depreciation}}{\text{Initial Investment}} = \frac{\text{Net Income}}{}$$

$$= \frac{\$43,750}{\$350,000} = 12.5\%$$

c. The formula for the payback period is:

$$\text{Payback Period} = \frac{\text{Investment Required}}{\text{Net Annual Cash Inflow}}$$

$$= \frac{\$350,000}{\$70,000*} = \underline{5 \text{ years}}$$

*$43,750 net income + $26,250 depreciation = $70,000.

2. a. A cost reduction project is involved here, so the formula for the simple rate of return would be:

Problem 14-23 (continued)

$$\text{Simple Rate of Return} = \frac{\text{Cost Savings} - \text{Depreciation}}{\text{Initial Investments} - \text{Salvage from Old Equipment}}$$

The reduction in costs with the new equipment would be:

Annual costs, old equipment............................		$85,000
Annual costs, new equipment:		
Salary of operator	$18,000	
Maintenance	4,500	22,500
Annual savings in costs.................................		$62,500

Thus, the simple rate of return would be:

$$\frac{\$62,500 - \$20,000^* = \$42,500}{\$260,000 - \$10,000 = \$250,000} = 17\%$$

$^*\$260,000 \div 13 \text{ years} = \$20,000$

b. The formula for the payback period remains the same as in part (1), except we must reduce the investment required by the salvage from sale of the old equipment:

$$\text{Payback Period} = \frac{\text{Investment Required} - \text{Salvage from Old Equipment}}{\text{Net Annual Cash Inflow}}$$

$$= \frac{\$260,000 - \$10,000 = \$250,000}{\$62,500^*} = \underline{4 \text{ years}}$$

*See part (2a) above.

3. According to the company's criteria, Machine B should be purchased. Machine A does not meet either the required minimum rate of return or the 4-year payback period.

Managerial Accounting

Problem 14-23 (continued)

Note: If the internal rate of return was being used, machine A would meet the company's 15% rate of return figure. The internal rate of return on machine A is about 17%.

Problem 14-25 (50 minutes)

1. The net cash inflow from sales of the detectors for each year would be:

	Year			
	1	**2**	**3**	**4-12**
Sales in units	4,000	7,000	10,000	12,000
Sales in dollars (@ $45 each)	$ 180,000	$315,000	$450,000	$540,000
Less variable expenses (@ $25 each)	100,000	175,000	250,000	300,000
Contribution margin	80,000	140,000	200,000	240,000
Less fixed expenses:				
Advertising	70,000	70,000	50,000	40,000
Other fixed expenses*	120,000	120,000	120,000	120,000
Total fixed expenses	190,000	190,000	170,000	160,000
Net cash inflow (outflow)	$(110,000)	$ (50,000)	$ 30,000	$ 80,000

*Depreciation is not a cash expense and therefore must be eliminated from this computation. The analysis is:

Cost of the equipment	$100,000
Less salvage value (10%)	10,000
Net depreciable cost	$ 90,000

$ 90,000 ÷ 12 years = $7,500 per year depreciation.
$127,500 – $7,500 depreciation = $120,000 cash fixed expenses.

Managerial Accounting

Problem 14-25 (continued)

2. The net present value of the proposed investment would be:

Item	Year(s)	Amount of Cash Flows	20% Factor	Present Value of Cash Flows
Investment in equipment......................	Now	$(100,000)	1.000	$(100,000)
Working capital investment	Now	(40,000)	1.000	(40,000)
Yearly cash flows	1	(110,000)	0.833	(91,630)
" " "	2	(50,000)	0.694	(34,700)
" " "	3	30,000	0.579	17,370
" " "	4-12	80,000	2.333*	186,640
Salvage value of equipment......................	12	10,000	0.112	1,120
Release of working capital	12	40,000	0.112	4,480
Net present value..............				$ (56,720)

*Present value factor for 12 periods....................	4.439
Present value factor for 3 periods	2.106
Present value factor for 9 periods, starting 4 periods in the future........................	2.333

Since the net present value is negative, the company should not accept the smoke detector as a new product line.

Problem 14-27 (30 minutes)

1. The net annual cash inflow from rental of the property would be:

Net income, as shown in the problem $40,000
Add back depreciation... 20,000
Net annual cash inflow $60,000

Given this figure, the present value of the cash flows associated with each alternative would be:

Item	Year(s)	Amount of Cash Flows	14% Factor	Present Value of Cash Flows
Keep the property:				
Annual loan payment.................	1-7	$ (30,000)	4.288	$(128,640)
Net annual cash inflow	1-15	60,000	6.142	368,520
Resale value of the property	15	500,000	0.140	70,000
Present value of cash flows				$ 309,880
Sell the property:				
Pay-off of loan.............	Now	$(180,000)	1.000	$(180,000)
Downpayment received	Now	250,000	1.000	250,000
Annual payments received...............	1-15	32,500	6.142	199,615
Present value of cash flows				$ 269,615
Net present value in favour of keeping the property................				$ 40,265

2. The company should be advised to wait for a better offer on the property. The reason is that the present value of the cash flows from selling the property is less than the present value of the cash flows from keeping the property.

Managerial Accounting

Further Aspects of Investment Decisions

15

Exercise 15-1 (10 minutes)

a. Management consulting fee $120,000
   Multiply by 1 – 30% x   70%
   After-tax cost .... $ 84,000

b. Increased revenues $50,000
   Multiply by 1 – 25% x   75%
   After-tax cash flow (benefit) $37,500

c.

Year	Undepreciated Capital Cost	CCA	Tax Saving	PV Factor 10%	PV of Tax Savings
1	$210,000	31,500	9,450	.909	$ 8,590.05
2	178,500	53,550	16,065	.826	13,269.69
3	124,950	37,485	11,246	.751	8,445.75

Exercise 15-3 (20 minutes)

1. The net present value of the new equipment would be:

Items and Computations	Year(s)	(1) Amount	(2) Tax Effect	(1) × (2) After-Tax Cash Flows	10% Factor	Present Value of Cash Flows
Cost of the new equipment	Now	$(65,000)	—	$(65,000)	1.000	$(65,000)
Net annual cash receipts..........	1-4	25,000	1 − 0.30	17,500	3.170	55,475
CCA tax shield*						12,577

$$* \frac{Cdt}{d+k} \times \frac{1+.5k}{1+k} \quad - \quad \frac{Sdt}{d+k} \quad \times \quad (1+k)^{-n}$$

$$= \frac{65,000 \times .3 \times .3}{.3 + .10} \times \frac{1.05}{1.10} \quad - \quad \frac{9,000 \times .3 \times .3}{.3 + .10} \quad \times \quad (1 + .10)^{-4}$$

$$= (\$14,625 \times .9545) - (\$2,025 \times .683) = \$12,577$$

Repairs to equipment**	3	(12,000)	1 − 0.30	(8,400)	0.751	(6,308)
Salvage value of equipment......	4	9,000	—	9,000	.0683	6,147
Net present value						$ 2,891

**Assumes repairs are expensed.

2. Yes, the equipment should be purchased. It will provide a return greater than the company's cost of capital, as shown by the positive net present value in (1) above.

Managerial Accounting

Exercise 15-5 (10 minutes)

1. The formula for the profitability index is:

    $$\frac{\text{Present value of cash inflows}}{\text{Investment required}} = \text{Profitability index}$$

    Applying this formula to the data in Exercise 15-4, we get:

	Project A	Project B
Present value of cash inflows:		
Net annual cash inflows	$33,610	$33,610
Tax savings from CCA (total)	9,078	—
Salvage value of the photocopier	2,335	—
Release of working capital	—	23,350
Total cash inflows (a)	$45,023	$56,960
Investment required (b)	$50,000	$50,000
Profitability index (a) ÷ (b)	0.90	1.14

2. An investment project with a profitability index of less than 1.0 is not an acceptable investment. The reason is that such a project has a negative net present value. (See Project A in Exercise 15-4.)

Exercise 15-7 (10 minutes)

1. The profitability index for each proposal would be:

Proposal Number	Present Value of Cash Inflows (a)	Investment Required (b)	Profitability Index (a) ÷ (b)
A	$126,000	$ 90,000	1.40
B	184,000	200,000	0.92
C	135,000	90,000	1.50
D	221,000	170,000	1.30

Managerial Accounting

Exercise 15-7 (continued)

2. The ranking would be:

Proposal Number	Profitability Index
C	1.50
A	1.40
D	1.30
B	0.92

Two points should be noted about the ranking. First, proposal B is not an acceptable proposal at all, since it has a profitability index of less than 1.0 (negative net present value). Second, proposal D has the highest net present value, but it ranks lowest of the three acceptable proposals in terms of the profitability index.

Problem 15-9 (20 minutes)

Items and Computations	Year(s)	(1) Amount	(2) Tax Effect	(1) x (2) After-Tax Cash Flows	12% Factor	Present Value of Cash Flows
Investment in new trucks	Now	$(450,000)	—	$(450,000)	1.000	$(450,000)
Salvage from sale of the old trucks	Now	30,000	—	30,000	1.000	30,000
Net annual cash receipts	1-8	108,000	1 – 0.30	75,600	4.968	375,581
PV of CCA tax shield						83,445

$$PV = \frac{Cdt}{d+k} \times \frac{1+.5k}{1+k} - \frac{Sdt}{d+k} \times (1+k)^{-n}$$

$$= \frac{(\$450,000 - \$30,000) \times .3 \times .3}{.30 + .12} \times \frac{1.06}{1.12} - \frac{\$20,000 \times .3 \times .3}{.30 + .12} \times (1+.12)^{-8}$$

$$= (\$90,000 \times .9464) - (\$24,000 \times .386) = \$83,445$$

Items and Computations	Year(s)	(1) Amount	(2) Tax Effect	(1) x (2) After-Tax Cash Flows	12% Factor	Present Value of Cash Flows
Overhaul of motors	5	(45,000)	1 – 0.30	(31,500)	0.567	(17,861)
Salvage from the new trucks	8	20,000	—	20,000	0.404	8,080
Net present value						$ 29,245

Since the project has a positive net present value, the contract should be accepted.

Managerial Accounting

Problem 15-11 (20 minutes)

1. The formula for the profitability index is:

$$\frac{\underline{\text{Present value of cash inflows}}}{\text{Investment required}} = \text{Profitability index}$$

The index for the projects under consideration would be:

Project 1: $567,270 ÷ $480,000 = 1.18
Project 2: $433,400 ÷ $360,000 = 1.20
Project 3: $336,140 ÷ $270,000 = 1.24
Project 4: $522,970 ÷ $450,000 = 1.16
Project 5: $379,760 ÷ $400,000 = 0.95

2. a., b., and c.

	Net Present Value	Profitability Index	Internal Rate of Return
First preference	1	3	4
Second preference	2	2	3
Third preference	4	1	1
Fourth preference	3	4	2
Fifth preference	5	5	5

Problem 15-11 (continued)

3. Which ranking is best will depend on Austin Company's opportunities for reinvesting funds as they are released from a project. The internal rate of return method assumes that any released funds are reinvested at the rate of return shown for a project. This means that funds released from project #4 would have to be reinvested in another project yielding an internal rate of return of 19%. Another project yielding such a high rate of return might be difficult to find.

The profitability index approach also assumes that funds released from a project are reinvested in other projects. But the assumption is that the return earned by these other projects is only equal to the cost of capital (or whatever discount rate is being used), which in this case is only 10%. On balance, the profitability index is generally regarded as being the most dependable method of ranking competing projects.

The net present value is inferior to the profitability index as a ranking device, since it looks only at the total amount of net present value from a project and does not consider the amount of investment required. For example, it ranks project #3 as fourth in terms of preference because of its low net present value; yet this project is the best available in terms of the amount of cash inflow generated for each dollar of investment (as shown by the profitability index).

Problem 15-13 (60 minutes)

1.

	Year				Total
	1	**2**	**3**	**4-10**	**1-10**
Tons of salt extracted and processed........	70,000	100,000	160,000	135,000	1,275,000
Contribution margin per tonne ($21 − $15 = $6)..........	x $6	x $6	x $6	x $6	
Total contribution margin..........	$ 420,000	$600,000	$960,000	$810,000	
Less fixed costs for salaries, etc........	530,000	530,000	530,000	530,000	
Net cash receipts (outflow)...............	$(110,000)	$ 70,000	$430,000	$280,000	

2. See the present value computations on the following page.

Problem 15-13 (continued)

Items and Computations	Year(s)	(1) Amount	(2) Tax Effect	(1) x (2) After-Tax Cash Flows	16% Factor	Present Value of Cash Flows
Cost of special equipment..........	Now	$(800,000)	—	$(800,000)	1.000	$(800,000)
Working capital needed.............	Now	(90,000)	—	(90,000)	1.000	(90,000)
Net cash outflow (above)	1	(110,000)	1 – 0.30	(77,000)	0.862	(66,374)
Net cash receipts (above)	2	70,000	1 – 0.30	49,000	0.743	36,407
Net cash receipts (above)	3	430,000	1 – 0.30	301,000	0.641	192,941
Net cash receipts (above)	4-10	280,000	1 – 0.30	196,000	2.587*	507,052
PV of CCA tax shield.................						143,945

$$PV = \frac{Cdt}{d+k} \times \frac{1+.5k}{1+k} \quad - \quad \frac{Sdt}{d+k} \times (1+k)^{-n}$$

$$= \frac{800,000 \times .30 \times .30}{.30 + .16} \times \frac{1.08}{1.16} \quad - \quad \frac{\$40,000 \times .30 \times .30}{.30 + .16} \times (1 + .10)^{-10}$$

$$= (\$156,521.74 \times .9310) - (\$7,826.09 \times .227) = \$143,945$$

Managerial Accounting

Problem 15-13 (continued)

Items and Computations	Year(s)	(1) Amount	(2) Tax Effect	(1) x (2) After-Tax Cash Flows	16% Factor	Present Value of Cash Flows
Cost to level and fill the land	10	$(275,000)	1 – 0.30	$(192,500)	0.227	$(43,698)
Salvage value of equipment (5% x						
$800,000)	10	40,000	—	40,000	0.227	9,080
Working capital released	10	90,000	—	90,000	0.227	20,430
Net present value						$(90,217)

*Factor for a 10-year annuity at 16%	4.833
Factor for a 3-year annuity at 16%	2.246
Difference	2.587

Problem 15-15 (20 minutes)

1. The formula for the profitability index is:

$$\frac{\text{Present value of cash inflows}}{\text{Investment required}} = \text{Profitability index}$$

The profitability index for each project would be:

Project A: $800,000 + $221,615 = $1,021,615;
$1,021,615 ÷ $800,000 = 1.28

Project B: $675,000 + $210,000 = $885,000;
$885,000 ÷ $675,000 = 1.31

Project C: $500,000 + $175,175 = $675,175;
$675,175 ÷ $500,000 = 1.35

Project D: $700,000 + $152,544 = $852,544;
$852,544 ÷ $700,000 = 1.22

Project E: $900,000 + $(52,176) = $847,824;
$847,824 ÷ $900,000 = 0.94

2. a., b., and c.

	Net Present Value	Profitability Index	Internal Rate of Return
First preference	A	C	D
Second preference	B	B	C
Third preference	C	A	A
Fourth preference	D	D	B
Fifth preference	E	E	E

Problem 15-15 (continued)

3. Which ranking is best will depend on Yancey Company's opportunities for reinvesting funds as they are released from a project. The internal rate of return method assumes that any released funds are reinvested at the rate of return shown for a project. This means that funds released from project D would have to be reinvested in another project yielding an internal rate of return of 22%. Another project yielding such a high rate of return might be difficult to find.

The profitability index approach also assumes that funds released from a project are reinvested in other projects. But the assumption is that the return earned by these other projects is only equal to the cost of capital (or whatever discount rate is being used), which in this case is only 10%. On balance, the profitability index is generally regarded as being the most dependable method of ranking competing projects.

The net present value is inferior to the profitability index as a ranking device, since it looks only at the total amount of net present value from a project and does not consider the amount of investment required. For example, it ranks project C as third in terms of preference because of its low net present value; yet this project is the best available in terms of the amount of cash inflow generated for each dollar of investment (as shown by the profitability index).

Problem 15-17 (40 minutes)

1. The incremental net annual cash receipts would be:

Incremental hours of use
(45,000 hours x 20% = 9,000 hours) .... 9,000 hours
Rental fee per hour .... x $7
Incremental revenues... $63,000
Less incremental cost of the maintenance contract........ 8,000
Incremental net annual cash receipts $55,000

Managerial Accounting

Problem 15-17 (continued)

2.

Items and Computations	Year(s)	(1) Amount	(2) Tax Effect	(1) x (2) After-Tax Cash Flows	10% Factor	Present Value of Cash Flows
Cost of the new carts	Now	$(350,000)	—	$(350,000)	1.000	$(350,000)
Maintenance deposit required...........	Now	(4,000)	—	(4,000)	1.000	(4,000)
Cash from sale of old carts:						
Sale price received	Now	110,000	—	110,000	1.000	110,000
Net annual cash receipts (above) ...	1-8	55,000	1 – 0.40	33,000	5.335	176,055
PV of CCA tax shield...........						63,821

$$PV = \frac{Cdt}{d+k} \times \frac{1+.5k}{1+k} - \frac{Sdt}{d+k} \times (1+k)^{-n}$$

$$= \frac{240,000 \times .30 \times .40}{.30+.10} \times \frac{1.05}{1.10} - \frac{\$35,000 \times .30 \times .40}{.30+.10} \times (1+.10)^{-8}$$

$$= (\$72,000 \times .9545) - (\$10,500 \times .467) = \$63,821$$

Cost to rewind motors	5	(90,000)	1 – 0.40	(54,000)	0.621	(33,534)
Salvage value of the carts (10% x $350,000)...............	8	35,000	—	35,000	0.467	16,345
Refund of maintenance deposit	8	4,000	—	4,000	0.467	1,868
Net present value						$ (19,445)

Problem 15-17 (continued)

No, the carts should not be purchased as shown by their negative net present value. However, other factors that should be considered include the image and prestige of the resort and the possible impact on overall resort revenues.

Managerial Accounting

Problem 15-19 (40 minutes)

Items and Computations	Year(s)	(1) Amount	(2) Tax Effect	(1) x (2) After-Tax Cash Flows	8% Factor	Present Value of Cash Flows
Alternative 1:						
Investment in the bonds...........	Now	$(200,000)	—	$(200,000)	1.000	$(200,000)
Interest on the bonds						
8% x $200,000)..................	1-24*	8,000*	—	8,000	15.247**	121,976
Maturity of the bonds..............	24	200,000	—	200,000	0.390**	78,000
Net present value						$ (24)***

*24 six-month interest periods; $8,000 received each interest period.

**Factor for 4% for 24 periods.

***This amount should be zero; the difference is due to rounding of the discount factors. (Since the bonds yield 8% after taxes, they would have a zero net present value at an 8% discount rate.)

Problem 15-19 (continued)

Items and Computations	Year(s)	(1) Amount	(2) Tax Effect	(1) x (2) After-Tax Cash Flows	8% Factor	Present Value of Cash Flows
Alternative 2:						
Investment in the business.....	Now	$(200,000)	—	$(200,000)	1.000	$(200,000)
Net annual cash receipts ($400,000 – $370,000 = $30,000)..........	1-12	30,000	1 – 0.35	19,500	7.536	146,952
PV of CCA tax shield						19,260

$$PV = \frac{Cdt}{d+k} \times \frac{1+.5k}{1+k} - \frac{Sdt}{d+k} \times (1+k)^{-n}$$

$$= \frac{80,000 \times .20 \times .35}{.20+.08} \times \frac{1.04}{1.08} - \frac{\$0 \times .30 \times .35}{.20+.08} \times (1+.10)^{-12}$$

$$= (\$20,000 \times .963) - \$0 = \$19,260$$

Recovery of working capital ($200,000 – $80,000 = $120,000).................	12	120,000	—	120,000	0.397	47,640
Net present value						$ 13,852
Net present value in favour of alternative 2						$ 13,876

Managerial Accounting

Problem 15-21 (18 minutes)

	Probability	Cash Flows A	B
		A	**B**
Investment Outlay	1.0	$30,000.00	$30,000.00
Net Cash Inflows:			
Pessimistic..............................	0.2	8,000.00	26,000.00
Most Likely..............................	0.6	10,000.00	11,000.00
Optimistic.................................	0.2	42,000.00	21,000.00

Project Life Span = 7 years   Firm's Cost of Capital = 10%
PV Factor (from Table 15-4) =   4.868

1.

	Pessimistic	**Most Likely**	**Optimistic**
A	$ 8,944.00	$18,680.00	$174,456.00
B	$96,568.00	$23,548.00	$ 72,228.00

2. Expected value for project A:
    $16,000.00

    NPV = $47,888

    The yearly expected value of $16,000 is then multiplied by the 10%
    annuity factor of 4.868 to give $77,888. From this amount we deduct the
    $30,000 investment to arrive at a NPV of $47,888.

    Expected value for project B:
    $16,000.00

    NPV = $47,888

    As with Project A the expected NPV equals $77,888 − 30,000 = $47,888.

3. *Project A:*

E_i	$\bar{E}$	$(E_i - \bar{E})$	$(E_i - \bar{E})^2$	P_i	$(E_i - \bar{E})^{2P_i}$
8,000	16,000	−8,000	64,000,000	0.20	12,800,000
10,000	16,000	−6,000	36,000,000	0.60	21,600,000
42,000	16,000	26,000	676,000,000	0.20	135,200,000
			VARIANCE =		$169,600,000

standard deviation = $13,023.06

Problem 15-21 (continued)

Project B:

26,000	16,000	10,000	100,000,000	0.20	20,000,000
11,000	16,000	−5,000	26,000,000	0.60	15,000,000
21,000	16,000	5,000	25,000,000	0.20	5,000,000
			VARIANCE =		$ 40,000,000

standard deviation = $6,324.56

Coefficient of Variation:

	A	B
standard deviation	0.814	0.395
expected value		

4. Project A is more risky than Project B, as evidenced by both the higher standard deviation and a larger coefficient of variation. The calculation of the coefficient of variation was not really necessary, because it does not provide any additional information compared to the standard deviation when expected values are the same as in this problem. Which project one would actually select depends on whether one is a risk taker or a risk averter. A risk taker may select Project A in the hope of higher returns, while a risk averter would probably choose Project B with less variability in its returns.

Managerial Accounting

Problem 15-23 (20 minutes)

	Year(s)	(1) Amount	(2) Tax Effect	(1) x (2) After-Tax Cash Flows	16% Factor	Present Value of Cash Flows
Cost of land	Now	$ (800,000)	—	$ (800,000)	1.000	$ (800,000)
Cost of new facility	Now	(600,000)	—	(600,000)	1.000	(600,000)
Cost of equipment	Now	(450,000)	—	(450,000)	1.000	(450,000)
Net annual cash receipts	1-10	525,000	1 – 0.45	288,750	4.833	1,395,529
Proceeds from sale of land	10	1,400,000	—	1,400,000	.227	317,800
Taxes paid on capital gain* on sale of land	10	600,000 $\times \frac{3}{4} \times$ .45 =	202,500	.227	(45,968)

PV of CCA tax shield:

on building $\dfrac{600,000 \times .10 \times .45}{.10 + .16} \times \dfrac{1 \times (.5 \times .16)}{1 + .16}$

$= 103,846.15 \times .9310$ 96,681

on equipment $\dfrac{450,000 \times .20 \times .45}{.20 + .16} \times \dfrac{1 \times (.5 \times .16)}{1 + .16}$

$= 112,500 \times .9310$ 104,738

Net present value .... $ 18,780

---

*Capital gain = $1,400,000 proceeds less original cost of $800,000. Three-quarters of this capital gain is taxable.

Service Department Costing: An Activity Approach

Exercise 16-1 (20 minutes)

	Service Departments			Operating Departments		Total
	X	Y	Z	1	2	
Overhead costs	$84,000	$67,800	$36,000	$256,100	$498,600	$942,500
Allocation:						
Department X: (5%; 20%; 50; 25%)*	(84,000)	4,200	16,800	42,000	21,000	
Department Y: (1/10; 2/10; 7/10)		(72,000)	7,200	14,400	50,400	
Department Z: (1/4; 3/4)			(60,000)	15,000	45,000	
Total overhead costs after allocations	$ -0-	$ -0-	$ -0-	$327,500	$615,000	$942,500

*Typically, allocations can either be shown in percentages, in fractions, or as a rate per unit of activity. Department X allocations, for example, have been shown as percentages above, but they could have been shown as 1/20; 4/20; 10/20; and 5/20 or they could have been shown as $70 per employee. Usually fractions will be used if percentages result in odd decimals. Both percentages and fractions are used above for sake of illustration.

Managerial Accounting

Exercise 16-1 (continued)

Supporting computations:

Department X allocated to:

Dept. Y	60 emp.	5%
Dept. Z	240 "	20
Dept. 1	600 "	50
Dept. 2	300 "	25
	1,200 emp.	100%

Department Y allocated to:

Dept. Z	10,000 sq. m	1/10
Dept. 1	20,000 sq. m	2/10
Dept. 2	70,000 sq. m	7/10
	100,000 sq. m	10/10

Department Z allocated to:

Dept. 1	10,000 MH	1/4
Dept. 2	30,000 MH	3/4
	40,000 MH	4/4

Exercise 16-3 (15 minutes)

	Arbon Refinery	Beck Refinery
Variable costs:		
1,080,000 litres x $0.075	$ 81,000	
520,000 litres x $0.075		$ 39,000
Fixed costs:		
60%* x $200,000	120,000	
40%* x $200,000		80,000
Total allocated costs	$201,000	$119,000

*The allocation of fixed costs is based on peak-period hauling needs for the two refineries.

Managerial Accounting

Exercise 16-5 (10 minutes)

Allocations should be based on the budgeted rate of $60 per employee, multiplied by the actual number of employees in each operating department during the year.

	(1) Budgeted Rate	(2) Actual Number of Employees	(1) x (2) Total Allocation
Cutting department..................	$60	500	$ 30,000
Milling department	$60	400	24,000
Assembly department..............	$60	800	48,000
		1,700	$102,000

The difference between the budgeted and actual cost per employee will be retained in the medical services department and not allocated to the operating departments. This variance, which totals $20,400 for the year as shown below, will be closed out against revenues at year-end, along with other variances.

1,700 employees x ($72 – $60 = $12) = $20,400.

Exercise 16-7 (15 minutes)

1.

	1	2	3	4	Total
Percentage of 19x7 sales	8%	40%	28%	24%	100%
Allocation of 19x7 fixed administrative expenses (based on the above percentages)	$ 72,000	$360,000	$252,000	$216,000	$900,000

2.

	1	2	3	4	Total
19x7 allocation (above)	$ 72,000	$360,000	$252,000	$216,000	$900,000
19x6 allocation	90,000	225,000	315,000	270,000	900,000
Increase (decrease) in allocation	$(18,000)	$135,000	$ (63,000)	$ (54,000)	$ -0-

The manager of department 2 undoubtedly will be upset about the increased allocation to the department but will feel powerless to do anything about it. Such increased allocations may be viewed by some managers as a penalty for an outstanding performance.

3. As stated in the text, sales dollars ordinarily is not a good base for allocating fixed costs. The problem is that sales dollars vary from period to period, and as a result can cause one department or division to be allocated costs because of what happens in *other* departments or divisions. In our illustration above, three departments remained static, and as a result, forced a greater allocation of costs onto the one department that showed improvement during the period.

Managerial Accounting

Problem 16-9 (30 minutes)

1.

	Machine Tools Division	Special Products Division
Variable costs:		
$0.50 x 90,000 machine-hours	$45,000	
$0.50 x 60,000 machine-hours......................		$30,000
Fixed costs:		
65% x $80,000..........................	52,000	
35% x $80,000..........................		28,000
Total cost allocated	$97,000	$58,000

The variable costs are allocated according to the budgeted rate per machine-hour multiplied times the budgeted number of machine-hours which will be worked in each division during the month. The fixed costs are allocated in predetermined, lump-sum amounts based on the peak-period maintenance needs in each division.

Problem 16-9 (continued)

2.

	Machine Tools Division	Special Products Division
Variable costs:		
$0.50 x 60,000 machine-hours	$30,000	
$0.50 x 60,000 machine-hours........................		$30,000
Fixed costs:		
65% x $80,000...........................	52,000	
35% x $80,000...........................		28,000
Total cost allocated.......................	$82,000	$58,000

Notice that the variable costs are allocated according to the budgeted rate per machine-hour and not according to the actual rate. Also notice that the fixed costs are again allocated in predetermined, lump-sum amounts based on budgeted fixed costs. Any difference between budgeted and actual costs is not allocated but rather is treated as a spending variance in the maintenance department:

	Variable	Fixed
Total actual costs for the month......................	$78,000	$85,000
Total cost allocated above.............................	60,000	80,000
Spending variance—not allocated..................	$18,000	$ 5,000

Managerial Accounting

Problem 16-9 (continued)

3.

Actual variable costs............................	$ 78,000
Actual fixed costs.................................	85,000
Total actual costs	$163,000

One-half of the cost, or $81,500, would be allocated to each division, since an equal number of machine-hours was worked in each division during the month.

4. There are two main criticisms: First, the spending variances should not be allocated since this forces the inefficiencies of the service department onto the using departments. Second, the fixed costs should *not* be allocated according to month-by-month usage of services, since this causes the allocation to one division to be affected by what happens in another division.

5. Their strategy probably will be to underestimate long-run average usage, in order to force a greater proportion of any allocation onto other departments. Top management can control strategy-ploys of this type by careful follow-up, with rewards being given to those managers who estimate accurately, and severe penalties assessed against those managers who underestimate long-run usage.

Problem 16-11 (25 minutes)

1. Beginning-of-year allocations of variable costs are based on budgeted rate multiplied by the budgeted level of activity. Fixed costs are allocated in lump-sum amounts based on the peak-period needs of the using departments. The computations are:

	Milling Department	Finishing Department	Total
Variable costs:			
20K x 10,000 meals	200,000K		
20K x 5,000 meals		100,000K	300,000K
Fixed costs:			
70%* x 200,000K	140,000		
30%* x 200,000K		60,000	200,000
Total cost allocated	340,000K	160,000K	500,000K

*The allocation percentages are based on peak-period needs.

2. a. End-of-year allocations of variable costs are based on the budgeted rate multiplied by the actual level of activity. Fixed costs are again allocated in predetermined lump-sum amounts based on budgeted costs. The computations are:

	Milling Department	Finishing Department	Total
Variable costs:			
20K x 12,000 meals	240,000K		
20K x 4,000 meals		80,000K	320,000K
Fixed costs:			
70% x 200,000K....................	140,000		
30% x 200,000K....................		60,000	200,000
Total cost allocated	380,000K	140,000K	520,000K

Managerial Accounting

Problem 16-11 (continued)

b. Any amount above the budgeted variable cost per meal and the budgeted total fixed cost would not be allocated to the other departments. The amount not allocated would be:

	Variable Cost	Fixed Cost	Total
Actual cost incurred during the year	384,000K	215,000K	599,000K
Cost allocated above	320,000	200,000	520,000
Cost not allocated (spending variance)	64,000K	15,000K	79,000K

The costs that are not allocated to the other departments represent spending variances that should be borne by the cafeteria.

Problem 16-13 (30 minutes)

1 . Yes, there is merit to the complaint. The company is using a variable base (lines of print) to allocate costs that are largely fixed. Thus, the amount of cost that is charged to a division during a given month will depend to a large extent on usage in other divisions. This is unfair, since inefficiency or a curtailment of usage in one division can result in shifts of costs from it onto the other divisions, even though the other divisions receive no more (and perhaps even less) service.

2.

	Lines of Print	Total Cost
May activity........................	200,000	$182,000
June activity.......................	150,000	179,000
Difference........................	50,000	$ 3,000

$$\frac{\text{Change in cost}}{\text{Change in activity}} = \frac{\$3,000}{50,000 \text{ lines}} = \$0.06 \text{ per line}$$

Fixed costs per month:

Total cost, May..	$182,000
Less variable cost (200,000 lines x $0.06).............	12,000
Fixed cost...	$170,000

Managerial Accounting

Problem 16-13 (continued)

3.

	Division			
	A	B	C	Total
May allocation:				
Variable cost:				
80,000 lines x $0.06.........	$ 4,800			
20,000 lines x $0.06.........		$ 1,200		
100,000 lines x $0.06.........			$ 6,000	
Fixed cost:				
40% x $170,000	68,000			
12% x $170,000		20,400		
48% x $170,000			81,600	
Total cost allocated	$72,800	$21,600	$87,600	$182,000
June allocation:				
Variable cost:				
75,000 lines x $0.06.......	$ 4,500			
30,000 lines x $0.06.......		$ 1,800		
45,000 lines x $0.06.......			$ 2,700	
Fixed cost:				
40% x $170,000	68,000			
12% x $170,000		20,400		
48% x $170,000			81,600	
Total cost allocated	$72,500	$22,200	$84,300	$179,000

Problem 16-15 (50 minutes)

a. i. **Direct Method**

Accounting dept. (AD) to Consulting: to AC 3/4 or $6,000
to LC 1/4 or $2,000
Legal dept. (LD) to Consulting: to AC 1/5 or $2,000
to LC 4/5 or $8,000

Income Statements

	Accounting Consulting	Legal Consulting
Revenue...........................	$30,000	$20,500
Individual costs	(6,000)	(14,000)
Allocated AD, LD..............	(8,000)	(10,000)
Net income......................	$16,000	$ (3,500)

ii. **Reciprocal/Cross Allocation Method**
AD = 8,000 + .5LD and LD = 10,000 + .2AD
AD = $14,444 and LD = $12,889
Allocating, AD to AC, $8,666; to LC, $2,889
LD to AC, $1,289; to LC, $5,156

Income Statements

	Accounting Consulting	Legal Consulting
Revenue	$30,000	$20,500
Individual costs	(6,000)	(14,000)
Allocated AD, LD	(9,955)*	(8,045)**
Net income	$14,045	$ (1,545)

---

*$8,666 + $1,289 = $9,955
**$2,889 + $5,156 = $8,045

Problem 16-15 (continued)

b. *MEMORANDUM*

DATE: Date of examination
TO: Managing Partner
FROM: Independent Consultant
SUBJECT: Performance of Consulting Service

The memorandum should note the following points:

i.   Only one month of activity has taken place; therefore, results will be very difficult to analyze. No comparisons are possible. Consequently, any analysis will be highly subjective and, recommendations should be handled carefully.

ii. The performance of the individual departments is different under the different approaches of cost allocation.

iii. The overall performance is satisfactory and since this "one-stop shopping" arrangement is in a sense a joint product set-up, the overall is more important than the artificial measurement of the parts.

iv. Some cost control procedures may be initiated, but these should be handled carefully, since we are dealing with professional staff and we would not want to suppress the creative element in their work. Therefore, the use of standard costing in such an organization may not be warranted.

(SMAC Solution, adapted)

"How Well Am I Doing?" Financial Statement Analysis

17

Exercise 17-1 (15 minutes)

1.

	19x2	19x1
Sales	100.0%	100.0%
Less cost of goods sold	63.2	60.0
Gross margin	36.8	40.0
Selling expenses	18.0	17.5
Administrative expenses	13.6	14.6
Total expenses	31.6	32.1
Net operating income	15.2	7.9
Interest expense	1.4	1.0
Net income before taxes	3.8%	6.9%

2. The company's major problem seems to be the increase in cost of goods sold, which increased from 60.0% of sales in 19x1 to 63.2% of sales in 19x2. This suggests that the company is not passing the increases in costs of its products on to its customers. As a result, cost of goods sold as a percentage of sales has increased and gross margin has decreased. Selling expenses and interest expense have both increased slightly during the year which suggests that costs generally are going up in the company. The only exception is the administrative expenses which have decreased from 14.6% of sales in 19x1 to 13.6% of sales in 19x2. This probably is a result of the company's efforts to reduce administrative expenses during the year.

Managerial Accounting

Exercise 17-3 (25 minutes)

1. Current ratio:

$$\frac{\text{Current assets,}\quad \$490{,}000}{\text{Current liabilities,}\quad \$200{,}000} = 2.45 \text{ to } 1$$

2. Acid-test ratio:

$$\frac{\text{Quick assets,}\quad \$181{,}000}{\text{Current liabilities,}\quad \$200{,}000} = 0.91 \text{ to } 1 \text{ (rounded)}$$

3. Accounts receivable turnover:

$$\frac{\text{Sales,}\qquad\qquad\qquad\quad \$2{,}100{,}000}{\text{Average accounts receivable,}\quad \$150{,}000} = 14 \text{ times}$$

$$\frac{365 \text{ days}}{14 \text{ times}} = 26.1 \text{ days (rounded)}$$

4. Inventory turnover:

$$\frac{\text{Cost of goods sold,}\quad \$1{,}260{,}000}{\text{Average inventory,}\qquad \$280{,}000} = 4.5 \text{ times}$$

$$\frac{365 \text{ days}}{4.5 \text{ times}} = 81.1 \text{ days to turn (rounded)}$$

5. Debt-to-equity ratio:

$$\frac{\text{Total liabilities,}\qquad\qquad\quad \$500{,}000}{\text{Total shareholders' equity,}\quad \$800{,}000} = 0.63 \text{ to } 1 \text{ (rounded)}$$

6. Times interest earned:

$$\frac{\text{Earnings before interest and income taxes,}\quad \$180{,}000}{\text{Interest expense,}\qquad\qquad\quad \$30{,}000} = 6.0 \text{ times}$$

7. Book value per share:

$$\frac{\text{Shareholders' equity,}\qquad\qquad \$800{,}000}{\text{Common shares outstanding,}\quad 20{,}000} = \$40/\text{share}$$

Exercise 17-5 (20 minutes)

1. Return on total assets:

$$\frac{\text{Net income} + [\text{Interest expense} \times (1-\text{Tax rate})]}{\text{Average total assets}} = \text{Return on total assets}$$

$$\frac{\$105,000 + [\$30,000 \times (1-0.30)]}{1/2\ (\$1,100,000 + \$1,300,000)} = \frac{\$126,000}{\$1,200,000} = \underline{10.5\%}$$

2. Return on common shareholders' equity:

$$\frac{\text{Net income} - \text{Preferred dividends}}{\text{Average common shareholders' equity}} = \text{Return on common shareholders' equity}$$

$$\frac{\$105,000}{1/2\ (\$725,000 + \$800,000)} = \frac{\$105,000}{\$762,500} = \underline{13.8\%}\ \text{(rounded)}$$

3. Financial leverage was positive, since the rate of return to the common shareholders (13.8%) was greater than the rate of return on total assets (10.5%). This positive leverage is traceable in part to the company's current liabilities, which may carry no interest cost, and to the bonds payable, which have an after-tax interest cost of only 7%.

   10% interest rate x (1 –0.30) = 7% after-tax cost.

Managerial Accounting

Exercise 17-7 (15 minutes)

1.

MIDWEST PRODUCTS, INC.
Income Statement
For the Year Ended May 31

Sales...	$800,000
Cost of goods sold...	500,000
Gross margin	300,000
Operating expenses	180,000
Net operating income	120,000
Income taxes (30%)...	36,000
Net income before extraordinary item	84,000
Extraordinary item: Fire loss, net of tax	(21,000)*
Net income	$ 63,000

*Actual fire loss...	$30,000
Less reduction in taxes at a 30% rate............	9,000
Fire loss, net of tax	$21,000

2. Earnings per common share:

On net income before the extraordinary item:	
$84,000 ÷ 20,000 shares..	$4.20
On the extraordinary item, net of tax:	
$21,000 ÷ 20,000 shares..	(1.05)
Net earnings per share	$3.15

Problem 17-9 (45 minutes)

			This Year	Last Year
1.	a.	Current assets	$2,060,000	$1,470,000
		Current liabilities	1,100,000	600,000
		Working capital	$ 960,000	$ 870,000
	b.	Current assets (a)	$2,060,000	$1,470,000
		Current liabilities (b)	$1,100,000	$ 600,000
		Current ratio (a) ÷ (b)	1.87 to 1	2.45 to 1
	c.	Quick assets (a)	$ 740,000	$ 650,000
		Current liabilities (b)	$1,100,000	$ 600,000
		Acid-test ratio (a) ÷ (b)	0.67 to 1	1.08 to 1
	d.	Sales on account (a)	$7,000,000	$6,000,000
		Average receivables (b)	$ 525,000	$ 375,000
		Turnover of receivables (a) ÷ (b)	3.3 times	16.0 times
		Average age of receivables:		
		365 ÷ turnover	27.4 days	22.8 days
	e.	Cost of goods sold (a)	$5,400,000	$4,800,000
		Average inventory (b)	$1,050,000	$ 760,000
		Inventory turnover (a) ÷ (b)	5.1 times	6.3 times
		Turnover in days: 365 ÷ turnover	71.6 days	57.9 days
	f.	Total liabilities (a)	$1,850,000	$1,350,000
		Shareholders' equity (b)	$2,150,000	$1,950,000
		Debt-to-equity ratio (a) ÷ (b)	0.86 to 1	0.69 to 1
	g.	Net income before interest and taxes (a).	$ 630,000	$ 490,000
		Interest expense (b)	$ 90,000	$ 90,000
		Times interest earned (a) ÷ (b)	7.0 times	5.4 times

Problem 17-9 (continued)

2. a.

MODERN BUILDING SUPPLY
Common-Size Balance Sheets

	This Year	Last Year
Current assets:		
Cash	2.3%	6.1%
Temporary investments	—	1.5
Accounts receivable, net	16.3	12.1
Inventory	32.5	24.2
Prepaid expenses	0.5	0.6
Total current assets	51.5	44.5
Capital assets, net	48.5	55.5
Total assets	100.0%	100.0%
Liabilities:		
Current liabilities	27.5%	18.2%
Bonds payable, 12%	18.8	22.7
Total liabilities	46.3	40.9
Shareholders' equity:		
Preferred shares, 8%	5.0	6.1
Common shares	12.5	15.2
Retained earnings	36.3	37.9
Total shareholders' equity	53.8	59.1
Total liabilities and equity	100.0%	100.0%

Note: Columns do not total down in all cases due to rounding differences.

Problem 17-9 (continued)

b.

MODERN BUILDING SUPPLY
Common-Size Income Statements

	This Year	Last Year
Sales	100.0%	100.0%
Less cost of goods sold..................................	77.1	80.0
Gross margin..	22.9	20.0
Less operating expenses	13.9	11.8
Net operating income	9.0	8.2
Less interest expense	1.3	1.5
Net income before taxes	7.7	6.7
Less income taxes	3.1	2.7
Net income	4.6%	4.0%

3. The following points can be made from the analytical work in parts (1) and (2) above:

The company has improved its profit margin from last year. This is attributable to an increase in gross margin, which is offset somewhat by an increase in operating expenses. In both years the company's net income as a percentage of sales equals or exceeds the industry average of 4%.

Although the company's working capital has increased, its current position actually has deteriorated significantly since last year. Both the current ratio and the acid-test ratio are well below the industry average, and both are trending downward. (This shows the importance of not just looking at the working capital in assessing the financial strength of a company.) Given the present trend, it soon will be impossible for the company to pay its bills as they come due.

The drain on the cash account seems to be a result mostly of a large buildup in accounts receivable and inventory. This is evident both from the common-size balance sheet and from the financial ratios. Notice that the average age of the receivables has increased by 5 days since last year, and that it is now 9 days over the industry average. Many of

Problem 17-9 (continued)

the company's customers are not taking their discounts, since the average collection period is 27 days and collection terms are 2/10, n/30. This suggests financial weakness on the part of these customers, or sales to customers who are poor credit risks. Perhaps the company has been too aggressive in expanding its sales.

The inventory turned only 5 times this year as compared to over 6 times last year. It takes three weeks longer for the company to turn its inventory than the average for the industry (71 days as compared to 50 days for the industry). This suggests that inventory stocks are higher than they need to be.

In the authors' opinion, the loan should be approved on the condition that the company take immediate steps to get its accounts receivable and inventory back under control. This would mean more rigorous checks of creditworthiness before sales are made and perhaps paring out of slow paying customers. It would also mean a sharp reduction of inventory levels to a more manageable size. If these steps are taken, it appears that sufficient funds could be generated to repay the loan in a reasonable period of time.

Problem 17-11 (25 minutes)

1. Net income to the common shareholders:

	Method A	Method B	Method C
Income before interest and taxes	$100,000	$100,000	$100,000
Deduct interest expense:			
10% x $250,000...................	—	—	25,000
Income before taxes..................	100,000	100,000	75,000
Deduct income taxes (30%)	30,000	30,000	22,500
Net income	70,000	70,000	52,500
Deduct preferred dividends:			
10% x $250,000...................	—	25,000	—
Net income to common shareholders	$ 70,000	$ 45,000	$ 52,500

2. Return on common equity:

	Method A	Method B	Method C
Net income to common shareholders	$ 70,000 (a)	$ 45,000 (a)	$ 52,500 (a)
Common shareholders' investment	$500,000 (b)	$250,000 (b)	$250,000 (b)
Return on common equity (a) ÷ (b)..............	14%	18%	21%

3. Methods B and C provide a greater return on common equity than Method A because of the effect of positive leverage in the company. Methods B and C each contain sources of funds that require a fixed annual return on the funds provided. Apparently, this fixed annual cost is less than what is being earned on the assets in the company, with the difference going to the common shareholders.

Method C, which involves the use of debt, provides more leverage than Method B, which involves the use of preferred shares, due to the fact that the interest on the debt is tax deductible, whereas the dividends on the preferred shares are not.

Managerial Accounting

Problem 17-13 (40 minutes)

1. Decrease   Sale of inventory at a profit will be reflected in an increase in retained earnings, which is part of shareholders' equity. An increase in shareholders' equity will result in a decrease in the ratio of assets provided by creditors as compared to assets provided by owners.

2. No effect   Purchasing land for cash has no effect on earnings or on the number of shares of common shares outstanding. One asset is exchanged for another.

3. Increase   A sale of inventory on account will increase the quick assets (cash, accounts receivable, temporary investments) but have no effect on the current liabilities. For this reason, the acid-test ratio will increase.

4. No effect   Payments on account reduce cash and accounts payable by equal amounts; thus, the net amount of working capital is not affected.

5. Decrease   When a customer pays a bill, the accounts receivable balance is reduced. This increases the accounts receivable turnover which in turn decreases the average collection period.

6. Decrease   Declaring a cash dividend will increase current liabilities, but have no effect on current assets. Therefore, the current ratio will decrease.

7. Increase   Payment of a previously declared cash dividend will reduce both current assets and current liabilities by the same amount. An equal reduction in both current assets and current liabilities will always result in an increase in the current ratio, so long as the current assets exceed the current liabilities.

8. No effect   Book value per share is not affected by the current market price of the company's shares.

9. Decrease   The dividend yield ratio is obtained by dividing the dividend per share by the market price per share. If the dividend per share remains unchanged and the market price goes up, then the yield will decrease.

Problem 17-13 (continued)

10. Increase   Selling property for a profit would increase net income and therefore the return on total assets would increase.

11. Increase   A write-off of inventory will reduce the inventory balance, thereby increasing the turnover in relation to a given level of cost of goods sold.

12. Increase   Since the company's assets earn at a rate that is higher than the rate paid on the bonds, positive leverage would come into effect, increasing the return to the common shareholders.

13. No effect   Changes in the market price of a share have no direct effect on the dividends paid or on the earnings per share and therefore have no effect on this ratio.

14. Decrease   A decrease in net income would mean less income available to cover interest payments. Therefore, the times-interest-earned ratio would decrease.

15. No effect   Write-off of an uncollectible account against the Allowance for Bad Debts will have no effect on total current assets. For this reason, the current ratio will remain unchanged.

16. Decrease   A purchase of inventory on account will increase current liabilities, but will not increase the quick assets (cash, accounts receivable, temporary investments). Therefore, the ratio of quick assets to current liabilities will decrease.

17. Increase   The price-earnings ratio is obtained by dividing the market price per share by the earnings per share. If the earnings per share remain unchanged, and the market price goes up, then the price-earnings ratio will increase.

18. Decrease   Payments to creditors will reduce the total liabilities of a company, thereby decreasing the ratio of total debt to total equity.

         Managerial Accounting

Problem 17-15 (90 minutes)

			This Year	**Last Year**
1.	a.	Net income	$ 280,000	$ 168,000
		Add after-tax cost of interest:		
		$120,000 x (1 – 0.30)	84,000	
		$100,000 x (1 – 0.30)		70,000
		Total (a)	$ 364,000	$ 238,000
		Average total assets (b)	$5,330,000	$4,640,000
		Return on total assets (a) ÷ (b)	6.8%	5.1%
	b.	Net income...	$ 280,000	$ 168,000
		Less preferred dividends.......................	48,000	48,000
		Net income to common (a).....................	$ 232,000	$ 120,000
		Average total shareholders' equity..........	$3,120,000	$3,028,000
		Less average preferred shares	600,000	600,000
		Average common equity (b)....................	$2,520,000	$2,428,000
		Return on common equity (a) ÷ (b)	9.2%	4.9%

c. Leverage is positive for this year, since the return on common equity (9.2%) is greater than the return on total assets (6.8%). For last year, leverage is negative since the return on common equity (4.9%) is less than the return on total assets (5.1 %).

			This Year	**Last Year**
2.	a.	Net income for common (a).....................	$ 232,000	$ 120,000
		Number of common shares (b)	50,000	50,000
		Earnings per share (a) ÷ (b)	$4.64	$2.40
	b.	Net income (a)......................................	$ 280,000	$ 168,000
		Common shares outstanding	50,000	50,000
		Converted common shares	40,000	40,000
		Total common shares (b)	90,000	90,000
		Fully diluted EPS (a) ÷ (b)	$3.11	$1.87
	c.	Common dividend per share (a).............	$1.44	$0.72
		Market price per share (b)......................	$36.00	$20.00
		Dividend yield ratio (a) ÷ (b)	4.0%	3.6%

Problem 17-15 (continued)

		This Year	Last Year
d.	Common dividend per share (a)	$1.44	$0.72
	Earnings per share (b)	$4.64	$2.40
	Dividend payout ratio (a) ÷ (b)	31.0%	30.0%
e.	Market price per share (a)............................	$36.00	$20.00
	Earnings per share (b)	$ 4.64	$ 2.40
	Price-earnings ratio (a) ÷ (b)	7.8	8.3

Notice from the data given in the problem that the average P/E ratio for companies in Hedrick's industry is 10. Since Hedrick Company presently has a P/E ratio of only 7.8, investors appear to regard it less well than they do other companies in the industry. That is, investors are willing to pay only 7.8 times current earnings for a share of Hedrick Company's shares, as compared to 10 times current earnings for a common share for the average company in the industry.

		This Year	Last Year
f.	Shareholders' equity	$3,200,000	$3,040,000
	Less preferred shares.............................	600,000	600,000
	Common shareholders' equity (a)...........	$2,600,000	$2,440,000
	Number of common shares (b)	50,000	50,000
	Book value per share (a) ÷ (b)	$52.00	$48.80

Note that the book value of Hedrick Company's shares is greater than the market value for both years. This does not necessarily indicate that the shares are selling at a bargain price. As stated in the text, market value is an indication of investors' perceptions of future earnings and/or dividends, whereas book value is a result of already completed transactions and is geared to the past. Thus, there is no necessary relationship between market value and book value.

Managerial Accounting

Problem 17-15 (continued)

			This Year	Last Year
3.	a.	Current assets	$2,600,000	$1,980,000
		Current liabilities	1,300,000	920,000
		Working capital	$1,300,000	$1,060,000
	b.	Current assets (a)	$2,600,000	$1,980,000
		Current liabilities (b)	$1,300,000	$ 920,000
		Current ratio (a) ÷ (b)	2.0 to 1	2.15 to 1
	c.	Quick assets (a)	$1,220,000	$1,120,000
		Current liabilities (b)	$1,300,000	$ 920,000
		Acid-test ratio (a) ÷ (b)	0.94 to 1	1.22 to 1
	d.	Sales on account (a)	$5,250,000	$4,160,000
		Average receivables (b)	$ 750,000	$ 560,000
		Accounts receivable turnover (a) ÷ (b)......	7 times	7.4 times
		Average age of receivables, 365 ÷ turnover	52 days	49 days
	e.	Cost of goods sold (a)	$4,200,000	$3,300,000
		Average inventory (b)	$1,050,000	$ 720,000
		Inventory turnover (a) ÷ (b)	4 times	4.6 times
		Number of days to turn inventory, 365 days ÷ turnover (rounded)	91 days	79 days
	f.	Total liabilities (a)	$2,500,000	$1,920,000
		Shareholders' equity (b)	$3,200,000	$3,040,000
		Debt-to-equity ratio (a) ÷ (b)	0.78 to 1	0.63 to 1
	g.	Net income before interest and taxes (a)..	$520,000	$340,000
		Interest expense (b)	$120,000	$100,000
		Times interest earned (a) ÷ (b)	4.3 times	3.4 times

Problem 17-15 (continued)

4. As stated by Marva Rossen, both net income and sales are up from last year. The return on total assets has improved from 5.1 % last year to 6.8% this year, and the return on common equity is up to 9.2% from 4.9% the year before. But this appears to be the only bright spot in the company's operating picture. Virtually all other ratios are below the industry average, and, more important, they are trending downward.

   Notice particularly that the average age of receivables has lengthened to 52 days—about three weeks over the industry average—and that the inventory turnover is 50% longer than the industry average. One wonders if the increase in sales was obtained at least in part by extending credit to high-risk customers. Also notice that the debt-to-equity ratio is rising rapidly. If the $1,000,000 loan is granted, the ratio will rise further to 1.09 to 1.

   In the authors' opinion, what the company needs is more equity—not more debt. Therefore, the loan should not be approved. The company should be encouraged to make another issue of common shares in order to provide a broader equity base on which to operate.

Managerial Accounting

Problem 17-17 (60 minutes)

1.

		19x2	**19x1**
a.	Net income	$ 525,000	$ 420,000
	Less preferred dividends	60,000	60,000
	Net income to common (a)	$ 465,000	$ 360,000
	Common shares outstanding (b)	100,000*	100,000*
	Earnings per share (a) ÷ (b)	$4.65	$3.60

*$500,000 ÷ $5 par value = 100,000 shares.

		19x2	**19x1**
b.	Net income (a)	$ 525,000	$ 420,000
	Common shares outstanding	100,000	100,000
	Conversion of preferred shares	150,000*	150,000*
	Total potential common shares (b)	250,000	250,000
	Fully diluted earnings per share (a) ÷ (b)	$2.10	$1.68

*$750,000 ÷ $10 issue price = 75,000 shares.
75,000 shares x 2 = 150,000 shares.

		19x2	**19x1**
c.	Cash dividends per share (a)	$1.80*	$1.40*
	Market price per share (b)	$60.00	$45.00
	Dividend yield ratio (a) ÷ (b)	3.0%	3.1%

*For 19x1: $140,000 ÷ 100,000 shares = $1.40.
For 19x2: $180,000 ÷ 100,000 shares = $1.80.

		19x2	**19x1**
d.	Cash dividends per share (a)	$1.80	$1.40
	Earnings per share (b)	$4.65	$3.60
	Dividend payout ratio (a) ÷ (b)	38.7%	38.9%

		19x2	**19x1**
e.	Market price per share (a)	$60.00	$45.00
	Earnings per share (b)	$4.65	$3.60
	Price-earnings ratio (a) ÷ (b)	12.9 times	12.5 times

		19x2	**19x1**
f.	Total shareholders' equity	$2,735,000	$2,450,000
	Less preferred shares	750,000	750,000
	Common shareholders' equity (a)	$1,985,000	$1,700,000
	Common shares outstanding (b)	100,000	100,000
	Book value per share (a) ÷ (b)	$19.85	$17.00

Problem 17-17 (continued)

		19x2	19x1
2. a.	Net income...................................	$ 525,000	$ 420,000
	Add after-tax cost of interest paid:		
	$120,000 x (1 – 0.30).......................	84,000	84,000
	Total (a)...	$ 609,000	$ 504,000
	Average total assets (b)	$4,467,500	$3,600,000
	Return on total assets (a) ÷ (b)	13.6%	14.0%
b.	Net income..	$ 525,000	$ 420,000
	Less preferred dividends.....................	60,000	60,000
	Net income to common (a)..................	$ 465,000	$ 360,000
	Average common shareholders' equity (b)	$1,842,500	$1,575,000
	Return on common shareholders' equity (a) ÷ (b)	25.2%	22.9%

c. Financial leverage is positive in both years, since the return on common equity is greater than the return on total assets. This positive leverage arises from (1) the preferred shares, which have a dividend cost of only 8%; and the bonds, which have an after-tax interest cost of only 8.4% [12% interest rate x (1 – 0.30)]; and the current liabilities, which may have no interest cost.

3. In the authors' view, the company's common shares are not an attractive investment. Even though most of its ratios equal (or are better than) the industry averages, the authors would not purchase the shares because of the large potential dilution from the conversion of preferred shares. Notice from the computations above that the effects of this dilution will be very great when conversion takes place. Undoubtedly other investors recognize this problem as well, since the shares have a low price-earnings ratio even though they have an unusually high return on common shareholders' equity.

Managerial Accounting

Problem 17-19 (40 minutes)

1. The income statement in common-size form would be:

	19x2	19x1
Sales	100.0%	100.0%
Less cost of goods sold	65.0	60.0
Gross margin	35.0	40.0
Less operating expenses	26.3	30.4
Net operating income	8.7	9.6
Less interest expense	1.2	1.6
Net income before taxes	7.5	8.0
Less income taxes	2.3	2.4
Net income	5.3%	5.6%

The balance sheet in common-size form would be:

	19x2	19x1
Current assets:		
Cash	2.0%	5.1%
Accounts receivable	15.0	10.1
Inventory	30.1	15.2
Prepaid expenses	1.0	1.3
Total current assets	48.1	31.6
Capital assets	51.9	68.4
Total assets	100.0%	100.0%
Liabilities:		
Current liabilities	25.1%	12.7
Bonds payable, 12%	20.1	25.3
Total liabilities	45.1	38.0
Shareholders' equity:		
Preferred shares, 8%	15.0	19.0
Common shares	10.0	12.7
Retained earnings	29.8	30.4
Total shareholders' equity	54.9	62.0
Total liabilities and shareholders' equity	100.0%	100.0%

Note: Columns do not total down in all cases due to rounding differences.

Problem 17-19 (continued)

2. The company's cost of goods sold has increased from 60% of sales in 19x1 to 65% of sales in 19x2. This appears to be the major reason the company's profits showed so little increase between the two years. Some benefits were realized from the company's cost-cutting efforts, as evidenced by the fact that operating expenses were only 26.3% of sales in 19x2 as compared to 30.4% in 19x1. Unfortunately, this reduction in operating expenses was not enough to offset the increase in cost of goods sold. As a result, the company's net income declined from 5.6% of sales in 19x1 to 5.3% of sales in 19x2.

Managerial Accounting

A1	B	C	D	E	F	G	H
2	**Problem 17-21** (45 minutes)						
3							
4	Koberg Company has just prepared the annual financial						
5	statements for 19A given below:						
6							
7				KOBERG COMPANY			
8				Income Statement			
9				For the Year Ended December 31, 19A			
10							
11	Sales revenue (half on credit)					95,000	
12	Cost of goods sold					46,000	
13							
14	Gross margin					49,000	
15	Expenses (inc. $3,000 interest expense)........................					33,000	
16							
17	Pretax income					16,000	
18	Income tax on operations (22%)					3,520	
19							
20	Net income..					12,480	
21							
22							

Problem 17-21 (continued)

```
23                          KOBERG COMPANY
24                            Balance Sheet
25                          At December 31, 19A
26
27                               Assets
28   Cash ....................................................................    20,000
29   Accounts receivable (net).....................................    30,000
30   Inventory ............................................................    40,000
31   Operational assets (net)......................................   100,000
32
33   Total assets.........................................................   190,000
34
35                             Liabilities
36   Accounts payable...............................................    50,000
37   Income tax payable ............................................     1,000
38   Note payable, long term ......................................    25,000
39
40                        Shareholders' Equity
41   Capital stock .....................................................    80,000
42   Retained earnings .............................................    34,000
43
44   Total liabilities and shareholders' equity .......................   190,000
45
46
47   ADDITIONAL INFORMATION:
48   Sales revenue for 19B................................................    100,000
49   Income tax rate ........................................................      22.00%
50   Portion of sales on credit..........................................      50.00%
51   Depreciation expense in 19B was ...........................      20,000
52   No long-term notes payable were paid during 19B........
53   Income tax that was unpaid at the end of 19B...............       1,500
54   Dividends paid during 19B.........................................      12,000
55   Additions to operational assets during 19B ...................      10,000
56   Inventory, January 1, 19A ..........................................      40,000
57
```

Problem 17-21 (continued)

58   REQUIRED: Using a computer spreadsheet, prepare forecasts of
59   the 19B income statement, cash flows and December 31, 19B
60   balance sheet. (Hint: Use 19A turnovers as estimates
61   for 19B)
62
63   SOLUTION AREA:
64
65   Accounts receivable turnover ratio ....   ?
66
67   Inventory turnover ratio ....   ?
68
69   To calculate the accounts payable turnover ratio we first
70   must calculate purchases for 19A as follows:
71
72   Cost of goods sold ....   ?
73   Add ending inventory, 19A ....   ?
74   Less inventory, Jan. 1, 19A ....   ?
75
76   Purchases for 19A..   ?
77
78
79   Accounts payable turnover ratio.....................................   ?
80
81

Problem 17-21 (continued)

82	KOBERG COMPANY	
83	Income Statement	
84	For the Year Ended December 31, 19B	
85		
86	Sales revenue	?
87	Cost of goods sold	?
88		
89	Gross margin	?
90	Expenses (same percentage as 19A)	?
91		
92	Pretax income	?
93	Income tax on operations..	?
94		
95	Net income..	?
96		
97		
98		

Problem 17-21 (continued)

	KOBERG COMPANY	
99		
100	Balance Sheet	
101	At December 31, 19B	
102		
103	Assets	
104	Cash	?
105	Accounts receivable	?
106	Inventory	?
107	Operational assets (net)............................	?
108		
109	Total..	-0-
110		
111	Liabilities	
112	Accounts payable.......................................	ERR
113	Income tax payable	?
114	Note payable, long term	?
115		
116	Shareholders' Equity	
117	Capital stock	?
118	Retained earnings	?
119		ERR
120		
121		
122		

Problem 17-21 (continued)

123	KOBERG COMPANY	
124	Statement of Cash Flows	
125	For the Year Ended December 31, 19A	
126		
127	Operating activities:	
128		
129	Net income...	?
130	Add (deduct) to convert to cash basis:	
131	Depreciation expense...	?
132	Accounts receivable increase.................................	?
133	Inventory increase..	?
134	Increase in taxes payable.......................................	?
135	Increase in accounts payable	?
136		
137		
138	Net cash from normal operations........................	-0-
139		
140	Financing activities:	
141		
142	Payment of cash dividends......................................	?
143		
144	Investing activities:	
145		
146	Additions to operational assets during 19B...............	?
147		
148	Net increase in cash..	?
149		
150		
151		
152		
153		

Problem 17-21 (continued)

154		
155		
156		
157		
158		
159		
160		
161		
162		
163		
164		
165		
166		
167		
168		
169		
170		
171		
172		
173		
174	SOLUTION:	
175		
176	Account receivable turnover ratio	3.167
177		
178	Inventory turnover ratio	1.150
179		
180	To calculate the accounts payable turnover ratio we first	
181	must calculate purchases for 19A as follows:	
182		
183	Cost of goods sold.................................. 48,421	
184	Add ending inventory, 19A 40,000	
185	Less inventory Jan. 1, 19A .... <u>40,000</u>	
186		
187	Purchases for 19A.. <u>40,000</u>	
188		
189		
190	Accounts payable turnover ratio	0.800
191		
192		

Problem 17-21 (continued)

193	KOBERG COMPANY	
194	Income Statement	
195	For the Year Ended December 31, 19B	
196		
197	Sales revenue	100,000
198	Cost of goods sold	48,421
199		
200	Gross margin	51,579
201	Expenses (same percentage as 19A)	34,737
202		
203	Pretax income	16,842
204	Income tax on operations..	3,705
205		
206	Net income..	13,137
207		
208		
209		

Problem 17-21 (continued)

210	KOBERG COMPANY	
211	Balance Sheet	
212	At December 31, 19B	
213		
214	Assets	
215	Cash	41,111
216	Accounts receivable	31,579
217	Inventory	42,105
218	Operational assets (net)...	90,000
219		
220	Total...	204,795
221		
222	Liabilities	
223	Accounts payable...	63,158
224	Income tax payable	1,500
225	Note payable, long term	25,000
226		
227	Shareholders' Equity	
228	Capital stock	80,000
229	Retained earnings	35,137
230		204,795
231		
232		
233		

Problem 17-21 (continued)

	KOBERG COMPANY	
234		
235	Statement of Cash Flows	
236	For the Year Ended December 31, 19A	
237		
238	Operating activities:	
230		
240	Net income	13,137
241	Add (deduct) to convert to cash basis:	
242	Depreciation expense...	20,000
243	Accounts receivable increase	(1,579)
244	Inventory increase	(2,105)
245	Increase in income taxes payable	500
246	Increase in accounts payable	13,158
247		
248		
249	Net cash from normal operations........................	43,111
250		
251	Financing activities:	
252		
253	Payment of cash dividends.....................................	(12,000)
254		
255	Investing activities:	
256		
257	Additions to operational assets during 19B...............	(10,000)
258		
259	Net increase in cash..	21,111
260		
261		
262	Note that the difference between the 19A	
263	and 19B cash account balance is..................................	21,111
264		
265		

Appendix
Pricing Products and Services

Exercise A-1 (10 minutes)

1. Absorption approach:

Direct materials	$ 6
Direct labour..	10
Variable and fixed manufacturing overhead	8
Unit manufacturing cost...	24
Markup: 50% x $24	12*
Target selling price...	$36

   *This markup must be adequate to cover the company's selling and administrative expenses, plus provide a desired profit.

2. Contribution approach:

Direct materials..	$ 6
Direct labour..	10
Variable manufacturing overhead..	3
Variable selling, general, and	
administrative expense	1
Total variable expenses..	20
Markup: 80% x $20	16*
Target selling price...	$36

   *This markup must be adequate to cover the company's fixed costs, plus provide a desired profit.

Exercise A-3 (15 minutes)

1.

$$\text{Markup percentage} = \frac{\text{Desired return on assets employed + Fixed costs}}{\text{Volume in units x Unit variable cost}}$$

$$= \frac{(10\% \times \$500{,}000) + \$400{,}000}{50{,}000 \text{ units} \times \$20}$$

$$= \frac{\$450{,}000}{\$1{,}000{,}000}$$

$$= 45\%$$

Target selling price:

Variable production costs	$19
Variable selling, general, and administrative expenses	1
Total variable expenses	20
Markup: 45% x $20	9
Target selling price	$29

Exercise A-3 (continued)

2.

$$\text{Markup percentage} = \frac{\text{Desired return on assets employed} + \text{Fixed costs}}{\text{Volume in units} \times \text{Unit variable cost}}$$

$$= \frac{(10\% \times \$500{,}000) + \$400{,}000}{30{,}000 \text{ units} \times \$20}$$

$$= \frac{\$450{,}000}{\$600{,}000}$$

$$= 75\%$$

Target selling price:

Variable production costs..	$19
Variable selling, general, and administrative expenses..	1
Total variable expenses..	20
Markup: 75% x $20	15
Target selling price..	$35

Exercise A-5 (5 minutes)

Sales (50,000 units x $65)	$3,250,000
Less: Desired profit (20% x $2,500,000).....................................	500,000
Target cost for 50,000 batteries	$2,750,000
Average target cost per battery ($2,750,000 ÷ 50,000)	$55

**Problem A-7** (40 minutes)

1. a. Supporting computations:

Number of jackets manufactured each year:

21,000 labour-hours ÷ 1.4 hours per jacket = 15,000 jackets.

Selling and administrative expenses:

Variable (15,000 jackets x $4).............................	$ 60,000
Fixed	474,000
Total...	$534,000

$$\text{Markup percentage} = \frac{\text{Desired return on assets employed} \times \text{Selling, general, and administrative expenses}}{\text{Volume in units} \times \text{Unit manufacturing cost}}$$

$$= \frac{(24\% \times \$900,000) + \$534,000}{15,000 \text{ jackets} \times \$40}$$

$$= \frac{\$750,000}{\$600,000}$$

$$= \underline{125\%}$$

b.

Direct materials...	$ 9.20
Direct labour	14.00
Manufacturing overhead....................................	16.80
Unit manufacturing cost	40.00
Add markup: 125% of cost to manufacture	50.00
Target selling price	$90.00

Problem A-7 (continued)

c. The income statement would be:

Sales (15,000 jackets x $90)......................		$1,350,000
Less cost of goods sold............................		
(15,000 jackets x $40)............................		600,000
Gross margin...		750,000
Less selling, general, and administrative expense:		
Shipping...	$ 60,000	
Salaries..	90,000	
Advertising and other..............................	384,000	
Total selling, general, and administrative expense		534,000
Net operating income		$ 216,000

Problem A-7 (continued)

The company's ROI computation for the jackets would be:

$$\frac{\text{Net operating income}}{\text{Sales}} \times \frac{\text{Sales}}{\text{Average operating assets}} = \text{ROI}$$

$$\frac{\$216,000}{\$1,350,000} \times \frac{\$1,350,000}{\$900,000} = \text{ROI}$$

16%	X	1.5	= 24%

2. a. Supporting computations:

Total fixed costs:
   Overhead (5/6 x $12 = $10 per hour fixed.
     $10 x 21,000 hours = $210,000*)................................... $210,000
   Selling, general, and administrative.................................... 474,000
     Total $684,000

  *Alternate computation: 5/6 x $16.80 = $14.00.
   $14.00 x 15,000 jackets = $210,000.

Variable costs per unit:
   Direct materials... $ 9.20
   Direct labour 14.00
   Variable manufacturing overhead (1/6 x $16.80) 2.80
   Shipping expense 4.00
     Total $30.00

Problem A-7 (continued)

$$\text{Markup percentage} = \frac{\text{Desired return on assets employed} + \text{Fixed costs}}{\text{Volume in units x Unit variable cost}}$$

$$= \frac{(24\% \times \$900{,}000) + \$684{,}000}{15{,}000 \text{ jackets} \times \$30}$$

$$= \frac{\$900{,}000}{\$450{,}000}$$

$$= \underline{200\%}$$

b.
Direct materials..	$ 9.20
Direct labour	14.00
Variable manufacturing overhead.......................	2.80
Shipping expense	4.00
Total variable expenses	30.00
Add markup: 200% of unit variable cost..............	60.00
Target selling price	$90.00

c.
Sales (15,000 jackets x $90)		$1,350,000
Less variable expenses		
(15,000 jackets x $30).....................................		450,000
Contribution margin		900,000
Less fixed expenses:		
Manufacturing overhead	$210,000	
Salaries	90,000	
Advertising and other	384,000	
Total...		684,000
Net operating income		$ 216,000

Managerial Accounting

Problem A-7 (continued)

3. If the company has idle capacity and sales to the retail outlet would not affect the company's regular sales, any price above the variable cost of $30 per jacket would add to profits. The company should aggressively bargain for more than this price; $30 is simply the rock bottom below which the company should not go in its pricing. As soon as the recession ends and regular sales pick up, the company should discontinue any special sales such as this and try to get its normal target selling price for all jackets.

Problem A-9 (50 minutes)

1. Supporting computations:

Number of pads produced per year:
100,000 labour-hours ÷ 2 hours per pad = 50,000 pads

Standard cost per pad:
$4,000,000 cost of goods sold ÷ 50,000 pads = $80 cost per pad

Fixed manufacturing overhead cost per pad:
$1,750,000 ÷ 50,000 pads = $35 per pad

Manufacturing overhead cost per pad:
$7 variable per pad + $35 fixed per pad = $42 per pad

Direct labour cost per pad:
$80 − ($30 + $42) = $8

Given the computations above, the completed standard cost card follows:

	Standard Quantity or Hours	Standard Price or Rate	Standard Cost
Direct materials	5 metres	$ 6 per metre	$30
Direct labour.........	2 hours	4 per hour*	8
Manufacturing overhead........	2 hours	21 per hour**	42
Total standard cost per pad...			$80

*8 ÷ 2 hours = $4 per hour.
**$42 ÷ 2 hours = $21 per hour.

Problem A-9 (continued)

2. a.

$$\text{Markup percentage} = \frac{\text{Desired return on assets employed} + \text{SG \& A expenses}}{\text{Volume in units} \times \text{Unit manufacturing cost}}$$

$$= \frac{(24\% \times \$3,500,000) + \$2,160,000}{50,000 \text{ pads} \times \$80}$$

$$= \frac{\$3,000,000}{\$4,000,000}$$

$$= 75\%$$

b.

Direct materials..	$ 30
Direct labour	8
Manufacturing overhead.......................................	42
Total cost to manufacture.................................	80
Add markup: 75%	60
Target selling price	$140

c.

Sales (50,000 pads x $140)...................................	$7,000,000
Less cost of goods sold (50,000 pads x $80)	4,000,000
Gross margin	3,000,000
Less selling, general, and administrative expense	2,160,000
Net income	$ 840,000

$$\frac{\text{Net operating income}}{\text{Sales}} \times \frac{\text{Sales}}{\text{Average operating assets}} = \text{ROI}$$

$$\frac{\$840,000}{\$7,000,000} \times \frac{\$7,000,000}{\$3,500,000} = \text{ROI}$$

$$12\% \times 2 = \underline{24\%}$$

Problem A-9 (continued)

3. a. Supporting computations:

Total fixed costs:

Manufacturing overhead...	$1,750,000
Selling, general, and administrative	
[$2,160,000 – (50,000 pads x $5 variable)]....................	1,910,000
Total fixed costs	$3,660,000

Variable costs per pad:

Direct materials...	$30
Direct labour	8
Variable manufacturing overhead...	7
Variable selling	5
Total variable costs	$50

$$\text{Markup percentage} = \frac{\text{Desired return on assets employed} + \text{Fixed Costs}}{\text{Volume in units} \times \text{Unit variable cost}}$$

$$= \frac{(24\% \times \$3,500,000) + \$3,660,000}{50,000 \text{ pads} \times \$50}$$

$$= \frac{\$4,500,000}{\$2,500,000}$$

$$= 180\%$$

b.		
	Direct materials..	$ 30
	Direct labour...	8
	Variable manufacturing overhead...	7
	Variable selling...	5
	Total variable expenses...	50
	Add markup: 180%	90
	Target selling price..	$140

Managerial Accounting

Problem A-9 (continued)

c. Sales (50,000 pads x $140)............................		$7,000,000
Less variable expenses		
(50,000 pads x $50)...................................		2,500,000
Contribution margin.......................................		4,500,000
Less fixed expenses:		
Manufacturing overhead...........................	$1,750,000	
Selling, general, and administrative..........	1,910,000	3,660,000
Net income...		$ 840,000